The Fifth Sun

THE TEXAS PAN AMERICAN SERIES

The Fifth Sun
Aztec Gods, Aztec World
By Burr Cartwright Brundage
Illustrated by Roy E. Anderson

University of Texas Press, Austin & London

The Texas Pan American Series is published with
the assistance of a revolving publication fund
established by the Pan American Sulphur Company

Library of Congress Cataloging in Publication Data
Brundage, Burr Cartwright, 1912–
    The fifth sun.
    (The Texas Pan American series)
    Bibliography: p.
    Includes index.
    1. Aztecs–Religion and mythology. 2. Indians of
Mexico–Religion and mythology. I. Title.
F1219.3.R38B7   299'.7   78-12562
ISBN 0-292-72427-6

To My Beloved Wife, Jini

Contents

In the year 13 Reed,
So they say, it first appeared.

The sun that now exists
Was born then.

This is the fifth sun,
Its date-sign is 4 Movement.

It is called Movement Sun
Because on that day it began to move.

The old people say
That in this age earthquakes will occur
And there will come starvation
And we shall perish.

       —ANALES DE CUAUHTITLAN

Introduction

In this work I present an outline of the world view of the Aztec people. I believe that the parts of this view add up to a comprehensive whole, though I am under no illusions that my approach will be accepted by all scholars in the field. Only recently Munro S. Edmonson wrote, "The world view of the Aztecs remains substantially problematic."

This book is not a monograph and should not be judged as such. It is a compendious handling of the subject of the Aztec appreciation of the universe and should serve as a reference work, as a work to enlighten scholars in other fields, and as a clearly written work for the intelligent layperson interested in such material. I have had these readers in mind throughout the writing of this book, which is why I have omitted almost all references in the text itself to contemporary scholarship. The layperson, the teacher, or the scholar in another field does not need such references.

The subject of how much documentation to introduce was difficult. The original draft of the work had over two hundred pages of notes, backing up virtually every statement. This was reduced progressively to the documentation appearing at the end of the book. Some of the notes remain lengthy, but these may be useful to the expert who wishes to look behind the statement in the text.

I have never hesitated to offer interpretations and analyses deriving from my own scholarship. Some of the interpretations are new, some are based on insights of other laborers in the vineyard. My insistence, however, on the *outrance* which marks Aztec religion might be considered new, as also might be my treatment of Tezcatlipoca and Huitzilopochtli.

The final test of the usefulness of any overview of the Aztec understanding of life and the world will in any case be the extent to which it explicates and is consistent with Aztec history. I have made only glancing references in the text (except in chapter 6) to historical concordances, for to have treated the relevancies of Aztec history *and* the Aztec world view would have necessitated a far longer and certainly an unwieldy book. Similarly with the subject of Aztec ritual. The first draft of this work contained several chapters on that closely related subject, but again considerations of length dictated a radical telescoping of this material. It is hoped that another volume will follow on this subject of the Aztec cult.

Now that volumes XII through XV of the *Handbook of Middle American Indians* are out, with their magnificent review and analysis of the bibliography pertinent to this subject, I do not need to offer an evaluation of sources. The sources upon which I principally leaned, however, can be briefly mentioned.

First there is the indispensable Bernardino de Sahagún, whom I used constantly, both in his *Historia general de las cosas de Nueva España* as well as in the twelve volumes of the Florentine Codex. The various volumes of translation and commentary on Sahagún in the series *Fuentes indigenas de la cultura Náhuatl: Textos de los informantes de Sahagún* were also used. Sahagún's towering importance can be seen not only in the references to him in the volumes of HMAI mentioned above but in the recent work edited by Edmonson, *Sixteenth-Century Mexico: The Work of Sahagún* (Albuquerque: University of New Mexico Press, 1974).

Diego Durán certainly came next. His *Historia de las Indias de Nueva España* was of great importance, especially in details relating to the Aztec gods.

Following these two I relied heavily for mythology on the old standbys: the *Anales de Cuauhtitlan*, the *Leyenda de los Soles*, the *Histoyre du Méchique*, and the *Historia de los Mexicanos por sus pinturas*. Other early sources drawn on extensively were Mendieta, Tezozomoc, Motolinía, Serna, Alarcón, Ponce, Pomar, and the three volumes of Garibay's *Poesía Náhuatl*.

Under the rubric of modern scholarship I have relied heavily on the five volumes of Seler's *Gesammelte Abhandlungen*, which has now been rendered eminently useful by the addition of an exhaustive index volume. The two volumes of Beyer's collected articles (*Mito y simbología* and *Cien años de arqueología mexicana*) were also useful as were, naturally, the twelve volumes (to date) of the *Estudios de cultura Náhuatl* published by the University of Mexico. Nor should I forget to mention Bodo Spranz' *Los dioses en los códices mexicanos del grupo Borgia*, a work of painstaking care and erudition.

Along with such sources and secondary works, I have consulted the pertinent codices. The codices are prime religious documents but, except in such cases as the Magliabecchiano, the Tudela, the Telleri-ano-Remensis, and the Vaticanus Latino, which have accompanying texts in Spanish or Italian, they require the greatest caution, for the interpretation of any particular scene is often questionable. I have perhaps been unduly reluctant to use them except where their meaning is fairly straightforward.

The American Philosophical Society aided in the production of this work with a grant for research in Mexico. I am most grateful for this aid. I am also in the debt of Professor J. Richard Andrews, whose *Introduction to Classical Nahuatl* (Austin: University of Texas Press, 1975) has been of great assistance. In addition, Professor Andrews has been most kind in responding to my request for help in the translation of certain of the Aztec names in this work. He has saved me from some egregious errors.

A word must be said about the illustrations in this book. Because a purely literary treatment of such a religion as that practiced by the Aztecs is inadequate to define its power and angularity, line drawings of some sort were judged by myself and the Press to be called for. I was most fortunate to interest the Florida artist, Mr. Roy E. Anderson, in this project. Mr. Anderson has made faithful copies of those parts of seven of the well-known codices which I designated to him, but he has nevertheless retained his own line in the process. He has also simplified the originals where details and shading would have been superfluous. The emblems which stand at the head of each chapter are taken from the Tonalamatl of the Codex Borgia to provide some consistency of style. The twenty-two larger illustrations scattered through the body of the text were chosen, however, not only from the Borgia but from Borbonicus, Cospi, Laud, Magliabec-chiano, Nuttall, and Vindobonensis. I wish to express my gratitude for Mr. Anderson's efforts. He has signally embellished the book.

The Fifth Sun

1. The World, the Heavens, and Time

The Four Directions and the Center

On a day in the past–perhaps somewhere around the year A.D. 1250 –the great Chichimec conqueror Xolotl solemnized his newly won possession of lands in Central Mexico formerly belonging to the Toltecs. He did this by dispatching four arrows from a mountaintop, one toward each of the four directions. A cable of dried grass, coarsely twined, was placed in the shape of a ring on the ground and burned, the ashes being scattered also to the four winds.[1]

This custom bears importantly on our survey of the world view of the Aztecs. Its interpretation seems easy. The Aztec universe was explicated, as throughout Mesoamerica, in terms of five directions: the center (where Xolotl's archer stood) and the four cardinal directions. The arrows shot from the Chichimec bow went forth to the four directions, each carrying the message of new possession. The burning ring of grass represented the circumambience of the edge of the world and the winnowing of the ashes added the peremptory notion of imperial frontiers.

The Aztec world then was not undefined. It had an undergirding of conceptual supports and a structure which was easily understood. The role which the five directions played in the lives of the Aztecs was basic.

When Aztec man put himself in the place of the rising sun, the path straight ahead of him led westward. This then was the orientation of the whole world. The north was defined as his right hand

and the south as his left hand. The four directions had been made explicit for him by the sun god himself, who, by first bringing day into the world, once and for all had proclaimed what was to be the correct orientation.

A myth enshrined this wisdom.[2] The four gods who were to aid in the appearance of the present or fifth sun had been sitting, just before his rising, in stygian blackness. They had fallen into a dispute as to which horizon would be honored by his first appearance; each god in his vigil therefore faced the direction he preferred and prophesied accordingly. Thus were the four directions each placed under a special patronage, while the fact that the sun rose finally in the east prescribed, as we have already seen, the final orientation of the universe.

This structure of the universe was also proclaimed in Aztec cult. At one point in the feast of the fire god four priests descended from his shrine, each carrying a blazing pine torch; they did reverence to each of the four cardinal directions (in the order east/north/west/south), after which the four brands were cast into the god's ever burning brazier.[3] In this ritual act the center of all things was defined as the abode of the central fire, with the four directions construed as emanations from that point.

To this fundamental structure of the universe all things had to conform. A city, for instance, could be laid out as a microcosm of the universe. Tenochtitlan, capital of the Mexican Aztecs, had as its focal area the temenos of the gods, an enclosed compound crowded with temples and other sacred buildings symbolizing the universal center. The principal temple, enshrining the two gods Huitzilopochtli and Tlaloc, was correctly interpreted as standing in the east and therefore being oriented toward the west. Four axial roads, leading east, north, west, and south, emanated from this focal area and thus pointed to the four quarters of the city. This was not merely an urban convenience for the Mexican Aztecs—it was a necessity imposed upon pious men everywhere who knew how to read the grand designs of the universe and who desired to conform to them in their works.

But there was more to the structure of the cosmos than just the extension of hallowed coordinates. Each of the five directions possessed a special name, color, and associated symbol, though these vary depending on the source we consult.[4]

The Aztecs considered that the node where the coordinates crossed was itself a direction—in fact it was considered the primary direction.

There, without any violation of its metaphorical meaning, the tetrad became pentad. Indeed the number 4 could not be considered fully meaningful by the Aztecs unless completed as 5. To the Aztecs this center was held by the most ancient of all the gods, the god of fire, whose name was Xiuhteuctli, Lord of the Year. He is located in the center quite obviously because the hearth, in all lands and in all times, has always been the point around which life has gravitated, and it was the fire god who postured and danced in the center of that hearth. Viewed geographically rather than metaphorically, his domain was in the center of the earth, deep underground; volcanoes were the vents through which his subterranean flames escaped.

Besides this ultimate manifestation in the earth's navel, Xiuhteuctli existed in four other transfigurations, each properly colored to conform to the directional system. In the year-end feast four victims, colored to correspond to the directions, were sacrificed. For purposes of that important event they were in quadruplicate the very person of the fire god. Each direction was sacred, but the peculiar quality of the center was its extreme venerability. While the fire god was in no sense an earth god, he was responsible for the rational ordering that gave meaning to the earth.

There were other sets of symbols associated with the five directions.[5] In addition to patron gods and colors, there were associated sets of birds, trees, dragons, and other animals and year symbols, all of which were used to further embellish the qualities of the five directions. Here then was the orderly structure of the cosmos.

The system expressed first the sacredness of the world. The earth upon which the Aztec walked, in whatever direction he might travel, in war or in peace, warned him of its divine probabilities and its inner purposes. However deserted and savage it might appear when he contemplated it, the world even beyond his own horizon presented much the same holiness as when he was at home in the center. If in the company of merchants he should walk for a thousand miles into the north, nothing would change in the somber face that direction showed him; its valleys and steppes would always be haunted by the larval dead. Should he travel east it was always toward blithe gods and good adventures. Thus the earth possessed a variously qualified holiness that was made clear in the climaxing metaphor of the four directions and the center.

Second, this system expressed the Aztec's closeness to the hub of things. He was always in or close to the center. He was of course aware that he could not move out along one of the directional axes and come upon that special mythic tree which there supported the sky or displayed in its branches the bird which further identified it. His only knowledge was that he inhabited the center and that the earth there was his home. This centrality gave the Aztec a sense of urgency and importance; things of moment could take place only in the center. This made him acutely receptive to divine demands.

Third, the system perfectly expressed that sense of spacious architecture congenial to the Aztec people. It was the opposite of that capriciousness of which there was already a sufficiency among gods and men. Answering his need to perceive the created world as orderly, this world scaffolding was indispensable to the Aztec. The four directions and the center assured him of the flawlessness of the entire structure.

The Sea and the Sky

Like many other peoples those of Mesoamerica believed that the earth floated in the midst of the sea. Mesoamerica lay like a lessening wedge of land between the Pacific Ocean and the Gulf of Mexico; to those on the shores, these bodies of water seemed to be endless. The sea was not a special element at all, nothing that one could contrast or compare with anything else, but a marvel:

> It is great. It terrifies, it frightens one. It is that which is irresistible; a great marvel; foaming, glistening with waves; bitter —very bitter, most bitter; very salty. It has man-eating animals, animal life. It is that which surges. It stirs; it stretches ill-smelling, restless.[6]

The sea was thought to extend outward and upward until—like the walls of a cosmic house—it merged with the sky, which then appeared to be the ceiling of a towering edifice.[7] Sea and sky were thus one substance, but the sea was more curdled; this explains the name given to the sea, "sky waters."[8] The sky therefore was known to contain waters which might in perilous times descend in deluges, annihilating men.

This indeed had happened once in the past when the sky collapsed upon the earth. It had been a difficult matter at that juncture for the gods to put the sky back and steady it again. This had been accomplished when four divine atlantes were posted at each of the world corners and two great world trees, probably aligned on an east-west axis, were erected to support the sky.[9] Other versions say there were four trees, one at each of the four heavenly corners.

This view of the sky as a great lake of waters overhead was based on observations commonly made by early men and was not unique to the Aztecs. Beyond this the Aztec priesthood had inherited a view which was theological and intellectual. This view they used to explain the function of the sky and its structural foundations in the earth.

According to this schema there were thirteen ascending levels which made up the whole.[10] The lowest level was defined as the abode of the god of fire and was centered in the earth. This level symbolized the idea of a hub from which all directions, including the upward direction, emanated. The surface of the earth counted as the first level and above this were the various heavenly terraces, each the abode of some astral or atmospheric presence or of one of the great gods. The uppermost tier was Omeyocan, the seat of divine authority. The sun, the moon, and the stars inhabited lower courses.

It is doubtful that this priestly construction counted for much with the average Aztec. In his assessment of the heavens it was the visible sun and the courses of the stars which gave him his crucial knowledge, not the speculations of the learned.

Like all Mesoamericans the Aztecs were vigilant observers of the heavens. Their ancestors, the wandering Chichimecs, considered the sun to be their father, and they drew attention to this affiliation by wearing on their backs an appropriate emblem, generally a sunburst of yellow parrot feathers. The sun was that celestial object excelling all others in lordliness and in the daily drama of his appearances and his exits. He was therefore a focal point of Chichimec mythology. He was called Tonatiuh, literally He Who Goes Forth Shining.

In the night skies there was no such splendor. Instead there was a richness of astral beings, crowding and wheeling about. The stars were their eyes. The Milky Way was a road across this sky and was presided over by two divinities: the male Citlallatonac, Starshine, and the female Citlalinicue, Star Skirt. Viewed in another sense, the Milky Way was itself the body of that Great Mother out of whose tenebrous womb had once poured the sun and the moon and the stars.[11] The constellations bore names and were watched as they threaded their way through the seasons. But no star possessed such magic as that planet which both foreruns and follows the sun. To the Aztecs the planet Venus was a warrior, a valiant champion whose challenges to the sun were dire and constant. The malevolence of

Venus was well known; he was called the Great Star. As for the moon the Aztecs condemned it as an ashen replica of the sun and as something of a coward. It could also be thought of as a basin that held in its expanding and contracting interior the waters of the sky. Considered as a deity the moon was Tlazolteotl, an ancient goddess of singular power found on the Gulf coast.[12]

Star lore formed a significant part of Aztec culture. The solemnity of the spangled vault of the night sky, the silences between the stars and along the galactic wheel, profoundly affected the Aztec. We can understand why the astral aspect of his religion was so compelling to him. In the night sky he could read, beside his own dooms, the frozen words of all the gods. Every large magnitude star and the constellations were identified with one of the gods, and the host of stars together could be thought of as demonic *tzitzimime*, monsters of death and destruction.[13]

The Ball Game

In the ruins of many ancient sites in Mesoamerica and even in our own Southwest, there appears an edifice called the *tlachco*, or ball court. It is of singular importance for our study of Aztec belief; a description of it is therefore in order.

In its classic form the *tlachco* was a narrow and extended gallery carefully leveled and often paved; its sides could be either shallowly sloped or perpendicular. The ends of the court were short transverse runways attached in such a way that the ground plan resembled a capital I. Entry into the playing area was made via transverses, either through breaks in the enclosing wall or down stairways from the spectators' ledge. Two sheds or small temples were often placed on top of the end walls and thus commanded a longitudinal view of the playing field below. Set into the ground directly in the center of the court was sometimes found a circular stone, while running through this from center wall to center wall was a painted line marking the limits for each team. Representations in the codices of the ground plan of the *tlachco* show it sometimes divided into four sections, each colored differently, for it too could conform to the cosmic orientation. Occasionally two stone rings, each perforated, protruded from the center of the side walls into the court. In most cases the whole playing field was sunken appreciably below ground level. Spectators sat

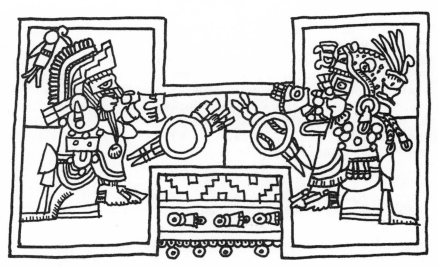

Two princes wagering in the tlachco *(Nuttall)*

or stood on the side and end walls and looked down on the sport. The game played in that court was *tlachtli*, an exhausting and often dangerous contest necessitating great skill.

Tlachtli has a very old history in Mesoamerica. According to the prevailing theory, the game originated in the Gulf lowlands. There men had learned to make resilient solid balls from the sap of the rubber tree. These burned fiercely and were primarily offered up as incense in certain cult performances. The most astonishing property of the ball, however–apart from the large volume of smoke it emitted when burning–was its mercurial movement when thrown, and from this feature a game early evolved which was closely tied into the religious cult. If the La Venta people of southern Vera Cruz (ca. 1250–900 B.C.) invented the game, as many think, then it could have been their merchants who not only carried it to the far corners of Mesoamerica but inevitably carried with it associated religious concepts. The sensational properties of the rubber ball–unlike anything else known–must have validated and heightened the impact of the cult. By 300 B.C. the game was fully developed.

As a result of the wide dissemination of *tlachtli* its rules changed radically in the course of centuries. At first thrown by hand, the ball was later propelled with bats. By the time the Spaniards appeared players were limited to bouncing the ball off their hips or knees, no other parts of the body being used. In this final stage of the game as few as two players could duel against each other, though as many as six might compete. The appearance of the courts also changed. At first they had simply been level fields marked by two symbolic standards placed at the ends of the long axis. Next they were encased in earth or masonry walls, and finally out of the walls protruded the stone hoops through which the players attempted to drive the ball. All such alterations must have reflected new understandings of the meaning of the game and therefore new cosmologies.

The Meaning of the Ball Game

The salient features of the *tlachco* are its narrowness and its pronounced length, plus the fact that it is generally sunken or given the appearance of being let down into the earth.[14] This is a significant form; it was undoubtedly thought to represent a straight runway or concourse in the underworld along which was fought out a contest involving the passage of a round flying object.[15] This flying object is the sun, here thought to be fallen under the western horizon and caught among nocturnal enemies. The conflict among the players in the ball game is equivalent to the attempt of the sun to struggle through the black sky of the underworld, to avoid entrapment, and to attain a heroic exit into the world above the earth. The two perforated stone rings will have symbolized the holes through which the sun entered the earth at evening and through which he emerged at dawn. If this theory is correct, *tlachtli* is a sacred drama depicting a natural tragedy: the nocturnal death and captivity of the sun.

What has confused some researchers has been the obvious equivalence between the *tlachco* and the night sky on the one hand and, on the other, the equally obvious equivalence between the *tlachco* and the underworld. The one might seem to prohibit the other.

Such is not the case. In the underworld the sun blunders through a thick and obscure sky peopled with enemies. This sky is indeed under the earth but it is not Mictlan, the abode of the dead; rather, it is a hippodrome through which—at full drive and at great odds—the wounded sun hurtles his way. This chthonic sky is nevertheless the night sky that smoothly rotates above our heads. They are one and the same. Thus the stars that swing up out of the east after the sun has set are by definition the sun's enemies. Like winking conspirators they throng around him in the darkness and subdue him. To us the firmament at night is a thing of beauty, but it was not beautiful to the Aztecs. In their close and suffocating silence the stars were thought of as dangerous influences.

The fact that the *tlachco* symbolized the night sky can be appreciated in the fact that before important games it had to be rededicated by a priest in a midnight ceremony.[16] As for its being also the underearth, we note not only the four equal areas of the court (each of the divisions or directions being separately colored when depicted in the codices) but the fact that the circular flagstone in the exact center of the court represented the nadir or middle point in the underworld and was appropriately called *itzompan*, "its end." Quetzalcoatl was said to have opened up this hole into the deepest part of the world.

There is another theory concerning the meaning of the game of *tlachtli*, based on the typical north-south orientation of the court itself: it represents the sun's *seasonal*, rather than his *diurnal*, peregrination. There is much in this theory to recommend it; certainly the peoples of Mesoamerica were vividly aware of the great solstitial rhythm.[17]

But we must now describe the role of the gods in relation to the game. Two divinities presided over it, one being the patron of the ball, the other being the patron of the court.[18] There can be little doubt that the one god represented the solar party and the other god represented the astral demons of the underworld or, if directionally interpreted, the exit from and the entry to the underworld.

In Tenochtitlan the god specifically involved in the game was that transfiguration of Huitzilopochtli known as Huitznahuatl, the Southerner, a name celebrating the former god's foray against the Four Hundred Southerners, the stars, at the time of his birth.[19] As the Mexicans grew to imperial stature, their god Huitzilopochtli took over some of the mythology of the sun and is thus, not unexpectedly, connected with the *tlachco*. A well-known variant of the myth of the gigantomachy, which we will comment on later, has Huitzilopochtli doing battle with the Four Hundred in a *tlachco*, defeating and then sacrificing them on the field. The Four Hundred are thus his enemies in the firmament of the underworld. On his feast day in Tenochtitlan the magnates gathered at ball courts to play *tlachtli* and victims were sacrificed there. Indeed, a shrine of Huitzilopochtli was inconceivable without an adjoining *tlachco*, itself considered to be a temple.

In Aztec myth a game of *tlachtli* that changed the course of the present aeon was once played between the gods Quetzalcoatl and Tezcatlipoca. During the game, which was to decide who of the two was to be the sun, Tezcatlipoca changed into a jaguar, thus achieving victory.[20] The appearance of the jaguar motif here is instructive, for that animal with its spotted coat represented to almost all peoples in Mesoamerica both the night sky glittering with stars and the interior of the earth.

We have seen that the *tlachco* was conceived to be a temple, and it should not surprise us that human sacrifice was involved. From various archaeological sources we know that in a special ritual performance of the game the captain of the losing team was beheaded over the center stone, his blood symbolically pouring down that conduit into the earth's bowels. It could be that this sacrifice was a reenactment of that death which the sun suffered at his nadir or an atonement for it. It could be that the losing team, in the very act of losing, was thought to have been transformed into a group of the sun's adherents, whereas the winning side became, on the same showing, the forces of darkness.[21]

Behind the *tlachco* and the contests that took place therein lay a most imposing conception. Indeed, as a product of the human imagination, the Mesoamerican ball game has seldom been surpassed. A choice had been presented to the Aztecs—to celebrate, as central in their religion, the march of the sun through the daylight hours, depicting him as unthreatened and unconquerable, or to stress the fateful and quixotic character of his course, ending in the extinction of light and life. The Aztecs, borrowing from their predecessors, chose the latter and thereby revealed their special feeling for the dark and the malign. They felt ritually at home in darkness. The statements they made about the cosmos were appreciative of its majesty, but they placed over the face of that majesty a mask of defeat and ill omen.

Time

Even more mysterious to men than the world itself are the nature and direction of its changes. The earth can be seen and walked upon, but time is never more than an impalpable reality at best. The impulsions of time are easily and everywhere apparent, from the sequence of the seasons to the birth and death of all organisms. Like a dark current it sweeps men along, and their complaints mean nothing to it. What men object to is its tragic directionality. They know that the essence of time is change and that this indeed is the structure of life, but they are shattered when they contemplate the fact that what begins in vigor marches only and always toward decay.

In their search for a formula that would more fully explain the character of time, the Aztecs isolated a profane and a sacred time, each with its separate calendar.[22] Let us begin with their concept of profane or, as we may well call it, natural time.

The Xihuitl or Natural Year

Xihuitl is the Nahuatl word for grass or a stem of grass, a branch, or leafage in general. Probably from this as a primary meaning were derived the following secondary meanings: the color green, the turquoise, and, finally, year. We can see how *xihuitl* could come to mean "year" if we suppose it to have been interpreted as "the time of verdure" or "the time of the new grass." The word would thus have been related to the experience of the Aztecs with the revolving year of nature, in other words with the recurrent spring. In the crude Aztec system of writing, the picture of the worked turquoise was the glyph for year. This year was our solar year of 365 days.

The basic datum we must begin with is the number 20, *cempohualli* or "one full count," referring to the total number of fingers and toes which a person possessed. The idea of a score contained the idea of totality, an implicit understanding that the number 20 cannot be, or should not be, exceeded, that it is in fact a closed or perfect number.

A natural year complete with two equinoxes is also a totality. It cannot progress beyond what the preceding year attained, thus becoming thereby something different. The year preceding it was a completed span of time and was without connections. Then another year began, taking its place but in no way indebted to it. The fact that the year is a totality meant that, to the Aztecs, the number 20 could aptly be applied to it in order to break it up and organize its inner structure. In our modern calendar we understand the year in a different fashion, namely in terms of a consecution of months or lunations. Thus we arrive at a number close to 12. The Mesoamericans applied the abstract number 20 to the year and by reckoning came out with eighteen periods of 20 days each, the whole equaling 360. Thus the perfect number 20 brought the Aztecs close to our year of 365 days but could not account for the 5 1/4 days left over. The fault was not in the *cempohualli*, which was by definition perfect, but in the incommensurable number of days remaining. Though necessary to complete the solar year, these days technically could not be counted. They did not exist in the *xihuitl* at all. They were therefore relegated to the status of *nemontemi*, five uncountable and unnamed days whose ominous and purposeless character derived from their lack of a patron deity. *Nemontemi* may be freely translated as "they complete the count of the year without profit."

The *xihuitl* was understood by the Aztecs very much as we understand our solar year. To them it was a series of eighteen groupings of twenty days each, roughly corresponding to our months, each group distinctively named and all following each other in an immutable order. Each set of twenty days had a special religious orientation which culminated in a great ritual on the last day of the twenty. It was in fact through the *xihuitl* that the gods participated in the activities of the community and decided whether to provide rain, to avert the hail, or to bring victory to the marching armies: it was the stage upon which they played out their roles. Thus, while the *xihuitl* accurately reflected the year in its length, it was also a priestly creation insofar as it was broken up into cultically oriented periods. Priestly manipulation is especially evident in the so-called divine year, composed of four of these solar years.[23] The rituals specified for the fourth year of this divine year were elaborate and stressed special penitential rites connected with Quetzalcoatl, the creator of the calendar.

A review of the solar year of the Aztecs is of interest. Herewith follows a list of the eighteen so-called months, each with their names and the deities especially honored therein.[24] Aztec cities were not necessarily consistent in selecting the month with which they began the year. In terms of our calendar this year can have begun on February 2, though a beginning as late as the March equinox is also indicated.

1. Cuauhuitlehua	Raising of Poles	Tlaloc
2. Tlacaxipehualiztli	Flaying of Men	Xipe
3. Tozoztontli	Little Vigil	Chicomecoatl and Tlaloc
4. Hueytozoztli	Great Vigil	Cinteotl and Tlaloc
5. Toxcatl	Drought(?)	Tezcatlipoca
6. Etzalcualiztli	Eating of Succotash	Tlaloc
7. Tecuilhuitontli	Little Feast of the Lords	Xochipilli
8. Hueytecuilhuitl	Great Feast of the Lords	Xilonen

9. Miccailhuitontli	Little Feast of the Dead	The ancestors and all the gods
10. Hueymiccailhuitl	Great Feast of the Dead	The Otomí form of Xiuhteuctli
11. Ochpaniztli	Sweeping of the Ways	Toci and Chicomecoatl
12. Teotleco	Arrival of the Gods	All the gods
13. Tepeilhuitl	Feast of the Mountains	The Tlaloque and Xochiquetzal
14. Quecholli	Roseate Spoonbill	Mixcoatl
15. Panquetzaliztli	Raising of the Banners	Huitzilopochtli
16. Atemoztli	Descent of Water	The Tlaloque
17. Tititl	Stretching	Cihuacoatl
18. Izcalli	Reawakening	Xiuhteuctli

In Central Mexico the first eleven of these months defined the agricultural part of the year, a time unit when the late winter frosts, problems of planting, weeding, and harvesting obsessed almost all sectors of the populace. As this season began Tlaloc, the god of rain, was appropriately honored first, followed immediately by that youthful god of the early spring, Xipe. Chicomecoatl, the mother of corn, dominated the central days of the planting period, but as the growing period began she was followed, curiously enough, by Tezcatlipoca. He can be there only because he was the god of contraries and reversals, the one who if rain were needed could deny it. There followed the period where judicious quantities of rain and sun were needed, so both Tlaloc and Xochipilli (the latter a solar god as well as a god of maize) were honored. Then as the ears of maize rapidly formed Xilonen, the maiden goddess who personified the sweet milkiness of the early ear, received her due. So far let us assume that the fields have survived but that, at any moment, unforeseen disasters could strike them, occasioned by the communities' neglect of the powers. Two of the months were therefore devoted to appeasing and feasting the departed dead, spirits who merge imperceptibly with the lesser gods. At this critical point the oldest and most venerable of the divine beings was also honored: the god of fire, master of the hearth and ultimate ancestor of all beings. Now came harvest home, a ritual wherein the several forms of the Great Mother were acknowledged, honored, and rewarded. Thus ended the agricultural portion of the year. All the gods at that point were supposed to have departed, having left behind a world emptied of the divine.

Seven months remained. They run, in terms of our calendar, roughly from the end of September to some time in February. If the preceding months all belonged to the farmers, these later ones belonged variously to other social groups—warriors, hunters, priests, adolescents, and women. Now that the primary task of filling the corncribs had been completed, the interests of various other parties and of the state could be consulted.

The remaining portion of the *xihuitl* began with the return of all the gods in a special and secret reentry into the community. We must keep in mind that, even though it was arbitrarily sliced up into twenty sections, the *xihuitl* was an integral event to the Aztecs, and this is why the twelfth month, the month that joined the two parts of the year, contained a ritual of all the gods. The *xihuitl* ended appropriately enough with a celebration of Xiuhteuctli, Lord of the Year, who thus sealed up his empire.

The Tonalpohualli *or Sacred Year*

In a succeeding chapter we will note that the Aztec gods were not understood to be a logically related class of beings organized as families, clans, or states. Considering the Aztec's abiding desire to serve and placate the gods this may seem unusual, for where man's interests are in question he has usually sought to institutionalize the society of divine beings along lines familiar to him.

To partly defuse the powers that ruled his universe and to make them more tractable, the Aztec fitted them into a conceptual framework inherited from his Mesoamerican past. He arbitrarily hacked out of the realm of time a portion which he called the *tonalpohualli* and to which he assigned authority to govern the gods and to constrain them to its mandate. This temporal answer to the problem of organizing the divine was most ingenious. By means of it the gods, both as a whole and individually, were made more comprehensible.

Thus for the Aztecs the gods did not form a body—they existed collectively because they were set within the *tonalpohualli*, which thus became their constitution. The *tonalpohualli* is the cadre within which a divine meaning is to be found. It is the charter of the heavenly state, the written constitution of the heavens, and, one might almost say, the central principle of coherence in the Aztec cosmos.

At a time in the remote past Mesoamerican priests had produced

Oxomoco and Cipactonal divining in a sacred enclosure (Borbonicus)

this amazing companion to the *xihuitl*. While the solar year stood unchanged as an essential computation, it was meshed into this new almanac, which was unrelated to the solar year or to any other natural period. To create this almanac the originating priesthood did not simply subdivide a recurrent period in nature. Instead they began with the sacred number 20, as had the inventors of the natural year, and added to it the number 13; from these two sacred numbers they built up a unique and wholly intellectual concept, a new entity of 260 days.

We have already described the number 20 and what it meant. Mesoamericans held the number 13 in equal if not greater veneration. An old theory accounting for this has been advanced by scholars, namely that the major gods were originally thirteen in number, thus defining that number as sacred.[25] If so, it must have been true in some civilization lost in the far distant past and thus would not necessarily be descriptive of the Aztec pantheon. Perhaps also related to the use of the number 13 in the *tonalpohualli* is the fact that the world and the sky were supposed to be arranged in thirteen superimposed layers. This idea the Aztecs had also inherited from the past. The earth was the initial level; above it were twelve others leading up to Omeyocan, the apical heaven where the high gods lived. In such a schema each level could well have been the abode of a god or a divine activity and thus thirteen named gods would have made up a full muster of all the terrestrial and celestial gods— though not of the chthonic ones.[26] If indeed the number 13 relates originally to such an orthodox list of deities we could understand its use in helping create this artificial world of divine time.

This peculiar chronology was produced by the revolution of the set of digits from 1 through 13 upon another set of twenty day-signs, each set maintaining a rigid order. Listed in their proper sequence the twenty day-signs were alligator, wind, house, lizard, snake, death, deer, rabbit, water, dog, monkey, grass, reed, jaguar, eagle, vulture, earthquake, knife, rain, and flower. The *tonalpohualli* was thus a geared rolling of the sacred number 13 on a set of twenty day-signs. Once one had checked off all possible permutations a period of 260 days was completed, each day of which had a distinctive name which was not duplicated in the *tonalpohualli*; for example: 1 Alligator, 2 Wind, 3 House, . . . 11 Knife, 12 Rain, and 13 Flower. The importance of this arrangement for us lies in its pure artificiality.

The twenty day-signs are of great antiquity and were obviously thought to be a complete count of the items in some sort of category, possibly naming divinities. In whatever culture the list was first put together, no doubt each sign, representing the fetish or the double (*nahualli*) of a god, was read as the name of that god. But by Aztec times some of the signs had become dissociated from these hypothetical antique deities, and new Aztec divinities were now assigned to the twenty signs as patrons.

Tonalpohualli means "the count of day-signs"; the word *tonalli* in the compound means "day-sign." The word for day was *ilhuitl* and was reserved for the days of the solar calendar. Whereas *ilhuitl* designates the days of the solar year as belonging to the whole community and therefore as public affairs, the word *tonalli* ends by designating the day as relevant only to the individual. The birthday or day-sign of a person was his *tonalli*, special and peculiar to him or to others born on that day.

It is apparent from what has been said above that there were twenty sets of thirteen days in each *tonalpohualli* and that each set began with a day-sign introduced by the number 1. Each month was usually under the patronage of two gods; occasionally a month had one patron god. These gods were in general identical with the gods associated with the *tonalli* day-signs, and they served to reinforce or enrich the augural properties of the thirteen days of each month.

What we probably have then, standing behind the Aztec *tonalpohualli*, are three sets of gods, one complete at thirteen and given in late days only as numbers, the other two complete at twenty and named (the one named as day-signs, the other as patron deities). On the surface the *tonalpohualli* appears to be a calendar. Underneath, however, it was a mystical and mathematically perfect dance of the gods, a quadrille whose incessant conjunctions and disjunctions produced all possible meanings and combinations of meanings.

The reader can now see what is involved in the *tonalli*. It was a person's fate and a powerful determinant of his actions. The reason it had such power was—as we have seen—that each of the 260 *tonalli* possessed its own distinctive quality, lent it by the three gods whose conjunction had originally formed it: the forgotten god behind the number of the day, the god connected with the sign of the day, and the god influencing all the days of the month in which it appeared.

According to an Aztec myth this is how the *tonalpohualli* came about.[27] In the days after the gods had created them, men considered their situation and saw that they lacked a rule or a calendar by which their lives could be regulated. They therefore referred the matter to the oldest of all the divine couples, Cipactonal and Oxomoco, who

lived in a sacred cave in Morelos. Oxomoco, the aged goddess, decided that on such a difficult and momentous decision it would be
best to consult her grandson, the wise Quetzalcoatl. The difficulty
was to settle upon a sign for the first day. Once that was done, all
the rest would fall into place. Because of her superior wisdom Oxomoco was chosen to make this all-important decision, and she chose
the Cipactli (the alligator or earth monster) because it had been the
first of all beings. So the first day in the *tonalpohualli* became 1 Alligator. The remaining signs were then easily filled in and the complete almanac of 260 days was painted in the *tonalamatl*, the book of
day-signs. The science of divining from that manual was passed
down to men by Quetzalcoatl.

The importance of this myth in the study of Aztec time has not
been stressed by scholars. On a historical level it can be interpreted
to mean that the priests of the city of Xochicalco in Morelos—where
the goddess Oxomoco was presumably worshiped—consulted with
the priests of Cholula—Quetzalcoatl's city—on a formulation (or a reformulation) of the *tonalpohualli* which from that point on was to become standard. If we consider the tale solely as a myth we cannot
fail to note that Oxomoco's presence is overriding. Oxomoco's consort, Cipactonal, is important only because of his name which, when
translated, means "the *cipactli* day-sign," in other words the first
day of the *tonalpohualli*. He is thus merely a symbol of that almanac
and of its divine properties. The goddess is thus seen to be the real
author of the almanac. It is even probable that her own date-name
was exactly this first day of the *tonalpohualli* and that in time it was
separated from her and worshiped as a connected divinity; ultimately, with a change of sex, the transfiguration became her consort.

We note that there is a corresponding myth of the creation of the
solar year, but it merely states that Tezcatlipoca and Quetzalcoatl
jointly created the *xihuitl* along with all other things. As we have
observed, the *xihuitl* existed only to measure the agricultural year
and to mark the proper places for the rituals of the many gods; it was
a practical social instrument. The *tonalpohualli*, on the contrary, was
the charter or the constitution of the whole numinous cosmos, clearly denoting that which was fortunate and desirable and that which
was unfortunate and hateful. The *tonalli* or day in this remarkable
register came ultimately to signify one's fate, fortune, or star.

The Calendar Round

Fifty-two years made up the Aztec century. It was called *xiuhmol-pilli*, "a bundle of years," which referred to the custom of marking the passage of each year by putting aside a peeled wand and, when the appropriate number of fifty-two had been accumulated, bundling them together into a fascine and ritually burying them. After which a new count would begin, accompanied by a corresponding sense of renewal.

The number 52 was arrived at by the merging of the natural year with the *tonalpohualli*. If they were fitted together and began revolving with their first days coinciding, at the end of fifty-two natural years their first days would again coincide. This fifty-two-year cycle is found in Mesoamerica as early as the middle pre-Classic and is sometimes referred to as the calendar round.

This cycle was more than just a convenience in reckoning for the Aztecs. Primarily it fulfilled their need to adequately define time. Today we settle for a bleak extension of years into the future, all undifferentiated, endless, without habitation. The Aztecs did not have our power to turn away from time; they prepared in the wastes of eternity stopping places where the spirit of man could briefly dwell before pressing on. Theirs was a very human response. It was a way of accumulating into a handy bundle the tribulations and sins of the years, which became supportable only because of the certainty that, at the end of the period, it could be put down, abandoned, and a new one taken up. The calendar round thus answered a deep and imperious need. Our own concept of a century cannot be considered comparable.

A bundle of fifty-two years produced a new series made up of four signs—rabbit, reed, knife, and house—and thirteen numerals. Each year was named after one of the four signs, repeated in the above order, along with attached numbers ranging from 1 through 13. Thus every calendar round began with the year 1 Rabbit and ended with the year 13 House. In other words there were four thirteen-year periods, each set beginning with a different one of the above signs. Each set of thirteen years was thought of as a single burden borne by the initial year of that set, which had to be either 1 Rabbit, 1 Reed, 1 Knife, or 1 House. Thus, as the round began, the year 1 Rabbit lifted his burden of thirteen years and carried it on his back down the road of time until, at the end of the thirteenth year, he set his burden down and gave way to 1 Reed, who correspondingly carried time onward, and so on in this fashion until after fifty-two years the four year-bearers had ended their journey and were ready to renew the relay. Such a way of viewing time as a portage was a high act of the imagination.[28] Integrating these divinized year-dates into the cosmic geography was the attribution of one of the four directions to each of the four year-signs. For instance, 1 Rabbit represented the south, 1 Reed the east, and so on around the circuit of the world. This closed the circle of time and space and made them a unit.

Time ran out at the end of the fifty-two-year period. Quite literally the Aztec supposed it to expire and be replaced—or not, as the case could be—by another series born out of the womb of night. If it were not replaced and time indeed expired, catastrophe ensued and the celestial demons descended to kill and eat the last of mankind. To deflect such an atrocity the Aztecs, on the last day of the calendar round, acknowledged the ending of time, broke all their household idols, and threw them into the rivers. The public ritual enacted at such times by Tenochtitlan and its neighboring Aztec cities was of a splendor not often achieved in human culture. We will consider this festival shortly.

Xiuhteuctli, Lord of the Year

Xiuhteuctli is one of the most interesting members of the Aztec pantheon.[29] We have already met him as the god of fire who, by his residence in the hearth, defines the center of all things and, as a necessary consequence, the four directions as well. He was the most ancient and venerable of all the gods and sacrifices were always made to him first;[30] it is this primigenial claim which gave him jurisdiction over time itself. He is always depicted as emaciated, bearded, deeply wrinkled, and bent over with extreme age. In ceramic representations he is seated cross-legged on the ground, his head and neck crushed down under the weight of a bowl in which ceremonial fire could be burned. This is the transfiguration of the god commonly referred to as Huehueteotl, the Old God. He was also called Our Father and sometimes Our Only Father. He was the father and mother of all the gods and consequently the source of their divinity. Newborn children were commonly passed through the flames of the hearth and lightly singed as a form of baptism and an acknowledgment of their filiation with the fire god.[31]

As the numen of the fire Xiuhteuctli was naturally identified with

Xiuhteuctli wearing the fire serpent as a backpiece (Borbonicus)

the hearth, the focus of all domestic concerns. Indeed he was treated as the family's most revered progenitor. At appropriate times he was serenaded with drums and song and addressed as "ineffable flower," while around the hearth jugs of the intoxicating drink *octli* would be placed, crowned and collared with garlands, each representing an ancestor come to share the communal meal.

Allied to this feeling for the god's centrality in the family was the picture the Aztecs had of him as living in the center of the earth, where he was supposed to inhabit a crenelated castle surrounded by a cloud of abyssal waters.[32] As we have previously mentioned he could be broken up into four avatars, colored blue, yellow, white, or red.[33]

The wrinkled Xiuhteuctli was worshiped with great pomp by the Aztecs in Tenochtitlan, where his divine hearth burned continually in front of Cihuacoatl's temple. The proximity of these two shrines in Mexico's sacred enclosure, that of earth and that of fire, explicated a fundamental symbolism in the Aztec's world: his belief that the nuclear fire dwelt in the earth and thus defined its universal center.

This homing quality of the god explains why he was a patron god of the merchant class. When the Aztec merchant adjusted his backframe, to which his goods were lashed, he was leaving the center and taking a perilous or unaccustomed direction. Success in barter and the merchant's life itself were thus to be defined only in terms of a radial excursion and a return to the hearth, the central fire.

Inasmuch as primacy and venerability were the peculiar characteristics of the fire god, he had become, if not a patron of the state, at least a kind of ultimate authority from whom the ruler drew his own prerogatives; indeed the blue diadem worn by Aztec rulers was the same as that depicted on the fire god's brow. Elections of princes and rulers were normally held on the god's birthday. New fiefs were granted and old ones confirmed on that day. Matchless in years and regal in his claims, Xiuhteuctli was the Aztec Cronus, the first king and the Lord of Time.

The connection between the fire of Xiuhteuctli and the sun was recognized, but he was never confused with that star. His two fixed festivals of the year may have originally celebrated the solstices, but this is not certain. We know that he could be referred to as the Prince of the Dawn and that he received offerings from every household just before sunrise but, though he was the vital principle of heat and fire in the sun, he was not the sun.[34] His abode was within the dark earth.

What interests us here is his connection with time. I suspect that what originally gave him his patronage over time was, quite simply, the putting to sleep of the paleolithic campfire as night fell and, with the first signs of dawn, the reawakening of that fire, the scrabbling aside of the ashes and the blowing on the tiny spark till it flamed again. This auroral act–almost synonymous with the sun's career– had been performed by men since the Old Stone Age and had, by Aztec times, become a symbol of renewal.

Today we seldom have to tend fires and therefore are no longer alive to the drama of the morning hearth. We do not serenade it as the precursor of all good things, indeed of life itself. If in our imaginations we can again evoke this periodicity of the fire at dayspring we can grasp why Xiuhteuctli became the god of time.

But Xiuhteuctli did not command time; he simply symbolized it in all its benign aspects. He alone of all the gods had never died in the four aeonic destructions of times past, and because of this he could be honored as Four Times Lord.[35] In short he was not a god of bleak eternity but a god of renewals. He did not condemn men to inhabit an abstract time that marched endlessly on whether they were there or not. Rather, as the familial numen in the Aztec fire, awakening each morning into life, he conveyed the sense of expressive intervals. Time under him was basically benevolent, and the average Aztec family lived in his ambience with gratitude and willing service. Every four years the people celebrated a recurrence of time in the month of Izcalli, which was dedicated to him; holding children by the hand, adults danced to symbolize their own rejuvenation. Children in fact were prominently displayed and ritually introduced into society in this quadrennial event, being provided with godparents, having their ears pierced, and indulging in group drunkenness for the first time. The annual fire festival during Izcalli, the Aztec new year's celebration, was said to have been the first of all feasts created by the gods. Though not the mightiest god in the Aztec pantheon, Xiuhteuctli was surely the best beloved.

The New Fire Ceremony

There is a hill near Culhuacan on the south side of present-day Mexico City called the Hill of the Star. On its summit once stood a terrace crowned by a famous shrine important to Xiuhteuctli. On this sacred spot–where legend said the god Mixcoatl first drilled fire[36]–there took place a ceremony at the end of each calendar round remarkable both for its staging and for its overriding importance in Aztec religion: that rite wherein the community of gods and men delivered themselves into the power of time and in fear and trembling awaited its verdict. The central feature of this performance was fire.

To the Aztecs, as we have noted, time moved in lustral bursts, each set self-contained. The world was known to be safe from destruction at any point within the calendar round; it was only at the expiration of one set, before the succeeding one began, that the world was vulnerable. At this juncture it was thought that the cosmic forces might cease and the sun, lost in the underworld, might not summon up the vitality to rise again, thereby preventing the inception of another set of fifty-two years. Universal death would then follow. The sign that this catastrophe was not going to happen, that the world would continue, occurred when it was seen that the Pleiades did not come to a halt on reaching the zenith at midnight but continued on in their course.

As this night of the world's danger began, a procession of priests, each clothed in the elaborate regalia of one of the great gods of Mexico and therefore representing the very person of that god, came out of the darkened city. Solemnly they marched southward down the Ixtapalapan causeway over the lake. This procession was called "they walk as gods." Some time before midnight these vicarial priests climbed the slopes of the sacred hill and took their appropriate stances around the altar. The gods themselves did not know what the outcome of time would be and their gathering here brought all the powers of heaven and earth to witness the event. Man himself in such an awful moment was insignificant.

At the appropriate time a distinguished captive of war—a ruler or at least a great captain—was sacrificed, his heart being ripped out and offered to the god of fire. In the cavity in the dead body a special fire priest then placed the sacred fire board and fire stick and, whirling the latter between his palms, elicited the first sparks of new fire. No words were spoken until the spark had been nourished into a flame. This fire was then applied to a great pile of fagots on the temple terrace which grew into a magnificent bonfire, signaling its joyful message across the night. Into this sacred fire was thrown the body of the sacrificed victim in commemoration of the birth of the sun out of the ashes of the god Nanahuatl, who had thrown himself into the fire and perished that the sun might come into being.[37] For many miles around in the blackness Aztecs of all walks of life had been waiting. On mountain peaks and rooftops, in some cases far off across the lake, they hailed the knowledge brought to them by the sight of the first fire of the new calendar round, the knowledge that they would be granted yet another fifty-two-year reprieve and that life would continue. Swift runners in relays carried the first torch taken from the new fire to the temple of Huitzilopochtli where, just before dawn, it too flamed up. From here it was dispensed to all the other gods in the Great Basin and from them to all individual homes. The ceremony was brought to an end when a bundle of fifty-two sticks, counters representing the just elapsed years, was buried in a specially designed altar.

Time was purified and Xiuhteuctli had once again shown himself beneficent.

The Five Suns

The bundle of fifty-two years sufficed for the average Aztec's understanding of time. A deeper look into the abyss, however, had been formulated by the priests, a theory of colossal proportions describing time not as a steady bearing forward of individual years or as lustral renewals but as aeonic bursts or "suns."

There were five of these suns or ages.[38] They were not cyclic, each repeating the other, but were unique and unrepeatable. They were limited in number—five was the maximum number. There will be no more. They have been alike only in that each was an imperfect cosmic experiment ending in collapse. The first four were past aeons; the fifth is the present one. Taken together they make up the complete history of time, of gods, and of man.

In the official version of the Aztec myth the first age was that of the Jaguar or the Earth Sun. There followed the Age of Great Winds, the Age of Fire, the Age of Floods, and the present age, the Age of Earthquakes. These ages are named after the cataclysmic events upon which each one closed or will close, and this fact is of importance in understanding the orientation of the Aztec mind, the first four corresponding to the four elements respectively: earth, air, fire, and water. To each age were assigned one of the five directions and the color therewith associated, thus locking the Aztec's spatial structure into the structure of time—a perfect fit—with the present age assigned to the center.

Each aeon was brought into being when a certain god died or

sacrificed himself to be reborn as the sun of that aeon. The aeons survived a variable number of years and then each disappeared entirely. Indeed so violent was the end of an aeon that all the gods making up its supernatural personnel disappeared with it (we must note that Xiuhteuctli was not included in this view of time). Between the end of one aeon and the beginning of the succeeding one there elapsed a stated number of years which do not properly belong to the realm of time; they are simply a way of counting no-time. The gods reappear as an aeon opens, but that is because they are parts of the cosmos; they certainly all die at the aeon's end. In other words –if we wish to interpret this philosophically–neither time nor the gods are eternal. The aeons are closely linked and, in five vast outbursts, they appear to be arranged in an ascending tale of cataclysms.

It will be worthwhile to recount the main features of this sequence if only to bring home the point that the Aztec lacked the concept of eternity and therefore of eternal repetitiveness.

The first god to become the sun was Tezcatlipoca, whose familiar animal was the jaguar. The light of this original sun was only a half light. People existed in this age but were finally destroyed by a race of misshapen giants. Food consisted of acorns and pine nuts. The giants were finally consumed by jaguars and the feeble sun was stricken from the sky.

The god who became the second sun was Quetzalcoatl. The food was now the seed from the mesquite tree, better than the previous acorns and pine nuts but still primitive. Great hurricanes finally disrupted all things. Men were picked up and blown through the sky into the forests; those who survived became monkeys.

Tlaloc became the third sun. In this aeon men raised a grain which was a forerunner of maize. Time ended when volcanic eruptions occurred and fire and cinders rained down out of the sky to consume the earth. In the general immolation men became birds.

Chalchiuhtlicue, goddess of waters, became the fourth sun. Men lived on a seed called *acicintli*. The ending of this age was of peculiar horror for, as an accompaniment to the gushing up of the hitherto impounded waters in the earth, the sky collapsed and fell upon the earth. In the ensuing floods men turned into fish.

The god Nanahuatl then sacrificed himself to become the present sun. Maize was grown for the first time, fire was domesticated, and the intoxicating drink *octli* was brewed. The full apparatus of culture appeared. The first people created were the Toltecs and with them war became endemic and a service to the gods. This aeon will end in earthquakes which will swallow all things, and the stars will be shaken down from the sky.[39] This will be the final end, and it will occur "when the earth has become tired, when already it is all, when already it is so, when the seed of earth has ended."[40]

2. Creation and the Role of Paradise

The Myths

Inheriting most of their concepts from a rich Mesoamerican past, the Aztecs could be accused of merely imitating others. Indeed they considered themselves to be no more than second-generation Toltecs and looked back to that tumultuous people as their model. They would have deplored any accusation of originality.

While they may have lacked true originality, however, the tissue of their thought was tough and many-colored. This feature can be seen especially in their concepts of creation, four of which interpenetrated all their mythology and were of outstanding importance. These four were creation from preexistent and demonic nature, creation by divine decision and collegial action, creation through blood sacrifice, and creation by victory in battle. Sometimes more than one of these models lies behind a single myth, thus leading to seeming contradictions in the narrative. We are not to suppose, however, that the Aztecs saw these four concepts as mutually exclusive. The myths in which they enshrined these concepts and which have come down to us offer proof of the intensity with which they had studied the miracle of creation. No peoples are ever without awareness of the fact of creation, but many do not take it very seriously. The Aztecs always looked backward and because of this they did take creation seriously.

The First Category of Creation Myths— Creation from Preexistent Matter

Cipactli was the personification of chaos or the unstructured matter out of which the cosmos was created. As we have already noted, this being was thought of as a leviathan, a monstrous alligator, a shark, or a sawfish, inhabiting the ocean as the first of all things. Cipactli in fact was the earth before it had been molded, bisexual and alone. When formed into a primitive version of the earth, this dragon was generally conceived as female and was known as Tlalteuctli, Earth Lady. Like Cipactli, she thrashed about in the bitter waters of chaos, and the Tlascalans believed she had never had a beginning.[1] Sometimes she was conceived as a colossal toad with mouths at all her joints, each running blood.

The myth states that Quetzalcoatl and Tezcatlipoca—here cast as demiurges—assumed the form of serpents.[2] Coiling themselves about Cipactli as she lay on the surface of the sea, they squeezed her into two parts. The upper part they elevated to make the sky, the lower part remained to become the earth. A variant of this myth tells us that the two gods entered her deflated body through her mouth and navel.[3] Four lesser demigods, let into the earth's center by the four directional roads, helped the two raise her upper part, which then became the sky. Under this sky they placed two trees, surrogates for Quetzalcoatl and Tezcatlipoca, and the four demigods then took up their stances at the four corners, acting as atlantes supporting the sky. From the hair of Earth Lady the gods fashioned trees and tall grasses, from her skin flowers and short grasses, from her eyes

Cipactli in the abyss with plumed serpent and marine life behind (Nuttall)

springs, from her mouth rivers and caverns, from her nose valleys, and from her shoulders mountains.

The choice of the two gods assigned the role of creators is of interest, for Tezcatlipoca represents darkness and Quetzalcoatl, as Ehecatl, represents air. They were the two invisibles. Though the matter of creation was gross, the manner was imponderable.

The Second Category of Creation Myths — Creation by Divine Decision

In the beginning, says this myth, there was only the high god who could be referred to as the Self-Created. More generally he was known as Tonacateuctli,[4] Lord of Sustenance. He is interchangeable with Tloque Nahuaque, whom we will discuss later. His venerability and authority are revealed in the codices, where he is always depicted as an old man with a beard. He was the creator and lord of all things and in Aztec times needed no sacrifices, temples, or cult statues.

He lived with his consort Tonacacihuatl, Lady of Sustenance, in a paradise in the highest of the thirteen heavens. Some said that he fashioned the waters from the sky and that he created the earth simply by breathing on it. But a Mexican version of the myth says that he deputed the act of creation to his four sons: the red and the black Tezcatlipoca, Quetzalcoatl (whom he created from his breath), and Huitzilopochtli.[5] Clearly the mythmakers here felt constrained to use the number 4 because of its reference to the fourfold structure of the cosmos. The myth, however, points out that the four immediately delegated their creative mandate to the two who are most clearly seen as complements: Tezcatlipoca and Quetzalcoatl.

In any case what distinguishes this myth is the feature that creation is the result not of sexual union, as is so frequently seen in mythology, but of a theistic decision, an idea in the divine mind which is then translated into demiurgic action by the gods (first four, then two gods). That this reflects a level of political culture wherein a ruler, such as the typical Mexican *tlatoani*, is vested with the plenitude of power which he in turn shares with four senators or princes is obvious to those who realize how mundane structures are often used as models for the structures of heaven. There is nothing unexpected about this picture of creation. What really invites speculation is why this version of the act of creation was not more clearly spelled out by the Aztecs. The order of the various steps, for instance, is haphazard—we are told that fire and half light were created first, then mankind was conjured up to act as a servant of the gods, then man's culture and the count of time, then death, then the vast bulk of the cosmos, earth, sky, etc., and finally the waters that make agriculture possible. Clearly there is some lack of focus here, an inability or a refusal to see creation as a matter of divine logic. Rather, the myth stresses the unqualified decision behind the act. The authority and omnipotence of the high god are indeed protected, but the content of his decision is obscured.

The Third Category of Creation Myths — Creation by Blood Sacrifice

In none of the other three categories were the Aztecs so adamant in their beliefs about the creative act: in this category, creation was defined very concretely. It was not an act *sui generis*, once and for all; rather it was an act of blood sacrifice that could always be repeated and indeed *had* to be repeated. Sacrifice was a mechanic, an inner logic of the universe, almost a god in itself. This concept permeated the whole of Aztec mythology, whether cosmogonic or otherwise. It was also the central preoccupation of the Aztec state.

It appears centrally in the Nanahuatl myth, where the god sacrifices himself by leaping into the fire so as to become the sun, thereby providing light and life for the world. I will comment fully on this later in the chapter; here I simply note the myth's central sacrifice motif.

Blood sacrifice—the method by which the stellar and the atmospheric parts of the cosmos came into being—established for the Aztec mind a corollary: the created cosmos was finite, its strength waned rapidly, and it must constantly be revivified. This renewal could be accomplished only by sacrifice, which thus became a ceaseless activity and an incumbency on those who desired the continuance of the cosmos.

Nanahuatl's original sacrifice was only the great exemplar; a series of sacrifices had to follow it. Gods, earth, and sky were entirely dependent on blood sacrifice to maintain them. Retroactively this defines the blood sacrifice performed in the creation of the sun and the moon as the precursor of necessity in a finite world. If there is to be life, there must be sacrificial death—all this is presented to us in a remorseless Aztec dialectic.

The Fourth Category of Creation Myths —
Creation by Victory

World mythology has several instances of this particular mode of creation. By conceiving of creation as a result of battle, men have taken their cue from the actions of the aggressive state. The second category, creation by divine decision, also looked to the chiefdom or the state as a model but focused on the element of authority. In this fourth and last category the element chosen to define the act of creation is sheer power, the power made evident in the state and in its heroic leader as he overrides all opposition. In this and similar myths of creation the opposition is generally thought of as a malevolent group of titans, numerous, deadly, and determined.

In the Aztec world this myth told of the birth of Huitzilopochtli and his glorious deeds. It ended with Huitzilopochtli's rout and destruction of the Huitznahua, the Four Hundred Southerners. The attack of Mixcoatl on the Four Hundred Mimixcoa is very nearly an exact replica of the tale, as we shall see later. These were originally astral myths—day dominating night and the stars—but they were early taken over and remodeled to the advantage of the state. The god of the day or the sun—in whichever fashion he was conceived—now could stand for a state or for a people, while the political enemies of the state assumed the role of the hostile stars and the other evil forces of night. The ordering of the cosmos, the moon's waning, the leaping forth of the sun from the womb of the earth, the cowering of the stars before the heroism of the dawn—all these were seen as the outcome of a great battle. War had decided an issue of creation.

A critic of this theory can very properly ask how such myths of battle relate to the creation. Creation in essence is an abstraction, whereas battle is a recurrent and visible fact of history.

The Aztecs could indeed view the act of creation intellectually or, in other words, abstractly, but such an explanation never satisfied them. It lacked the drama and the realism of the struggle of tribes and the confrontations of city-states, all of which were so much a part of Aztec culture. Warfare and what resulted from it became a way of life so pervasive, so absorbing, that it infected all other areas of their thought. It was known that a new order and a novel structure of society always appeared out of the victory which followed a crucial battle. To all intents and purposes a true reordering had taken place, sufficiently sweeping to be called, if not creation, at least a re-creation.

The Myth of Star Skirt and Her Children

The astral and the atmospheric loomed large in Aztec cosmology. The night sparkling with stars seemed sufficiently "other" to be the pristine home, the dark source, of all being. The myth in which the Aztecs set forth this understanding cannot therefore be omitted from this survey of their cosmogony.[6] The tale is of significance in any probing of the Aztec mind, for it also talks about man's role in a universe born of night and filled with gods. In the scheme which we have introduced above, it belongs in both the second and the third categories of creation myths, but it goes beyond them in giving a full rationale of the intentions of the gods, the nature of the cosmos, and, finally, man's standing in that cosmos. It is without a doubt the most crucial of all the Aztec myths.

We have already noted the presence of a high god in Aztec mythology, often called Tloque Nahuaque and considered, for certain purposes, to be unique. This god could be and often was divided into two transfigurations, male and female counterparts, as in the case of the gods called the Lord and Lady of Sustenance. We shall be dealing with these gods at more length later.

There was another of these ethereal couples, the male Citlallatonac, Starshine, and the female Citlalinicue, Star Skirt. In the myth under consideration, the female is especially featured. She was the Great Mother of the stars and as such was peculiarly incarnate in the Milky Way.[7] The stars were thought to number 1,600, which was simply four times the number of the Mimixcoa or the Huitznahua–groups of nocturnal gods conquered by the sun in his several avatars. The number 1,600 can be best translated as "innumerable."

Enthroned in the Milky Way Star Skirt was the source of all wisdom, and she communicated with other beings through her messenger, a hawk. All the stars were gods and she had borne them all. Even the two great creator gods, Quetzalcoatl and Tezcatlipoca, were her sons. It was about her that there was told this tale, one of the most majestic and frightening myths of the Aztec world.

In the beginning Star Skirt bore the *tecpatl*, the flint knife, the first thing, itself a god. The *tecpatl* was the knife used by the Aztec cult in human sacrifice. At its birth this sacred object fell out of the night sky onto Chicomoztoc, the legendary site in the north claimed by the Aztecs as their original home. From the *tecpatl* forthwith sprang the 1,600 gods. At first these divine beings lived deprived of such services as should have been theirs by right. Finally they sent forth the hawk with a petition to the all mother asking that she provide humans to serve them not only as domestics and slaves but also as food. In her wisdom the venerable goddess sent down word to her children that they should acquire the bones of a former race of men, presently in the land of the dead, and revive them. After they had considered this well, the 1,600 gods ordered that Xolotl, a god with knowledge of the underworld, should be the one to undertake the errand; he was warned to hasten lest the Lord of the Dead, after releasing the bones, should change his mind. Xolotl descended into the underworld and secured the precious bones but, as predicted, was hotly pursued by the Lord of the Dead, who had granted the bones as a whim and then changed his mind. On his flight back into the world of light and life, Xolotl stumbled and the bones were shattered. Nevertheless he brought them back, imperfect as they were, and the gods surrounded them and performed autosacrifice over them. Their sacrificial blood dripping on the dry bones brought forth first a male child, later a female. There being no human mother to suckle them, Xolotl raised them on the milk of the maguey. Thus appeared the race of men, who henceforward would serve the gods.

That the Aztecs should have given the *tecpatl*, a cult instrument, such a central place in the myth of the creation of gods and men seems to us egregious; superficially it appears to be a reversal of the commonly acknowledged role of cult. Cult is generally thought to be a reality secondary to the divine. It takes what is already given, namely the supernatural, and only then does it respond to it, imitate it, or attempt to influence it. Yet in this myth of Star Skirt and her children all is reversed, for here cult, symbolized by the sacrificial knife, precedes the gods and indeed produces them. Here the knife is the ultimate principle in the universe. If we erase the high god or the goddess from the picture we can see that sacrifice as a central cultic act was of a holiness superior to that possessed by ordinary gods. The deities that haunted the cosmos were all thought to be subject to the overarching logic of blood sacrifice. Having been born out of it they must inescapably submit to all its mandates; their divinity can only be tested against it.

The Aztecs inherited this sanguinary feature of their religious life from the Toltecs, but they seem to have carried it to an obsessive extreme. It is this inordinate feature of the myth which strikes us first and which lends it such a horrid and fascinating aura.

The myth begins with the highest authoritative level of godhead, that of Star Skirt and the *tecpatl*, her *modus operandi*. It then drops to the level of gods, describing them as incomplete. They lacked service and therefore they lacked dignity. This introduces us to the third and lowest level—that of men—whom we now understand as being clearly menial. Even this level of being, however, is created by sacrificial means, the effusion of blood by the gods. All things are subject to the *tecpatl*.

The Physical Sun

There is one god, the sun, whose myth belongs in both the third and the fourth creation categories. He was a distinctive deity and is called in one of the sources the solitary god. In the eyes of the Aztecs there was something about the sun which expressed the very essence of divinity, some characteristics that seemed to be a special revelation of godlike power.

The sun's name was Tonatiuh, He Who Goes Forth Shining. Behind the name is the concept of a heroic emergence from the darkness. Besides this personal name, appellations describing his career in detail were frequently applied to him. He was the Resplendent One or the Heavenly Marksman, a title which referred to him as a warrior who shoots his rays through the vast spaces of the sky.[8] Above all he was the Eagle, symbol of drifting flight, of kingly disdain of those beneath, and of sudden and swift predation. As the eagle rises on the updraft of the morning air and as he plummets down to strike his prey, so does the sun rise and finally swoop down and disappear from our sight. The sun's journey from dawn to dusk was an eagle's flight.

The sun was loosely thought to inhabit a house far out in the eastern waters, a veritable castle of delights, of dancing and the sounds of drumming, of conch trumpets and jangling rattles.[9] In the halls of that palace fluttered and sang the most beautiful birds in the world: these were the souls of warriors waiting for the supreme moment of the day. At dawn the sun emerged from this house, escorted by the full retinue of his warriors, men who had died on the field of battle or perished bent over the stone of sacrifice. At that moment the sun was the Jeweled Prince, young and fresh at the beginning of his adventures, swaggering and basking in the adulation of his troops as they whirled about him, shrieking their war cries and clashing their shields.[10]

Having passed the zenith the sun's flight rapidly weakened and he became He Who Swoops like an Eagle.[11] At the end of his course, as the Earthbound Sun, he was swallowed by the earth monster.[12] Defeated, he has now become Yaomicqui, one who has died at the hands of the enemy, though alternatively he could be thought of as having been captured by the Evening Star and sacrificed. Thus the concept of the sun's journey as a coursing over the battlefield is brought to its expected conclusion.

In the underworld the sun became the Night Sun, and he moved through the galleries under the earth accompanied by the dead, shedding for them a gloomy and grotesque light.[13] He had become a blind, stumbling, and wrinkled monster. All this until his rejuvenation once again at dawn.

But there was a more explicit and, indeed, dramatic myth of the death and resurrection of the sun. We know of this only in a Tarascan, in other words a non-Aztec, version.[14] However, this version is quoted in our source by people speaking the Aztec tongue, and we have every right to presume that it was well known to the Aztecs, probably having come down to them from their Chichimec past. The tale runs as follows.

The old and declining sun agreed to play a game of *tlachtli* with the night. The sun was vanquished and, according to custom, was sacrificed. Later his posthumous son was subsequently raised as a foundling. When this youth discovered the truth of his parentage, he searched for his father's burial, located the bones, and bore them away on his back. On this journey he stopped to shoot some quail, during which incident the old sun's bones were transformed into a deer which sprang away into the north, its pelt streaming forth rays.

There is an Aztec myth that speaks to the same effect.[15] Here the sun, who could be conceived as a deer and was called Piltzinteuctli, played *tlachtli* with Xolotl, who in this tale was the Evening Star. Defeated, the sun fell into the House of Night but rose victorious after another game had been played in the underworld. Nothing is explicitly said in this myth of Piltzinteuctli's vindication by a son; but his name, Lord of Princes, might imply a solar filiation. Among the Totonacs on the coast, in this same vein, it was foretold that a son of the sun would someday come to renovate the world.[16]

To the Aztecs the physical sun thus had two careers: his diurnal race, which had a beginning and an ending and was thought of as a procession over the battlefield, and his nocturnal saga, which revolved around his defeat in the ball game. The mystery of the sun's rising is thought of as the reincarnation of the dead sun in the person of his son and successor. Each day's sun, therefore, is different, though connected by descent with the previous one.

The Sun as the Measure of Doom

Like all the other gods the sun had a date-name which commemorated the day he had been born and therefore represented his destiny. This was the day *naui olin* or 4 Movement.

Olin means "it moves" (or, as a noun, "that which has moved"), as the earth moves in a quake. Because of the lordliness of this date-name (which also became a transfiguration of the sun) it was adjudged to belong particularly to the elite knightly class, and the day was celebrated by them with great solemnity. The day was of such

The glyph 4 Movement

good augury that any man born under its sign was certain to become a ruler or, at the very least, a magnate.

But there is another meaning behind the name Four Movement.
This was the knowledge that when this present sun, the fifth and
last in the sequence of suns, should crash down into the darkness
it would occur on a day 4 Movement. Thus the very fact that the
sun bore that name was also an earnest of the doom that awaited
him.[17] On that day of the *tonalpohualli* and on the preceding four
days, therefore, all the people in Mexico drew blood from their
bodies, thus sacrificing part of themselves to strengthen the sun and
to stave off his predicted disastrous end.

By tying the world's end to the birthdate of the present sun, the
Aztecs were contradicting their belief that the world would end only
on the final moment of a fifty-two-year cycle. Ostensibly these are
different dooms, yet on closer inspection both are variants of the
same thing. In the first instance the sun was to fall out of the sky,
leaving behind only darkness; in the second he would simply fail
to rise again out of the underearth. In either case it is the failure of
the sun which extinguishes the age. The sun was not necessarily
the pivot of time, but within time he provided the concrete spectacle
of impending doom.

The Aztecs' sense of the impermanence of things was very acute:
the threat of nothingness constantly menaced them. Night and darkness seemed more powerful essences than the light of day and in the
end would win out. Though Tonatiuh was so great a conqueror,
even his days were numbered.

The Primal Sun Myth

The Aztec saw the sun as a warrior before all else—the solar rays
being his darts. The first act performed by him after creation was to
be characteristic of the violence which so clearly marked him. Nevertheless this conquering sun was not always so resplendent and his
full mythology is sometimes surprising.

We recall from the previous chapter that there were five aeons,
each designated as a special sun. Under the name Four Movement,
Tonatiuh is the present or fifth sun. The myth we are concerned with
relates the appearance of this final sun.[18]

In the nothingness that followed the extinction of the fourth aeon,
four gods, each connected with one of the cardinal directions, de-

The descent of warrior spirits from the home of the sun (Nuttall)

cided upon a mighty act of creation. They realized that it was up to them to call into being a sun which would give light to the darkness and would rise and set to provide the divisions of time. For this purpose they gathered in the city of Teotihuacan, the Place Where the God Was Created, which had been the seat of a civilization of the preceding aeon but was now ruined and empty.

The creator gods knew that such a work as theirs could succeed only as a result of some supreme sacrifice, and to this end they piled up a great bonfire. They then debated who among them would cast himself onto the pyre to become, by that sacrificial death, the regnant sun. None of the four dared to face the heat of the fire. They finally accepted the offers of two gods, Nanahuatl, the Ulcerated One, and Teucciztecatl, He of Teucciztlan, who both volunteered their lives.

Nanahuatl came from an ancient and high lineage of gods. However, he was distinguished by his poverty and his hideous deformities—his whole body was covered with running sores. Because of this the gods turned first to the god from Teucciztlan. Four times this god rushed toward the fire and four times he retreated, unable to face death in the flames. At this point the wretched Nanahuatl showed himself of superlative bravery: he threw himself into the fire to perish and become the sun. In a final and bitter emulation the god from Teucciztlan threw himself into the flames and became the moon, a lesser luminary.

Now in the darkness the four creator gods waited for Tonatiuh's appearance. But the red glow of dawn surrounded the entire horizon and none could be sure which was the east, the place of appearances. The effects of this disorientation were increased when it was discovered that the sun had become imperious and was challenging the gods by refusing to move. In return for his rising he demanded their hearts and blood as his food and drink. This so angered the Morning Star, the most baleful of the innumerable gods and their great champion in this first cosmic contest, that he replied to the sun's defiance by confronting him. But the sun was an even more practiced warrior than he. The great duel between them continued until the sun finally struck down the Morning Star, who fell defeated into the icy underworld.

By his initial refusal to light the world and by defeating their champion, the sun thus overpowered the gods and himself assumed their sovereignty. The entire roster of divinity, 1,600 gods, thereupon submitted to the sun and allowed themselves to be sacrificed. It was the god Xolotl who assumed the role of sacrificer, and when his gruesome task was completed he sacrificed himself.[19] Placated and strengthened by such an infusion of blood, Tonatiuh now rose above the eastern horizon and began the first day.

The main outline of this fascinating myth is clear and does not require much commentary. It is the old, old story told in every part of the world of the battle between the sun and the stars or between day and night. Here its dramatic quality is increased by describing it as an event of the first and therefore of the archetypal day. The periodicity of the sun's rising is here submerged and seen as a single, once and for all event where the sun, or the day, is victorious. But this merely outlines the scenario; certain elements in the story need further comment.

The first element is the placement of the myth in Teotihuacan, the well-known archaeological site just outside present-day Mexico City. In shaping the primal sun myth the Aztecs cast this ruined capital as a dead city of the fourth aeon. The beacon fire that formerly must have burned throughout every night on the top of the Pyramid of the Sun in Teotihuacan becomes the divine hearth into which

Nanahuatl hurled himself. This leads us to suggest, when we interpret the myth cultically, that it explicated the New Fire ceremony which, as we have seen, was designed to strengthen and placate the sun so he would rise to usher in another cycle of fifty-two years.

The second element to consider is the importance of orientation in the myth. The four creator gods are each assigned a direction. There is quarreling among them as each one vies to face the direction in which the sun will first appear; it was in fact the orientation of each of the four gods at that sunup which defined once and for all the four directions. In the myth mention is made of four dawns, each in one of the four quarters, to point up the chaotic conditions before the uprearing of the sun. By insisting on the orientation of the sun as one of his most distinctive features, the myth is strictly conforming to that elaboration of symbolically rich compass points so congenial to the Aztec mind. As it turned out, the new creation faced the west.

A third element is the reduction of the universal conflict between the sun and the stars to one confrontation, that between the sun and one star in particular, the planet Venus in its two phases: the Evening Star and the Morning Star.[20] The Morning Star incorporates in himself the totality of stars and he becomes the gigantic symbol of all that is dangerous, dark, and cold. His demonic quality is well brought out when we learn that the darts he hurls turn to frost as they fall to earth and that he becomes in the underworld the god Cetl, the personification of ice.[21] The Evening Star was to metamorphose and to become, by an art of self-sacrifice, the sun himself. Thus, in spite of its unpretentiousness it carries the true splendor.

A fourth element has to do with the theology of the sun cult, namely the emphasis in the myth on the total sovereignty of the sun over all the other gods, whether it is the four creator gods or the 1,600 stellar beings. In the myth Tonatiuh faces down all the gods and then causes them to be sacrificed. I strongly suspect that this powerful statement points to the military orders in the Aztec states, the knights who especially worshiped Tonatiuh and who celebrated his rites in ways forbidden to commoners. It was to the advantage of this elite class–the eagle and jaguar warriors–to claim supremacy for their god over all others; in this they would simply be reinforcing their own claims to dominion in the temporal sphere even as the sun ruled for the purposes of the myth over the cosmos. It is interesting to note that nowhere else in Aztec mythology is complete sovereignty claimed for any god, even though there were several high gods and Great Mothers who might well have made that claim.

The fact that this myth was particularly the possession of the knights further explains the pivotal role played in it by sacrifice. For in the Aztec world the knight was the person most liable to be captured on the field of battle and later sacrificed. His whole life was a preparation for sacrifice, whether he died on the battleground or, spread-eagled over the stone of sacrifice, yielded up his heart to the sun. The entire myth turns on the point of sacrifice.

These then are the most obvious elements in the myth. There is also one especially difficult question. This concerns the identity of Nanahuatl. Who was he and why did the Aztec mythmakers attribute the creation of the sun to such a deformed god?

Nanahuatl was the pustulous god of the Aztecs, patron of all those with diseases of the skin. His very name means "pustule" or "ulcer," and he had a shrine in Mexico called Netlatiloyan, Where People Are Hidden. Gold was the excrement of this god and it was thought to be a specific medicine. In the fourth aeon Nanahuatl had lived in Tamoanchan, the Olympian home of the gods, and he had been involved in securing the first maize with which gods and men are sustained. He came, as we have noted, from distinguished parents.[22] His father was the deified blade of sacrifice, Itzpapalotl or Obsidian Knife Butterfly, here unexpectedly considered to be masculine. His mother was the goddess of the maize-bearing earth. He had, however, been raised by another divine couple representing the union of sun and fruitful earth. Sahagún vaguely connects Nanahuatl with Xipe, the springtime sun, but it is much more likely that he is Xolotl, the Evening Star.

Behind the myth was reality. What the ancients of Mesoamerica saw, as all men do, was the Evening Star plunging down into the vast fires of the sun after he had fallen below the horizon. This was thought of as an act of the will. Insignificant when compared to the sun, the Evening Star yet managed, by immolation in those fires of darkness, to be born again as a new and rejuvenated sun. The star's insignificance and impotency are celebrated in the deformity and disease of the god Nanahuatl, who in turn, as stated above, was a transfiguration of Xolotl. It was not birth, as animals and men know it, which renews the sun but death in his darkening fires. Behind the myth there was thus a powerful sense of the identification of the sun and the planet Venus. In the myth they could be understood as three separate divine beings. But the truth is that they were one. If thought of as the evening sun, he dies. If thought of as the Evening Star, he is sacrificed. If thought of as the sun at dawn, he duels his alter ego, the Morning Star, to a compelling victory. In any case out of the underworld will come a transformed and pristine sun. The myth of the fifth sun is the most magical tale in the whole corpus of Aztec myth, for it is an unsurpassed *reductio ad unum*.

It may seem difficult to make a connection between Nanahuatl and the glorious Tonatiuh, who would become his transfiguration in the fifth aeon. Yet the myth does not try to hide the connection between the unblemished hero and the disfigured one; rather it insists on it.

Paradise

In all ages man has delighted in exercising his talents for fantasy in his depictions of paradise. The fragile and often harsh conditions of his life have given him the incentive to dream of a vanished glory. His need to create an Eden and paint it in loving colors is simply a commentary on his own incomplete nature and broken accomplishments.

Paradise is always a corollary to the concept of creation. Men have occasionally thought of the creation of the cosmos as a total and an unsullied act. This is usually made concrete by the mythmakers either in the action of a "good" creator (as in Genesis 1) or as occurring in a "good" and pure place (as in Genesis 2). It is this latter concept which gives rise to paradise. A heavy emphasis on paradise, however, commonly led mythmakers to suppress the creator and to define the misery of man as the result of an original alienation, either temporary or permanent, from paradise. The Aztecs did not believe this.

Tamoanchan was one of the common names for the Aztec paradise. The etymology of the word was a puzzle to the Aztecs and is even less clear today.[23] Like the garden in Eden, Tamoanchan had an earthly locus: the Aztecs more or less agreed that it had been in the area comprised by the present state of Morelos. Some scholars today assign it even more precisely to Xochicalco.[24] This site, with its marvelous vistas and its extensive pre-Aztec ruins, is in every way worthy of the claim made for it. It was once a fortified city and a ceremonial center contemporary with the last days of Teotihuacan and the floruit of Tula. The remains indicate that it had been a particularly holy site and a point of convergence for important cultural and religious influences from as far off as Mayaland. By the time of the Aztecs it had fallen away from its glory and was only vaguely remembered. What few things the Aztecs remembered of it, however, gave them the opportunity to romanticize it and cast it in the role of an earthly paradise. Even Tula did not attain such a high dignity.

So in the nature of things the Aztecs mythologized Tamoanchan. To this place, they said, were brought the bones out of which men were created, and here the newly formed children were nourished by Xolotl. It was the place of origin for all men, but they could not lay claim to it afterward. It had not been theirs to possess in the first place.

Rather it belonged to the gods. It was a never-never land where the lovely Xochiquetzal, the Earth Mother or Precious Flower, was perpetual mistress. Around her were maidens or nymphs, along with buffoons and dwarves to entertain her. All manner of delights surrounded the young goddess there, and in her enjoyment of these she was well protected from all rude intrusions. This holy retreat could be thought of as far off to the south, situated on the top of a mountain so high it almost touched the moon.[25]

There was another depiction of Tamoanchan which is of interest. In some sources it was said to be the abode of the Lord of Sustenance and his consort, situated in the highest of the thirteen heavens. There all the gods were created and there they had once lived in original blessedness, subsisting on maize, the holy food. In the center of this land of eternal summer and flowing waters stood a tree whose boughs were not supposed to be broken or its flowers plucked.[26] Exotic birds caroled among its leaves without ceasing. All was joy in this world until the gods unaccountably defied the injunction of the Lord of Sustenance: they desecrated the tree by tearing off long sprays of its blossoms and thus destroyed its pristine beauty. For this breach of the divine command the gods were cast down out of Tamoanchan to take up various stations allotted to them in the underworld, on the earth, and in the sky.

The myth could be told in even more detail. One version recounted that it was the deity Obsidian Knife Butterfly who alone disobeyed the divine command, for which she was hurled down to earth to become the demonic being she is.[27]

This myth looks remarkably like the story of the garden of Eden

and the expulsion of Adam and Eve. The question of possible con-
tamination through the early friars therefore legitimately arises.
However, the notable feature of this Aztec myth is that it is concerned not with the fall of man from grace as in the biblical tale but
with the fall of the gods—or of a single god who is surrogate for
the rest.

We interpret the Aztec myth of paradise in the following way:
joy and loveliness are the proper and pristine state of things, and
the loss of this state was a demonic act, the first such, and resulted
in the present order of things. Nothing is said about the possibility
of the gods ever recovering their first innocence. Salvation from the
present order of things, in fact, seems to be impossible even for these
divine beings. The corollary of this is that man inherits from his
divine superiors a world worsened by *their* wicked actions—and this
will henceforth be the immutable structure of the cosmos.

Tamoanchan is intimately associated with that curious couple we
have already had occasion to notice, Cipactonal and Oxomoco. The
confusion which envelops them in our sources stems from two facts.
It would seem that they were once, in some remote period, high
gods no different from the Lord and Lady of Sustenance. If so, they
rightfully belong in paradise. On the other hand they were so anti-
quated by the time of the Aztecs and so overlaid by later levels of
myth that they had dwindled to almost human stature and, as first
progenitors (like Adam and Eve), had assumed the role of culture
innovators. They are still situated in Tamoanchan, but it too has been
brought down to a more earthly level identified as a specific city.
As a result of the diffusion of Toltec culture these two deities had
been taken in pre-Aztec times into the Mayan area, where they are
later found among the Quiché as the Grandfather and Grandmother.[28] Cipactonal in fact is found as far south as Nicaragua.

Cipactonal and Oxomoco are said to have lived in the first aeon
long before the flood.[29] Myth thus insists on their great age. Cipactonal, in fact, is said to have been created in the first dawn. All
men are descended from these two.[30] They had lived in paradise but
had been cast out in the great expulsion mentioned above (Oxomoco
being at this point identified as the goddess Obsidian Knife Butterfly).[31] This part of the myth relates to the antique status of these two
as gods.

In turning to their connections with the cave in the earthly Tamoanchan, we find that they are the first humans and are thought to
have been infinitely wise. As culture heroes they created the world

of civilized man, giving him knowledge of herbs and curing, of the mining and polishing of turquoise and other precious stones, of the ascertaining of the fates, of the casting of lots to discover the divine will of the gods, of the stars, of the painting of religious books, and finally of a proper respect for fire.[32] But it was as lords of the *tonalpohualli* that they were best known. The count of the days was their great work.[33]

The paradise to which the warrior aspired was quite different from Tamoanchan. It was a closed and very private society; only men of the knightly orders–the eagle and jaguar warriors–could hope for entry, and even in this group only those who had died well, who had sacrificed prisoners, or who themselves had been captured and sacrificed could qualify.[34] That knight who had died earning glory for himself and giving sustenance to the sun was rewarded by inclusion in the contingent which escorted the star of day at his dawning. After four years of bravura display in this otherworld, he became a cloud or a fiery bird singing raptly in the dawn.

We may briefly note two other elysian paradises which the Aztecs inherited. The best known was Tlalocan, the Place of Tlaloc. This was a paradise contrived by an agricultural people whose culture revolved around rain and drought. Naturally enough Tlalocan is situated on an Olympian height, for it is there the rain clouds gather.[35] In Tlalocan the storm king ruled and the only mortals who inhabited it were those who came by invitation, as it were, for the god favored those who drowned, who were struck by lightning, who died of dropsy or diseases of the skin, etc. These fortunate dead lived happy lives in this Mesoamerican Avalon and their brows were wreathed with ever fresh garlands.

Cincalco was a variant of Tlalocan, though to the Mexican Aztecs it had a very specific locale.[36] The promontory of Chapultepec, which jutted out into Lake Tezcoco just west of the island city of Mexico-Tenochtitlan, was thought to be that rock through which one gained entrance to the otherworld of Cincalco, the House of Maize. The water gushing out from the base of the rock had caused the original sanctity of the place and had conjured up ideas of arcane caverns within, well stored with waters and the good fruit of the earth. In the world within the rock there was thought to be continuous feasting in the presence of the legendary Toltec ruler Huemac, reported to have disappeared into the interior of the rock after the fall of the Toltec state. Huemac, however, was not solely the Toltec hero in Cincalco but was also a transfiguration of Tlaloc, and his palace there was guarded by doorkeeper gods.

When we consider these various paradises we can see a constant theme: men do not inhabit paradise unless, as in the case of Tlalocan, they are selected by the god himself or, as knights, they have repeated the original solar sacrifice. These alone are the fortunate ones.

3. The Quality of the Numinous

The Masks of God

In the language spoken by the Aztecs the word for god was *teotl*. The glyph they used to evoke this word was the picture of the sun. Consonant with this is the fact that, when used alone, the word generally had reference to the sun–who is thus dignified as "the god." In compounds the word *teotl* has secondary meanings of that which is difficult, vast, awesome, and dangerous, or it may have the meaning of genuineness and rareness.[1] The word basically expressed the extravagant whether in good or ill, and from this we might theorize that the demonic was a main ingredient in the Aztec concept of godhead. We shall be discussing farther on when an Aztec god is a distinctive being and when he is a numinous essence. The line between them is difficult to draw.

In the early part of the year 1519, at an anchorage probably off the Tabasco coast, the first formal meeting between the ambassadors to Moteuczoma II and the party of Hernando Cortés took place. Because the year 1519 happened to be approximately the same as the year 1 Reed (Ce Acatl) in the Mexican calendar, a catastrophic interpretation was placed on this meeting by the contemporary peoples of Mesoamerica, the Aztecs in particular viewing it as ominous. Ce Acatl was the date-name of the god Quetzalcoatl, and according to an old prophecy it was also the year-date when that god would return from his exile in the east to reinstitute the glories of the Toltec empire. Because of this calendrical coincidence Cortés was thought by Moteuczoma to be the very person of Quetzalcoatl or, barring that, to be at least his lineal successor. The sacred was crowding closely in upon the Aztecs.

Moteuczoma's response on being informed of the portentous landfall was to send Cortés the regalia of four gods: Xiuhteuctli, Tezcatlipoca, Tlaloc, and Quetzalcoatl.[2] These pieces of regalia included costly scepters, shields, and war bonnets in gold, silver, turquoise, mosaics, rare woods, and feathers of all sorts. These were classed by the Spaniards as gifts, but they were not that at all: they were tokens of submission to the divine powers.

Two things should be noted here. According to one source the regalia of Quetzalcoatl was first offered directly to Cortés, while the rest of the items were deposited at his feet.[3] A superficial interpretation of this could be that it was simply a matter of fit; if the Aztecs should be mistaken and the god was not Quetzalcoatl, he would be one of the other three and could easily select his proper regalia.

But it is probably more than that. The number 4 recalls for us that the most prominent Aztec deities easily divided themselves into four transfigurations, to return again to singleness in the understanding of their worshipers when unity was more appropriate. Could it be, in this most serious crisis of the Aztec world, that the four gods, however disparate we know them to have been, were thought of for purposes of homage as a mere quadruplicate transfiguration of a single divine being? And, if so, was this divine being a named god or was he the essence of godhead, undifferentiated and numinous?

I know of no statement in any of our sources that the four gods—Xiuhteuctli, Tezcatlipoca, Tlaloc, and Quetzalcoatl—were related to each other as, for instance, were the Four Tlaloque or the four avatars of Tlazolteotl. Nevertheless, I think it significant that the first great confrontation should have brought forward these particular gods. If a scholar today were asked to select the four preeminent male gods of the Aztecs, he would almost certainly indicate these four. If they represented the fullness of deity not only in the number 4 but also in their conglomerate jurisdiction and powers, then we might be dealing with a concept of the numinous that stands behind the Aztec pantheon and washes all the gods in its colors.[4]

This concept is not in any sense to be confused with monotheism, as if one god, here unnamed, split into four forms for easier service and comprehension. Rather it suggests a type of pantheism where the pantheistic essence splits and assumes various masks, each identified and unmistakable. This style of religious thinking may well provide us with an explanation of what happened on the coast of Tabasco in 1519. It may be one of the keys to a more correct understanding of Aztec godhead.

One of the salient features of certain of the Aztec gods is their seeming ability to absorb other gods or at least to possess themselves of portions of their powers and prerogatives. To understand this, we must discuss one of the cardinal points in Aztec thought: the power of the mask. The Aztecs carried the principle of the mask to extremes; they saw it as a medium by which the gods lost their separateness and merged into communities.

I am using the term "mask" here in a very broad sense.[5] It is meant to include face paint, vestments, and all the other regalia. The Aztecs had a very concrete, hard-edged picture of each of their gods, who were in general anthropomorphically conceived. Visual perception played the same role in Aztec religion as does dogma in the history of western religions. The Aztec gods, in brief, were thought to be adequately defined by their attire. The fire god, for instance, was known to be painted all over yellow and to have his face crossed by two black bars. He wore the special turquoise diadem of sovereignty. On his back he carried a paper replica of the fire dragon, and he brandished a peculiar curved baton. His turquoise pectoral was a stylized butterfly, the symbol of fire. He and only he had the right to be thus arrayed; he could never be mistaken for another god when so invested. For the Aztecs the mask, by its power of definition and localization, was as impressively divine as the god himself.

The corollary of this is that whatever god wore the regalia of another god, or a part of the regalia, effectively wielded the powers proper to that god, or at least a part of his powers. We can present this another way by saying that the mask is the fully defined and true god. The godlike essence behind the mask will then represent the concept of the numinous which is not brought into focus until it has acquired a mask. The regalia of Tezcatlipoca, for instance, we know to have been adored as if it were the god himself.

There was thus what we might call a mask pool in Aztec religion. The parti-colored divine essences dipped into this pool and selected their own attributes, thus becoming recognizable gods. But the pool was held in common. Gods other than Quetzalcoatl could wear his wind jewel and wield the special magic that went with it. Other gods could adorn themselves with Tezcatlipoca's smoking mirror whenever they exercised the power it symbolized. At first glance this appears to be a chaotic and shifting world, but it is not. The various items of the divine regalia continued to symbolize the same things no matter what gods assumed them.

The Principle of Divine Transfigurations

In some instances a god was thought to become another god, in effect taking over his whole regalia along with all its attached powers. This transfiguration could be simply for the purpose of one mythic episode, as when Xolotl takes Quetzalcoatl's place in the myth of the recovery of the bones of men, or it could be a permanent duplication, as in the case of the Tlascalan deity Camaxtli, who is known to always be the god Mixcoatl. It is impossible to understand the Aztec pantheon without a grasp of such divine transfigurations.

Some of these transfigurations were initiated when charismatic rulers or priests died and were later shaped into demigods, patterned after the deities with whom they had formerly been connected. Camaxtli's worshipers, for instance, preserved his ashes as relics, which leads us to suspect that he had once been a leader of a tribe which worshiped Mixcoatl. Transfigurations could also arise when foreign gods were added to the pantheon.[6] The priesthood would have been well aware of any similarities that marked the cults and myths of Aztec and of alien gods and so could have regularized the transfigurations. In such an event no doubt the Aztec god would have acted as the model, while the imported god would have been considered for certain purposes as his transfiguration. For example, Xipe is generally thought to have originally been a sun and fertility deity from the Pacific coast of Mesoamerica, where he was known as Yopi. The Aztec theologians cast him (when he was not thought of as purely himself) as a transfiguration of the red or diurnal aspect of Tezcatlipoca, named Tlatlauhqui Tezcatlipoca, this latter deity being himself a transfiguration of the black or nocturnal aspect of Tezcatlipoca, namely Yayauhqui Tezcatlipoca.

When one goes carefully over the roster of the Aztec gods, it can be seen that they are either models or transfigurations of models or —as in the case of the red Tezcatlipoca—they are both at once. Here one might venture the opinion that there existed a concept that the god was seldom himself alone inasmuch as he existed in a continuum of divine beings, all of whom were linked in a wavering pattern of transfigurations. As a matter of fact, since the gods were all allotted birthdays (which in the *tonalpohualli* always themselves possessed divine characteristics and ominous meanings), each was born with an initial transfiguration. And, in such an entangling network, it was relatively easy for deities to shift their sex. Oxomoco, a goddess of divinatory skills, and her consort Cipactonal occasionally appear reversed in sex. Obsidian Knife Butterfly appears reversed in sex, and other examples could be cited.

The ramifications of such a system can be extremely confusing. Let us take the case of Tonacateuctli, Lord of Sustenance, by way of illustration. He is the patron deity of the first day-sign in the Aztec calendar and thus represents beginnings. He is ancient and had once been known as the god who had created the earth by blowing on it. His jurisdiction is a general one over the sky, over the waters it contains, and over the heat of the sun in summer–all this adding up to his reputation as a bringer of abundance. In his highest or model manifestation he stands for first things, and he is accordingly depicted in the codices as extremely aged. But even there he is split in two, giving rise to a female counterpart and consort, Tonacacihuatl, Lady of Sustenance–one of his important transfigurations. Like him she appears as the providential source of human life. At this high level of abstract authority and primacy the Lord of Sustenance may also appear transfigured as the ancient god of the Milky Way, the spouse of the stellar mother goddess Star Skirt.

In his model form as the master of beginnings the Lord of Sustenance almost automatically becomes associated with human procreation. Thus his next transfiguration appears as Two God, a deity also concerned with first things. From this latter god we can derive the transfigurations Two Lord and Two Lady, the gods in the thirteenth heaven who send children down to earth to be born.[7] This is a purely intellectual concept concerning the origin of children, but it has an obvious counterpart in the sexual act on earth. The Lord of Sustenance, therefore, insofar as he represented essential heat, could assume the shape, colors, and posture of Xochipilli, the youthful god of sexuality and the rising sun.[8] Also, as the creator of children, the Lord of Sustenance may appear in iconography wearing the Huaxtec headdress generally reserved for Quetzalcoatl. More remote from this line of reasoning, the Lord of Sustenance may be transfigured into a god with jurisdiction over the vast northern lands of the Gran Chichimeca, considered by the Aztecs to have been their ancestral home. In this transfiguration he may be referred to as Master of the Steppe, the Snarer, or Owner of the Mountains, a spread of titles which would seem far more appropriate to Mixcoatl.[9]

Such a list of transfigurations for one god makes clear the Aztec concept of the numinous as a continuum of divine activity. No one god can ever become all the other known deities or even a majority of them, but all can become at least one other god and sometimes more. Tezcatlipoca, for instance, is the most prolific of the model gods in spawning transfigurations; he can appear as at least fourteen other deities with an almost equal number of epithetical and date variations also available to him. Mictlanteuctli, Lord of the Dead, is apparently limited to a single important transfiguration, that of the god Tzontemoc, though many other gods can take on Mictlanteuctli's regalia.

A continuum is the opposite of a formal association of parts. It implies wholeness of quality and singleness of essence, and it therefore rejects structuring, which is the articulation of parts. The Aztecs felt a need to see their gods in various transfigurations, and this was allowable because they could also experience the divine as a numinous autonomy, pure and undifferentiated. Their priests therefore never evolved a pantheon or theater of the gods where each was restricted to one shape for eternity. Though the masks were many, the divine world was one.

But how then did the Aztecs really conceive of their gods?

Granting our contention that the divine world was a numinous continuum, this still did not drive the Aztecs to doubt the basic separateness of their gods. While Huitzilopochtli might assume the bearing and jurisdiction of Mixcoatl at times, while Xipe could appear as a form of Tezcatlipoca, nevertheless there was always a recognizable, indelible godhead. To make such a statement is to lay oneself open to the charge of inconsistency, for it would seem that the Aztecs understood their gods as either insubstantial shadows fleeting forever over the face of a numinous backdrop or as concrete beings individually named and shaped, where the numinous simply becomes a convenient pigeonhole into which the overly clever scholar slips them all.

I believe that we can more easily grasp the Aztec principle of divine transfigurations by first realizing that the gods were not so much substantial entities as qualities. Tezcatlipoca is in his essence the master quality of darkness and unknowability; thus he can appear concretely as a god of war, or a god of mockery, or of feasting, or as an enemy of Quetzalcoatl. Xipe is the master quality of vernal renewal and budding; thus he appears as the sun god, or as a dying young god, or as a god of agriculture. Tonatiuh is the master quality of the martial and the heroic, and thus he can appear as the god of warriors, or as the rising or setting sun, or as the sun conquered by the night. Tlazolteotl is the quality of femaleness; thus she appears as the Earth Mother, as a goddess of sexuality, as the mistress of spinning, and so forth.

It is because the gods were understood to epitomize certain qualities that they moved so easily from one transfiguration into another, for a quality by definition is shapeless and within limits can take on various disguises. But, though shapeless, a quality need not be without precise definition.

Thus to the Aztecs the numinous was qualified. Though it was one thing and only one, it was shaded and made iridescent by qualities. These shadings could be treated as detachable and were then symbolized in concrete regalia.

The qualities of all things were of the essence, according to the Aztecs' way of thinking. The narrowness of things, their sharpness, their flatness, their harmoniousness or their oppositeness, their filthiness or their freshness, their atrociousness or their domesticness—these were real. No matter how visually dramatic or colorful an object might appear to him, the Aztec sought its reality not in the physical object itself but in the quality which could be verbalized out of its form. Xiuhteuctli might well be the hearth fire, plainly visible to all, but as a god he was really the quality of all that was well oriented and comfortable.

In these ways the Aztec was a spiritualist who, in the world of appearances, abstracted their auras and deified those. He believed ardently in the gods and worshiped them as idols. He liked the sense of knowing their shapes and colors. But he was also aware that they might freely pass these shapes about among themselves. Their essences, their qualities, these alone were inalienable. In this fact lies the explanation of the relationship of the Aztec gods to the numinous.

Idols and Ixiptla

Like the Toltecs from whom they inherited so much, the Aztecs were known far and wide for their idolatry.[10] In our sources there are frequent references to the multiplicity of Aztec idols. The plastic genius of the Aztecs indeed created a vast world of images, perpetrating them in numbers far exceeding those of previous epochs.[11] The Aztecs appear to have been a people compelled to insist on the visible presences of their gods. In the conceptualization of these presences they went to extremes of detail. Elaboration of detail is certainly one way a people can try to harness their gods. The state not only proliferated images in the temples but displayed them at crossroads in and outside cities and in countless shrines everywhere. Great stone idols towered on mountaintops and in every house lares and penates abounded in their frozen multitudes. To the Aztec the day was like a great cathedral and every minute in it was a niche railing in an idol.

But the Aztecs had a special type of idol which differed radically in that it was animate and incarnate. This was the *ixiptla*, "image" or "representative," a person who wore the regalia, acted out the part of the god, and then was sacrificed.

In the understanding of the Aztecs the gods moved of their own volition among men. In other words their presences were not conjured up by men. Rather the world was a stage common to both men and gods and therefore, once the gods had assumed their masks and had taken concrete forms, they were at home on earth. Men and gods, however disparate in qualities, lived together in territorial symbiosis. The gods could and did inject themselves into static idols in order to maintain a constant presence and a daily cult of service. Among men, however, they moved dynamically as *ixiptla*, entering homes on ceremonial occasions, ascending and descending the temple stairs, dancing in public, receiving the liberality of their worshipers and blessing them, cohabiting with young women reserved for them, feasting, etc. In every case the chosen humans wore all or a sufficient part of the regalia of the god in question to be able to dispose of his powers. The *ixiptla* was considered to be the god in person.

These incarnations, so pervasive a part of the religious scene, supported the concept of the power of the mask. Charged with its own potent magic, the *ixiptla* was the earthly mask of the god, who in a sense broke out into vivid physical activity. A people such as the Aztecs would certainly have been drawn to symbolize the god in action, if for no other reason than pure theatricality. The extra confidence given them by the living presence of the gods was of incalculable support to them in their piety.

Every major god or goddess had his or her *ixiptla*. In the Feast of the Flaying of Men, for instance, each ward in the city of Mexico dressed a slave as the *ixiptla* of the particular deity of that ward.

Before the sun had set each one had been sacrificed. On the other hand, the famous *ixiptla* of Tezcatlipoca acted out his part for an entire year, at the end of which, universally honored, he was destroyed. Even the god of death on his special feast day was impersonated by an *ixiptla* who was duly sacrificed.[12]

The Pantheon

I have referred to the "pantheon" of Aztec gods as if they comprised a society constituted somewhat after the manner of the gods of Greece. At the same time I have defined them as numinous, that is to say, as parcels of a single homogeneous divine power. I have further noted the role of the mask in magically evoking separate and recognizable gods out of this shadowy force. Obviously the word "pantheon" does not adequately cover such concepts.

With a few exceptions the members of the Aztec pantheon were not grouped in clear family situations. This is curious and raises the question, Why should it be so? The answer is that, whenever the Aztec needed a structuring principle for the purpose of organizing his gods, that principle could be instantly derived from the nature of the Aztec cosmos, which was made up of a center and four partitions. This principle of fiveness (and its associated principle of fourness) was utilized by the Aztecs in arranging their deities in preference to the principle of the nuclear family, namely father, mother, and progeny. To the Aztecs the idea of fiveness was a universal metaphor and could be used to define any form whatsoever. The nature of the gods could certainly be best revealed in the application of this principle.

For example, Tlazolteotl, patroness of sex, can be represented as a veritable Dea Syria, naked and single, or she can appear as a group of four sisters. A cluster of demonic females called the Goddesses or the Princesses is said to have numbered five. The rain god Tlaloc could be thought of as surrounded by a court of four Tlaloque, each dispensing a different kind of rain. And we have already met the four avatars of the fire god. Gods such as those who performed the original creation or certain deities of war could be grouped in fours. These examples illustrate a kind of architecture in the Aztec pantheon.

What we are being told, however, is that the Aztec pantheon *as a whole* was not organized. It was not even conceived to be an im-

Tlaloc wielding lightning and thunderbolt (Laud)

perial state in the heavens, a pattern we might well have expected; among the Aztecs the weakness of the idea of the state probably prevented such an idea. We do note, as we have mentioned above, a tendency to assemble the great gods in a cluster of thirteen, implying all the gods, but that is a reflection of the sacred number 13 in the Aztec calendrics and does not further define the gods included in the list. Again, if we interpret the day-signs of the *tonalpohualli* as the symbols or *nahualli* of an original twenty gods long precedent to the Aztecs, we would have a kind of submerged pantheon whose principle of selection had been the number 20. And 20 is 4 multiplied by 5.

We must then admit that the Aztecs, in spite of the great profusion of gods whom they served, felt little need to subsume their deities under any constitutional rubric other than the *tonalpohualli*. The application to the cosmos of the rule of the five directions was rigid enough to assure them that chaos had been thwarted. A god was thus thought to walk among men either as one individual or as one accompanied by four avatars.

One thing, and one thing only, contradicts the impression of a disjunction in the society of gods. Almost without exception they are clad in gaudy battle array. In the codices they are shown striding menacingly about, shaking their darts and displaying armorial bearings on their shields. Gods of banqueting and entertainment wear warriors' accouterments. The grim god of the city of Mexico was specifically a god of the melee and his grandmother was patroness of war. One of Tezcatlipoca's most important transfigurations was the armed Enemy. A specific goddess guided the fortunes of those who fell in the fray. Quetzalcoatl's mother, Shield Hand, was among other things a goddess of war. These examples are sufficient to illustrate a concept which united the gods in a superficial way: in varying degrees all the gods participated in a cosmic commonality of threat and bloodthirstiness.

But we must accept the fact that, while the intensely warlike orientation of the typical Aztec state had its effect on the gods and their appearances, even it did not serve as a truly integrating factor in making the Aztec pantheon one institution. The pantheon remained a disjunction of beings, and in this sense we can say it was modeled upon the upper level of Aztec society, formed of knights striving for a sacrificial end or for individual renown.

The Historic Background of the Pantheon

Two cities loomed in the background of Aztec life: Teotihuacan and Tula. In a later chapter we will comment upon the religion the Chichimecs brought down with them from the steppe. Here we merely wish to note that it was the capital city of Tula which cast its religious spell over the unsophisticated Chichimecs, just as earlier it had been the immemorial city of Teotihuacan which had overawed and civilized the Toltecs.

The Toltecs were the spiritual ancestors of the Aztecs. It was probably they who began the stress on stellar elements in Mesoamerican religion, as a consequence of which they must have considerably enriched the mythology and expanded the cult.[13] They were undoubtedly the ones who added to the Chichimec stock of gods the all-important figure of Tezcatlipoca, a deity symbolizing lordship and treachery. And it was the Toltec Quetzalcoatl, the god of the Morning Star and of warriors, who predominated in the Aztec pantheon rather than the Quetzalcoatl we see earlier at Teotihuacan, the god of tornadoes and water-bearing winds.

One can rather artificially project four historic strata of Aztec gods. The gods derived from the Chichimecs can be seen as the formulations of the shaman's mind, those of Teotihuacan were probably called forth by the pomp of the sacerdotal, while those of Tula appeared out of the mysteries of elite secret societies or warriors' lodges. A fourth and eclectic level, added later, included those gods conquered or otherwise met with in the violent outthrusting of the Aztec world. Thus chronologically assembled, the gods formed no pantheon but only a motley crowd. The Aztecs felt no need to recognize the society of gods as a brotherhood; rather they concentrated on the iconographic elaboration of each god.

Perhaps it was the above historic layering which prevented the Aztec gods from being divided into two parties eternally confronting each other, as is sometimes the situation in polytheisms, with good versus evil, light versus darkness, deistic versus demonic. Some observers have professed to see in Aztec thought and religion a thoroughgoing dualism.[14] I myself fail to see this. The Aztecs had no concept of an Armageddon, a day when the gods of the army of the day and the gods of the army of the night should ultimately clash. Even the struggle in the *tlachco*, which would have provided a most tempting scenario for an Aztec Armageddon, was never so used in myth.

Thus we look in vain for a developed sense of celestial drama among the Aztecs, a feeling for a high morality trapped in the clutter of ignorance and evil. Aztec thought dwelt rather on the autonomy of the individual god, which necessarily precluded that god from ever adopting a principle of good or evil. There were, in brief, no good gods and no evil gods in the pantheon. They were simply figures who, however much they may have mingled in the priestly ceremonies, were members of no self-conscious society.

An easy way for us to explain this would be to write off the Aztec pantheon as "primitive" or "barbaric," but this explains nothing. The Aztec would certainly have been able to construct a pyramided society of the gods had he seen any advantages to it. For him to have imposed upon them a social order, such as a dualism or a graduated hierarchy, would have contradicted everything he believed about them. The numinous to him was of an order wholly different from the totality of social man. It needed only the mask to free it from its matrix and give it individual definitions for all men to see and declare. But each god, once he had been so defined, then stood discrete and alone.

The Demonic

An aspect of godhead powerfully present in Aztec religious thought is the demonic. To most students of Aztec cult, in fact, it is even repulsively present. A spectacular cult performance well illustrates this.[15] Two priests clad in the freshly flayed skins of women just sacrificed in the fire god's feast slowly descended the pyramid steps, brandishing the defleshed arm bones of the victims and braying as if demented. Meanwhile the crowd waiting at the bottom chanted over and over: "Now our gods are coming!"

The intention in this performance was quite obviously to underscore that aspect of divinity which we generally refer to as the demonic. Inasmuch as the source of the demonic was always the supernatural—however much it may have been symbolically manipulated by men—it is proper to consider it here.

Sculptural representations as well as paintings in the codices give us a clear picture of how the Aztec envisaged the demonic. Let us take as examples those supernatural beings called the *tzitzimime*, conceived either as one, Tzitzimitl, or as a collective four.[16] These particular demonic beings lived in the night sky and were a constant threat to men, especially during eclipses. One source has it that in the far distant past they were originally stars and fell from their noble stations to become four lords in the underworld. But more commonly it was thought that, with the final destruction of the world, the *tzitzimine* would appear to initiate the shambles in which the last men were to be destroyed. One representation shows Tzitzimitl as a skeleton with talons instead of hands and feet and with every bony joint defined as a skeletal mouth.[17] The monster has a rattlesnake for a penis, wears earrings of human hands and a necklace of bloody hearts alternating with hands. The hair is madly disheveled. Generally the *tzitzimime* are said to be women; in fact they are even called female demons. When viewed in the singular Tzitzimitl is an eerie goddess in the night sky.

Besides gods who were deliberately cast as demons, we find the quality of the demonic was widely shared by almost all the gods.

Tzitzimitl wearing a necklace and a diadem of hands and hearts (Magliabecchiano)

If we are correct in asserting that religions, wherever found, see deity as creative, sustaining, and demonic all at once, then I believe it follows that Aztec religion powerfully emphasized the latter, perhaps more than any other known religion.

It is in the fantasies of Aztec religious art that we come face to face with that overpowering demonic sense of the Aztec people. The Aztec artists strove with rare consistency to depict the gods as shocking. Though anthropomorphically conceived, however, the gods are still not presented to us as comprehensible. They are buried under a plethora of symbols and rendered inanimate by severe and rigid stylization. We are not asked to reply to the majesty of Huitzilopochtli, the sexuality of Tlazolteotl, the largess of Tlaloc, or the familial warmth of Xiuhteuctli. Rather we are placed in front of the grotesque, the absurd, the impossible, even the disgusting, and through these means we are asked to appreciate the nature of the gods. Our Aztec artist never portrays the graceful, the lively, or the lilting in life. Harsh angles and coarse figurations are preferred. Blood, bones, excrement, and serpents are excessively depicted to heighten the sense of the unclean, the uncanny, and the perilous.

Though the Aztec was in no sense a naturalistic artist, he managed to portray with feeling the awful urgency of the gods. They are more often shown in crisis than in statuesque poses. They engage in agonistic affairs; there are great fallings down and stabbings; there are duels in the *tlachco*, hurlings of darts, and orders given for chastisement—in fact a complete range of volcanic energy is depicted as normal for the gods. This is evident even to the most casual student in the pages of the screenfold codices.

Nowhere, however, are the gods shown grouped in titanic factions or cabals, opposing or reinforcing each other in open conflict. The confrontations are always between individual gods. Their contests are outgrowths solely of their individual demonic vitality, not of any issues which separate them. The only gods understood as joined under a common banner in Aztec myth are the Four Hundred Mimixcoa (who are enemies as well as doubles of Mixcoatl) and the Four Hundred Southerners (who are hostile to Huitzilopochtli as well as being his brothers). The Aztecs apprehended so keenly the quality of vitality in their gods that their tendency was to depict them in all the heroism or tragedy of a singular and stupendous action. What they were concerned with, in other words, was the emphasis of demonism, that superhuman and arbitrary blazing forth of energy, as the most distinctive characteristic of the divine.

The Nocturnal

Also characteristic of Aztec religion is its mood of darkness. This is not just a subjective feeling; it is a specific emphasis which can be documented and is a concomitant of the Aztec emphasis on the demonic. The nocturnal element better embeds the Aztec numinous than does the diurnal. Night, which is "other" and hostile to man, is congenial to the Aztec divine.

A central myth in Aztec lore, as we have seen, is that of the five suns. Though solar in character, this myth begins and ends with darkness. It insists on the episodic character of light and ends with a prediction of the annihilation of the fifth and final sun. Thus the myth is not a paean of victory—"Hail! holy light"—but a statement that night encases the light and is its inevitable shell. The fifth sun will finally be stolen by Tezcatlipoca, the very spirit of darkness.[18]

We shall see later that Tezcatlipoca is the dominant god of the Aztec pantheon. He has two major personifications—the red Tezcatlipoca and the black—the former standing for the diurnal sun, the latter for the sun in the underworld. Our sources insist that the latter, the nocturnal sun, is the primate one.[19] The two can be shown confronting each other in the *tlachco*.[20] But the *tlachco*, as we have already seen, is a symbol of the astral underworld and the night sky. From this we understand that, whatever the outcome of the cosmic confrontation, the field of action is defined as being clearly in favor of the black Tezcatlipoca.

When we consider the gods en masse, we find that they were popularly thought to have originally been the stars in their multitudes, the 1,600.[21] They either fell to earth or were sent down by the Great Mother, the Milky Way. In any case their beginnings were nocturnal. Even the most ancient and beneficent of them all, the god of fire and the original light, sits at home in the blackness of the underearth.

We are talking here about an emphasis. Naturally there were Aztec supernaturals who exemplified the light of day, and sometimes even its gladness, but the fascinated mind of the Aztec dwelt more easily on things of the night and in that direction his gods tended to lean.

A summary consideration of Aztec cult brings forth the same point. The nightly service of the gods was at least as important as the daytime ritual devoted to them, probably more so. In Tenochtitlan the god was censed four times during the day; at night he was censed five times.[22] Indeed it is fair to say that most acts of worship acquired greater efficacy through being performed at night.

Midnight was a parlous time in the temple compound. A vast uproar of conch trumpets, horns, and drums broke forth to mark the time of the sun's dark nadir, and the priests then busied themselves cutting their flesh and offering the drippings of their blood to the deities. For this occasion they were painted with *teopatli*, the "divine salve" of Tezcatlipoca, a preparation which enchanted and immunized them against the fears of the night.[23] Even in the daytime cult the priests were painted with soot (a substance greatly revered), thus carrying on the nocturnal emphasis.

An Ordering of the Gods

It is still necessary, however, for the researcher to speak of the Aztec gods in categories—otherwise all will continue to be obscure. I have therefore, quite arbitrarily, set up four rubrics under which we can rationally (though not neatly) include all the gods.

In this system gods will be considered explanatory, affective, providential, or focal—or combinations of any of the four. By explanatory gods I mean those gods who were apprehended as a result of the needs of the inquiring intellect. Affective gods are those whose essence is their ability to move men, not to thanksgiving or the like, but to passions and ebullitions. Providential gods preside over the material aspects of men's lives, nourishing, clothing, housing, training, curing them, etc. The last category of gods, which I will call focal, answers to man's social needs, his sense of identity, of locale, and of belonging.

In such a scheme I am making no attempt to necessarily keep a god and his transfigurations under the same rubric. Some gods could well occupy multiple niches—I have in such cases assigned them to the one which appears to be stressed in their cult and mythology. For instance I class Huitzilopochtli as a focal god, but his most common transfiguration, Painal, the Runner, I would place among the affective gods. Another example is Quetzalcoatl, who was the patron god of the city of Cholula and would thus be a focal god. He also brings rain and so could be classed as providential. I place him, however, under the rubric of explanatory gods because of his preeminent role as a culture hero and a priest. Mixcoatl as the first to drill fire could be classed as providential, but his powerful connections with war make it more logical to class him as affective. What follows are short discussions of these four categories with comments on certain of the more important gods assigned to them.

The Explanatory Gods

In Tezcoco, most regal and largest of all the Aztec cities, was a temple built by the great ruler Nezahualcoyotl which was dedicated to a most unusual Aztec god, one said to have had no idol.[24] The pyramid had several levels representing the ascending stages of the heavens. On the terrace the shrine was painted black and decorated with stars. This signified not only that the god in question lived above the highest heaven but that, like the night, his mind and his deeds were unknowable. Although this god, Tloque Nahuaque, was acknowledged in all Aztec communities of note, the speculative turn of mind of the great ruler made Tloque Nahuaque the particular possession of Tezcoco. Nezahualcoyotl is reported to have composed over sixty hymns in his honor.

Tloque Nahuaque is reputed to have originally been a Toltec god, and this is indeed quite probable. His name is epithetical and literally means He Who Is the Owner of Near and the Owner of Close, which we can transpose more simply into the Immanent One. Everything we know about him suggests that over a long period he had been crystallizing out of the god Tezcatlipoca as a valid philosophical abstraction. He was a basic intellectual symbol for deity per se; the lack of a well-defined cult devoted to him and the absence of any attempt to create a mask for him bear this out. The only temple known to have been built for him was the one in Tezcoco.

He was known by many other names: Our Lord, He through Whom We Live, the Hidden and Impalpable One,[25] the Self-Created, Creator of Men, Teacher, Lord of Creatures, Lord of Heaven and Earth, and others. We can see from these titles that he was the epitome of a high god, one having the attributes of supremacy and inscrutability which we in the biblical tradition normally attribute to Jehovah. But because there was no mask that distinguished Tloque Nahuaque, because he had no visibility, he was not really a god at all as the Aztecs defined them. He was rather the appearance of the undifferentiated numinous that stands behind and supports all the gods.

This type of religious refinement was difficult for the Aztecs to maintain. Occasionally they would put an already existing mask on the Immanent One, thus making him more congenial to their ways. At such times he was identified with Tezcatlipoca or, less often, with the Lord of Sustenance. Thus contaminated he could acquire the shifting colors of these gods while never wholly becoming either one of them, for they stood for opposing concepts—Tezcatlipoca for the mocking and the enigmatic, the Lord of Sustenance for origination and maintenance. All we are saying here is that the two gods, especially Tezcatlipoca, are occasionally referred to as Tloque Nahuaque. Viewed from this angle, Tloque Nahuaque appears to be an authentic god. He was a friend of man and yet, acting as Tezcatlipoca, he intended man's destruction. He mocked men and saw to it that all things decayed. Yet he protected the land of Anahuac. In brief he merely reproduced the particular characteristics—whether arbitrary, heroic, or patronizing—of clearly defined gods, especially Tezcatlipoca, while imputing some of his supremacy to them.

The conception of the Immanent One gave the Aztecs answers to questions which always arise when men are confronted by the problem of a multiplicity of gods. No one can fail to be impressed by the Aztec achievement here. Nevertheless it is surprising that the concept had not established itself well before this time in a latrian form of worship and an appropriate cult. I suspect again that the inadequacy of the Aztecs' sense of empire had something to do with hampering such a religious development. The concept of the Immanent One remains an important intellectual achievement, but it was a lonely one. It bore no fruit.

Much more concretely realized than this isolated aspect of deity are the paired lord and lady gods. These couples could be graphically depicted, whereas there is no certain representation of Tloque Nahuaque. Their role in Aztec mythology is to explain phenomena in terms of ultimate derivation and ultimate authority, and for this reason they are always conceived as being old. They are also alike in all being residents of the uppermost heaven. One might deduce from this that the Aztecs did not feel that a simple affinity with the earth could automatically supply a god with powers of origination. To be a high god and to stand as a fountainhead a god had to be empyreal. The best known of these paired gods were the Lord and Lady of Sustenance, Two Lord and Two Lady, and Cipactonal and Oxomoco.

One other god should be mentioned under this rubric because of his role as a demiurge, a culture hero, and a prime actor in Toltec history. This is Quetzalcoatl. Because of the difficulty of analyzing him and because of the richness of his associations, he will be considered at length in a later chapter.

The Affective Gods

The greatest god of this group is Tezcatlipoca, in myth the adversary of Quetzalcoatl. As in the case of the latter, however, we will devote a later chapter to him.

This rubric includes most of the daunting and horrifying gods in the Aztec pantheon, some of whom will be considered in the chapter on the Great Mother and her transfigurations. No other people in history surpassed the Aztecs in the elaboration and promotion of such gods. Even the gigantic demons in East Asian temples look almost insipid when compared to the famous Coatlicue, whose effigy has caused thousands of beholders to turn away shuddering. We have mentioned such predatory goddesses before, deities who give men nothing but exist as wholly "other" and are wholly baleful. In the case of Mictlanteuctli, Lord of the Dead, and Mictecacihuatl, Mistress of the Dead, we have typical affective gods whose images can be matched in the plastic records of many other cultures but who nevertheless have a peculiarly livid quality. Mictlanteuctli is often known as Tzontemoc, the Head-Downward Descender, a designation which refers to the tumbling of his victims into the underworld.[26] His consort could be shown as a hideous woman with a bare skull for a head, dancing on the open jaws of earth as it gulps down swaddled corpses.

The god of the Morning Star is another such prodigy of terror; he is depicted as a warrior dueling with the sun and is generally painted with the vertical red stripes of sacrifice. Sometimes he has a death's-head. The first rising of this planet was always an ominous event; it was attended by great dangers to certain categories of people and −as in the god's ability to cause drought−even to nature itself. The Morning Star was singled out to represent a whole range of fears that afflicted men. The god of frost was shown as a faceless being with a huge curved obsidian knife blade, deeply serrated along its cutting edge, arising from his head.[27] Huitzilopochtli's sister, killed and decapitated in myth, is shown only as a head with the eyelids lowered in sullen death.

We could enumerate many more divine beings who fall into this category. The extremism which marked the Aztec character produced tensions that had to find relief in such depictions.

The Providential Gods

In this category belong those Aztec deities who, supporting the people in their daily lives, were generally closest to them. Here was the many-breasted Mayahuel, the beloved goddess of the maguey, from which was brewed the intoxicating *octli*. Surrounding her were the Dionysian gods of drink itself, a group called the Four Hundred Rabbits, widely worshiped throughout Mesoamerica. There was Chicomecoatl, Seven Snake, goddess of harvests and of maize in particular. There was the goddess of salt; the god of games, banqueting, and good living; the god who guided merchants and brought them luck; there were Jade Skirt and Blue Skirt, great goddesses of standing and running waters; there was Amimitl, whose skills were passed on to the hunter and the fisherman.[28] There were innumerable others.

Perhaps the most venerable of the providential gods was Tlaloc, the mountain king who brought the life-giving rain. He was of great antiquity and was modeled on a most ancient deity who had been worshiped by the La Venta people on the Gulf coast.[29] These people later took him up-country and created for him a hill sanctuary and pilgrimage center at Chalcatzinco, in the present state of Morelos. By Teotihuacan times, much later, this god was appearing in two transfigurations, showing respectively jaguar and crocodile characteristics.[30] His name in Nahuatl means He Who Is Recumbent on the Earth, a reference to the fact that he is the conceptualized mountain.[31]

His appearance was unique and, in the eyes of the first Spaniards, supremely hideous. Under his nose he wears a buccal mask displaying multiple fangs. Around each eye he wears a circular hoop. In one hand he carries a tomahawk of jade representing the thunderbolt or, alternatively, a writhing serpent as a symbol of lightning; in the other hand he carries a jug out of which he pours the rain. While the rain is his to command, he is definitely not a sky god but, rather, the numen of the raised earth or mountain. His home in fact is to be sought on the high crags of mountains or in caves in the sides of those mountains.[32] Out of such caves and down from the crags he pours the swollen clouds, which then march out to lower over the land. Thus he is first the god in the mountain, the Jovian dispatcher of the storm, and only after that the lord of seed and verdure and plenty.

Every mountain around which rain clouds gathered was a Tlaloc. Following a tradition already old when they moved into the area, the Aztecs looked to the sierra on the east side of the Great Basin as a habitat peculiarly his—it is still known today as Mount Tlaloc.[33] For this reason the Aztec city of Tezcoco which lay at its feet had control over the god's cult and indeed commanded an amphictyony of Aztec cities which shared a ritual undoubtedly going back to Toltec and Teotihuacan origins. This particular Tlaloc was given preeminence, for he engendered the clouds which rolled down to drench the Basin with rains and to gully its sides. But any mountain with sufficient height was conceived to be the home of rain; each was named and they were grouped into a college of gods referred to in the plural as the Tlaloque.[34] They could also be thought of as four. The concept of the Tlaloque, however, included not only mountains but wind, water, fog, reed beds, and so on. Thus they symbolized not so much water as its vitalities and its many manifestations.

The cult of mountains played an impressive role in Aztec religion. In fact, in the Nahuatl language, a mountain is considered grammatically to be an animate creature, a very god of being, sentient and impending. More often than not the mountain was female. Long and arduous pilgrimages were taken to caves in certain mountains reputed to be particularly holy. In the calendar there was an annual Feast of the Mountains that was moved from one peak to another so that all the mountains rimming the Basin might be equally honored. Popocatepetl was indisputably the lordliest of them all; there was a famous cave with an attached shrine on the southern slope of that monarch of mountains.[35]

Within the mountains, as in covert and locked containers, lay pools of water. Out of the mountains came the life of the people in the form of black clouds and watercourses that pelted down the slopes to pass through the corn lands and among the cities. On the appropriate feast days the people molded dough images of the various mountains cast as Tlaloque; these were roughly made to resemble children, and for eyes and teeth seeds and beans were pressed into the dough. They were referred to as the Green Mountain Gods and at the end of the ceremonies they were symbolically killed and eaten.

The Tlaloque were mythically conceived. They were deformed and dwarfish beings, probably thought of as small editions of Tlaloc himself. They lived in a great palace of four halls in Tlalocan, the terrestrial paradise, each of the halls representing one of the four directions.[36] In the inner patio which the halls surrounded there were four tubs, each containing a different kind of rain or weather. On Tlaloc's orders the appropriate one of the Tlaloque would fill his great jug and pour it out over the world. The thunder was the sound of their jugs breaking. In that paradise–vaguely to the east and lost among the mountaintops–it was always green summer.

But, however Tlaloc might enjoy himself in his mountain garden, he often turned his anger against the people. Then the Tlaloque retired, each into his cave, and sent forth no more cloud bundles. In the days of the Aztec emperor Moteuczoma I, there occurred a catastrophic four-year drought in which thousands perished. At such times the people stared helplessly at the dry mountains and the brazen sky, and Tlaloc became the greatest and indeed the only god. Out of such a terrible confrontation between the irate deity and his people came moving supplications. One depicts how the Tlaloque have done away with their sister, the goddess of maize, how "she feebly drags herself along, she is covered with dust, she is covered with dust, she is covered with cobwebs, she is utterly worn and weary."[37] People everywhere are dying in the famine and children are hollow-eyed, the complaint continues. Even the birds collapse. "They topple over and lie prostrate on their backs, weakly opening and closing their beaks." The breast of Mother Earth has dried up and the Tlaloque have carried away all green things, locking them away in Tlalocan. So people cry out to the mountains, "O Gods, our Lords, make haste!"

I have taken some pains to present Tlaloc to the reader. He is without doubt the most encompassing of all the providential gods, and he is representative of them all because his role is that of a provider or a withholder. Frightening as his mask may be to us, he did not–as did Tezcatlipoca–seek out an individual to overawe him, shatter his life, or whimsically shower blessings upon him. Tlaloc brought to whole societies abundance or starvation–not himself.

As we have said, Tlaloc was the outstanding providential god, but there was another not far behind him in overall importance. This was Totec, Our Lord, who had two especially important transfigurations: Xipe and Yohuallahuan. The name Xipe may well mean He with the Phallus.[38] How far he goes back in time we do not know, but we do know that he was worshiped in many parts of Mesoamerica, principally in the south. The fact that the skins of persons sacrificed to him were worn by officiants was one of the spectacular features of his cult.

It is difficult to be as precise about Xipe's divine jurisdiction as we were in the case of Tlaloc. He appears to have been the Aztec Adonis, the stripling god who represents the first flowers of the new

Xipe as the red Tezcatlipoca (Borbonicus)

year and then dies in the bloom of his life.[39] He was certainly thought of as a young god to whom the first spring flowers were offered. We also know that he had close connections with other flora, especially the verdure and fruit of the zapote tree.[40] His very presence blessed babies, as befitted a god of rejuvenation. He and his priests carried the rattlestaff, a cult instrument producing fertility, and we know that appeals were made to him to bring forth fruit of all kinds. At some point during his festival the victim who represented him was hung up on a frame of poles and shot to death with arrows, to allow his fructifying blood to drip down upon a round stone symbolizing the earth. The arrows, the blood, and the earth symbol used in this grisly ceremony are to be interpreted sexually. So important is human sacrifice in Xipe's cult that the stone over which his victims were destroyed was even deified, thus becoming one of his transfigurations; this derived god's name was Itztapaltotec, Our Lord the Flat Stone.

Another line of evidence reveals Xipe as a transfiguration of the sun.[41] One of his names was Red Mirror,[42] and his great festival took place at the vernal equinox. His *nahualli* or double is said to be the eagle, a solar bird. In his festival the sun is certainly prominently involved, while only the most valiant of war prisoners were sacrificed in his cult, as is also consonant with the worship of the sun.

It is nevertheless difficult to see him clearly, and perhaps we do not have to choose between the two alternatives. It may be best to view him as the deification of spring, a time when sun, rain, and fresh verdure were all compounded. At any rate Xipe is a god who offered man the early fruit and goodness of the earth. Durán presents him as a "universal god."

The Focal Gods

I have already discussed the most obvious and certainly the earliest of all the focal gods, fire. Fire as the hearth from which the four directions lead has no peer as a fundamental sign of man's location upon the earth, providing the primitive family and the band with three crucial elements: orientation, identification, and territoriality.

There was a further type of focal god among the Aztecs, one who served people organized at a higher social level than the family. These were the national, tribal, and city gods[43]–mascots who brought luck to the society and summed up its essential constitution. Because the Aztecs were never a single united nation but lived in separated cities, no one god stood over and protected them all. But every Aztec city did possess its own deity, considered to be either the city founder or the first ancestor. The city of Huexotzinco, for instance, was centered around the hunting god Camaxtli. Cholula worshiped Quetzalcoatl; Cuitlahuac worshiped Amimitl; Cuauhtitlan worshiped Mixcoatl; the Tepaneca cities worshiped Otonteuctli; Mexico, as is well known, worshiped Huitzilopochtli. All these gods could be referred to as "the heart of the people" or simply by local designations: He of Huexotzinco, He of Cholula, etc.

The true nature of these focal gods becomes apparent when we learn that their shrines were in part small armories, for in the attics of these shrines were stored darts, swords, clubs, and other weapons of war. It was customary in Aztec warfare for an attacking force to drive first for the beleaguered city's focal shrine. The loss or successful defense of this symbol of the people's heart was always decisive for the outcome of the battle, and the weapons housed in the shrine could be turned to good account in a last-ditch imbroglio; however, should the image of the focal god be seized or destroyed, the people's will to fight automatically collapsed.

It is apparent that the focal gods were essentially different from the divinities in the other three categories, for they appeared and disappeared, waxed and waned, as the political situation indicated. Thus no focal god could be exported; he could only be captured. Needless to say a god well known in one of the other categories might also act as a focal god, as Quetzalcoatl did in Cholula; in that case we have to consider the focal form of the god as a transfiguration of his more universal form.

The Pattern of Aztec Mythology

All these gods had to be thought about and presented, where needed, in mythological narrative. Mythology is a relatively late exercise in man's religious life, and not all of it is intended to be serious, but it is always a reasoned attempt to explicate the numinous, to force the unknowable into the open where it may be conveniently grasped. Like other peoples, the Aztecs stressed certain things and neglected others in their mythology, and these seeming vagaries may tell us much. It is worth our while to dip, however briefly, into the subject.

One can discover in Aztec mythology eight cycles, defined here as major by having one or more surviving variants. We have presented these eight in the following list. The order in which they are arranged derives, of course, from western logic and is not meant to represent any Aztec system. The cycles are named after the deity principally concerned. The first six form a series that, taken together, fully describes the role of the supernatural, the central four of that series (numbers 2 to 5) being exclusively astral. The seventh cycle concerns Aztec man's appreciation of the structure of his corporate life. The eighth and last cycle stands somewhat apart from the others, offering as it does a detailed world view which focuses on man. There is a certain grandeur about these tales which, owing to the exotic names and the unfamiliar references, may be difficult to present. My interpretations are designed to enable the reader to grapple more effectively with their larger meanings. Let me then briefly discuss these cycles, cautioning the reader, however, that there exist contradictory versions of many of the events related. Some of the myths have already been described; others will be mentioned later in the book.

1. The Cipactli cycle. This cycle is basic to Aztec cosmogony and is unrelated to any which follow. The Cipactli monster is a being or a status precedent to all the gods. He is an oceanic dragon designed to symbolize preexistent and formless matter, neither earth nor ocean exclusively but both. The four creator deities depute two of their number, Tezcatlipoca and Quetzalcoatl, to act as demiurges who create heaven and earth from the monster's body. Four lesser gods are then selected to hold up the sky. Quadruplicity and the separation of opposites are the two forming elements in this cycle. The theme is the nature of the beginning.

2. The Citlalinicue cycle. This begins an interesting series of four stellar cycles. The goddess Citlalinicue can be thought of concretely as the Milky Way or the epitome of all the stars. She is cast, however, as the august mother of all the gods, and she sits in the seat of authority in the highest heaven with her consort. The two divide their dominion over the universe, she giving oracular commands to all female beings, he to all male beings. She bore the stone knife from which sprang the 1,600 gods—all the gods that ever were—under the leadership of Xolotl. This cycle presents the night sky as the ultimate seat and source of divinity—and therefore of authority. This authority is exercised through the female/male dichotomy, the female sex predominating.

3. The Nanahuatl cycle. The gods gather in Teotihuacan to see who will sacrifice himself by leaping into a fire to become the sun. Only two volunteers are found, Nanahuatl and Teucciztecatl, the first of whom becomes the sun, the other the moon. But Nanahuatl, now Tonatiuh, refuses to rise unless fed with sacrificial hearts and blood. Enraged at such presumption, the god of the Morning Star attempts to slay him but himself succumbs in the duel. The rest of the gods now give over their collective sovereignty to Tonatiuh and allow themselves to be sacrificed. The sun thereupon triumphantly rises in the east. The theme of this cycle is blood sacrifice, the mechanism by which the great astral movements in the universe are maintained; its provenience out of an astral context is made explicit.

4. The Mixcoatl cycle. Sun and Mother Earth produce the first gods, all stars, the Four Hundred Mimixcoa. These gods become unruly and refuse to provide their parents with food. In retaliation the divine parents produce five additional Mimixcoa led by the hero Mixcoatl. These five ambush and defeat the Four Hundred (a contradictory variant has the Four Hundred murdering Mixcoatl, which allows his son, the Morning Star, to avenge him by destroying them). That combat and the subsequent sacrifices provide the divine parents with the hearts and blood necessary for life. Mixcoatl then embarks upon a career of hunting and war, carrying on his back the deified knife of sacrifice. He meets the earth goddess, and they produce their famous son, Ce Acatl, the Morning Star. The outstanding theme of this cycle is heroic war as an ultimate command from the heavens. The personages are modeled on astral prototypes; warfare is thus a main activity of the stars.

5. The Xolotl cycle. This is the last of the stellar cycles. Xolotl is an aspect of the planet Venus, generally interpreted as the Evening Star. He plays ball in the *tlachco* against the sun in the underworld and is depicted as defeating and sacrificing him. When the 1,600 gods decide to send one of their number into the underworld to retrieve the bones of the men of the preceding aeon in order to re-create them, Xolotl is selected for that mission. His familiarity with the underworld is also attested in the myth where he abducts the young goddess Xochiquetzal and takes her down into the underworld to ravish her. The theme of this cycle is the underearth, both as the home of the planet Venus and as a field of action for celestial beings.

6. The Xochiquetzal cycle. The core tale places the goddess Xochiquetzal in a verdant paradise as the wife of the sun (or of Tlaloc).

She is stolen and taken into the underworld. Her husband and lover himself descends into the darkness to seek her. Alternating with this is the tale of the wonderful tree planted in paradise, the fruit of which is aphrodisiac. Xochiquetzal eats this and is thus the first female to succumb to sexual temptation. Her expulsion from paradise follows, whereat the tree withers and breaks in two. The theme of this cycle is the tragic loss of paradise, interpreted as the earth's loss of fruitfulness in the fall season and the retreat of the sun southward.

7. The Quetzalcoatl cycle. This is the most heterogeneous of all the cycles but clearly reveals the basic theme of priestly wisdom and the validation of human culture, this probably coming from Quetzalcoatl's character as the god of air. Quetzalcoatl is born in the highest heaven and there given his cultural commission by the Two Gods. Alternatively he is born to Mixcoatl and the Earth Mother. He is credited with creating men and women and brought into cultivation maize and the maguey, two of the great staples. He invented the calendar and patronized all crafts and commerce; he was the archpriest and gave men rituals and penances. Quetzalcoatl was far traveled and had fundamental connections with the east, the land of learning. His rule in Tula was an age of wonders and, when he left, culture decayed. His cycle also includes his adventures as Ce Acatl, the Morning Star, and the fascinating story of his temptation, exile, and prophesied return.

8. The Tonatiuh cycle. This is the only cycle in Aztec mythology which is anthropocentric; in it even the various species of animals are derived from men. It is a true history, speculative, evolutionary, catastrophic, and logical. Its great age is attested by the extreme dislocation of the order and the details of the five ages in the surviving versions. The sun rules each of the five divisions of time, representing the overriding principle of light, but in each age he appears under a different transfiguration: Tezcatlipoca, Quetzalcoatl, Tlaloc, Chalchiuhtlicue, and Nanahuatl. Each age ends with the extinction of the sun. The struggle between Tezcatlipoca and Quetzalcoatl is given as the reason for the end of each age, but this is secondary to the true dynamic, which is simply the working out of the Aztec motifs of quadruplicity and quintuplicity. In the process of moving from the first age to the fifth, man is shown to have moved through a series of increasingly civilized foods, from acorns to maize. The two themes of the cycle are the spasmodic and limited nature of human history and the ultimacy of the present age. What is significant is

the fact that the gods are treated as mere *dei ex machina*, wholly subordinate to time.

Having presented these eight cycles we must note some curious omissions: why are no cycles attached to such important deities as Xipe, Tlaloc, or Xiuhteuctli? It may be that the very antiquity of these gods finally stripped them of their original mythology. More likely, their cults were antithetical to narrative elaboration. But we do not really know. We would certainly expect to have these three important deities more prominently displayed in the mythology.

Tezcatlipoca is another matter. I have listed no cycle opposite his name because he is an active agent in almost all of them. He permeates the entire mythic mixture, giving it a homogeneity, a tincture of dark grandeur, a kind of Renaissance terribilita. To single him out would falsify his real role in the mythology: that of a common denominator.

When we consider all the cycles together we can see how one-sidedly Aztec man presented the cosmos. There is no cycle of important myths relating to maize, which is astonishing considering that maize culture absorbed so much of the Aztecs' energy in ritual. There is nothing here on the control of water, nothing suggested by the rich lacustrine life the Aztecs lived. There is nothing on the far-flung commerce which became an important part of the Aztecs' economy. It is not, of course, that these areas were far removed from their interests but that they modeled their storytelling upon astral movement, interpreting it through the central motifs of war and human sacrifice.

The Aztecs were fascinated by the great solar triumph and tragedy: the sun's fierce and unexpected rising, his splendid journey, and his fall into the underworld, where he battled with the demons of the night and, with it all, the constant and sinister presence of a challenger, a duelist as bellicose as he. It is as if the mythic substratum from the Aztecs' hunting and gathering days as Chichimecs had been too recent and too deeply engrained to be swept aside by a peasant mythology centering on maize and the manipulation of water.

Thus Aztec mythology had something like an organizing principle. It is fatuous to attempt to reduce a people's mythology to an overriding formula, for man's eternal delight in storytelling and embellishment would effectively demolish such an assumption, yet it is certainly true that Aztec mythology is remarkably single-minded.

4. Tezcatlipoca

Description

The great Franciscan friar Sahagún has given us an appreciation of the Aztec gods in which, to characterize them, he paired them with the gods of the classical world.[1] Among the male gods, for instance, Huitzilopochtli is Mars, Painal is Mercury, Quetzalcoatl is Hercules, Tezcatzoncatl is Bacchus, Huehueteotl is Vulcan, and Tlaloc is Neptune. Among the females Chalchiuhtlicue is Juno, Chicomecoatl is Ceres, Cihuacoatl is Venus, and Teteoinnan is Diana.

At the head of this pantheon and taking the place of Jupiter, Sahagún placed Tezcatlipoca, Smoking Mirror. It is of interest that Sahagún felt that a further statement was needed about this god: he added, "This wicked Tezcatlipoca we know is Lucifer, the great devil who there in the midst of heaven, even in the beginning, began war, vice and filth." To have equated Tezcatlipoca both with Jupiter, king of the gods, and with Lucifer, the demonic archangel, may at first glance appear contradictory. But Sahagún was right. His dual identification leads us directly into a closer analysis of this sinister deity.

Tezcatlipoca is generally depicted as a warrior armed with atlatl, darts, and shield. He carries a war banner which may be blazoned with his peculiar device, the smoking mirror. He wears knee cuffs of jaguar skin. His body and limbs are black (or red in the case of his alter ego) and are dimly painted with circles, sometimes with lines. His face is the color of gold with three black stripes crossing it—one over the brows, one across the nose, and one across the chin.

He wears the double heron feathers of the Aztec warrior in his hair and has, strapped on his back, a towering feathered backpiece. What most distinguishes him, however, is the mirror he wears as an ornament in his hair, while another replaces a severed foot. A large ring hangs around his neck as a pectoral.

The Dark Mirror

The name Tezcatlipoca has generally been translated as Smoking Mirror, and we may keep that meaning here as adequate.[2] The god, also known as Lord of the Mirror, is intimately bound up with that object in which one sees the world reflected. In the city of Mexico there was a shrine dedicated to Tezcatlipoca called the House of Mirrors.[3] There the walls were hung with circular reflecting plaques which symbolized the god.

The looking glass is of respectable antiquity in Mesoamerica. In La Venta times concave mirrors made of polished magnetite were worn hanging from the neck as sacred pieces of jewelry. The concavity of the mirror's surface caused appreciable distortion, and one could expect a person gazing into it to be shocked or frightened at his reflection.[4]

In Toltec legend the end of droughts could be foretold by a mirror, no doubt a mosaic surface of black obsidian (commonly known as *tezcapoctli*, "mirror smoke")[5] Tezcatlipoca was said to have stolen this mirror and secreted it for a time, thus withholding relief from a serious famine then in progress. But even more sinister powers of the magic mirror were called into play in Tula when Tezcatlipoca persuaded Quetzalcoatl to gaze into it; the mirror revealed that mild deity to be repulsive and misshapen beyond belief. It was this meretricious self-revelation which helped to finally destroy Quetzalcoatl; in fact, the eerie Tezcatlipoca carried the title Tezcatlanextia, He Who Causes Things to Be Seen in the Mirror. Thus Tezcatlipoca's mirror was one of his most trenchant weapons; with it, if he so desired, he could undermine any truth. In one late text it is referred to as his "magic mirror," for it had the property of continuously bringing faces onto its dark surface, faces which could be seen through rolling smoke.[6] One important Nahuatl text says that it "clouds up all over like shadows on its surface." No doubt the fact that this mirror is generally shown smoking is a reference to such aspects of occultism.

When Tezcatlipoca, in one of the wandering legends, led the Huitznahua southward on their long trek into history, he guided and encouraged them with oracular visions from his sacred mirror? These Aztec people finally settled in Tezcoco, across the lake from Tenochtitlan, and installed this mirror in the temple they built for the god. In it one was supposed to behold, if not one's own image, then the image of the dark god himself.

But besides wearing the smoking mirror as a hair ornament and as an artificial foot, the god also wore a variant of it as a pendant about his neck. This was his *tlachialoni*, his spyglass, a burnished and perforated round plate or ring through which he peered to behold whatever he wished while himself remaining undiscovered.[8] The ring was probably supposed to represent another eye. By means of it Tezcatlipoca could look into the hearts of men, thus uncovering their most secret intentions.

It is apparent that Tezcatlipoca was a seer, that he had prevision and instruments for gaining hidden knowledge. This clairvoyance is unique, for no other god is so described. Even the paired high gods do not share Tezcatlipoca's uncanny and penetrating powers.

Tezcatlipoca as Shape Shifter

Tezcatlipoca had several facets to his personality, but I believe him to have been originally and most persuasively modeled on the American Indian shaman. The accretions of centuries have naturally obscured this shamanic archetype to some extent. But he is still there, behind the scenes. By any analysis Tezcatlipoca was an invisible and omniextensive god, a sorcerer, a trickster, a manic, a seer, and a shape shifter—all these pertain to his shamanic origins and they are still crucial elements in his later appearances. He does not, however, function as a socially cohesive force or as a reassurance to his people —as did the typical shaman in the primitive band or tribe—rather he deals mockingly and menacingly with men. He was almost exclusively the practitioner of black magic, as one might guess from the fact that he was left-handed.[9] If the nodal being upon which Tezcatlipoca was modeled was indeed the shaman, it was not that shaman who was accustomed to mediate between the people and the supernatural but the sorcerer of disruptive magic and furtive mind.

Tezcatlipoca prominently retains one characteristic of the shaman that is diagnostic—his ability to take other forms. Many Aztec gods take varying shapes at will, but Tezcatlipoca excels them all. Among his common doubles, we could mention the skunk, the monkey, and the coyote. This latter animal was that form of Tezcatlipoca worshiped above all by the Otomí, who considered him to have been their tribal progenitor or totem.[10]

In the above guise he was called Huehuecoyotl, Drum Coyote, a reference to the fact that he was a patron of singing and dancing.[11] Everything we know about this ancient Chichimec animal god shows him also to have been modeled on the shaman; in fact anyone born under his sign in the *tonalpohualli* was destined to become a chieftain, a singer, or a medicine man. He was a trickster like Tezcatlipoca and like him cast discord among men. There can be little doubt that the coyote, sly, contriving, implacable, and gloriously resonant in the night, provided for the Aztecs an example of the shaman's *nahualli* or double. As such he was naturally brought into conjunction with Tezcatlipoca.

But the guise most commonly associated with Tezcatlipoca was the jaguar, an animal known to be an evil omen. The echo of this predator's coughing roar in the deep barrancas was nerve-racking and always menacing. The jaguar was in fact so symbiotic with Tezcatlipoca that we must emphasize the connection between the two.

Of all the Mesoamerican fauna, the great spotted cat was the most formidable. He was associated with nighttime and deep coverts, with sudden death, with power and arcane wisdom. It was because of these qualities, patent to all who knew him, that we find him among the Maya particularly equated with the sorcerer. In the Mayan tongue the word *balam* means both jaguar and sorcerer, while in two of the Aztec myths we see Tezcatlipoca changing himself into a jaguar. Quoting from Sahagún, we can see why this link between the sorcerer and that animal seemed so natural to the Aztecs and their congeners. The Aztecs said of the jaguar (pointing it out as endowed most especially with superior vision):

> It is a dweller of the forests, of crags, of water; noble, princely, it is said. It is the lord, the ruler of animals. It is cautious, wise, proud. It is not a scavenger. It is one which detests, which is nauseated by dirty things. It is noble, proud. . . . And by night it watches; it seeks out what it hunts, what it eats. Very good, clear is its vision. In truth, it sees very well; it can see far. Even if it is very dark, even if it is misty, it sees.[12]

In Aztec symbolism, the spotted pelt of the jaguar represented the night sky, this coinciding with the animal's nocturnal nature.

As a god in his own right the jaguar was Tepeyollotl, Heart of the Mountain.[13] The animal's matchless power and stealth seemed to perfectly duplicate, or at the very least to suggest, the attributes of Tezcatlipoca. The lord of animals was most certainly a worthy counterpart in nature to the Aztec Jupiter.

The Black Tezcatlipoca

Blackness was always associated with Tezcatlipoca. To the Aztec nighttime was filled with phantoms and goblins and all of these could be indiscriminately identified with Tezcatlipoca. As one example, he might appear to men caught out in the dead of night as a horrible being called the Night Ax:[14] a headless man with a dreadful wound in his chest which kept opening and slamming shut, each time with a spine-tingling thud like that of an ax hurled into a tree. Such apparitions evidenced the demonic part of Tezcatlipoca's nature; he could be appropriately called the god of ill omen.[15]

Of the four Tezcatlipocas, the black Tezcatlipoca was the greatest (though not the firstborn) of the sons of the goddess. This underlines the fact, easily gathered from other signs, that black is the god's most congenial and native color. In cult this was indicated not only by his statue, which in one instance was made of shining black obsidian,[16] but by a special body paint worn by the priesthood of Tezcatlipoca and compounded from tobacco, narcotic mushrooms, poisonous snakes, and scorpions all ground up in a thick paste of soot. This body paint was put on by the priest only after sunset and possessed the property of rendering him fearless as he wandered among the high crags on his cult errands. In Tezcoco Tezcatlipoca's *ixiptla* or human surrogate, who presented people with the actual presence of the god, strolled through that city playing his flute, but only after dark.

The emphasis on blackness and impenetrability is obvious, and we cannot go far wrong in seeing Tezcatlipoca as night personified, a keenly conceptualized rendering of men's fears and insecurities. Inasmuch as the night is manifest most clearly in the thick bed of stars overhead, so Tezcatlipoca was thought of as the night sky. He is thus depicted in the codices playing in the *tlachco* against those who represent the powers of day. And we are not surprised to discover that by night he haunted crossroads, always dangerous and ill-starred places. It is probable that the god Yohualteuctli Yacahuitztli, Lord of the Night, the Sagacious One, was a transfiguration of his.

There is an impressive depiction of the black Tezcatlipoca in the *Selden Roll*, where he is called One Jaguar, an appropriate date-name.[17] He is shown as a warrior painted black, ensconced in the interior of the earth and wielding sacrificial knives. Thus did the artist symbolize the lethal effects of this god upon the present cosmos. The end of time too will be within this god's dark power, for we are told that when the fifth aeon has spent its days it will be he, the black Tezcatlipoca, who steals the sun away and plunges all things into eternal night.

He has a somewhat ambiguous opposite, the red Tezcatlipoca, said to be his brother and also a designation for the Tlascalan god Camaxtli (himself a transfiguration of Mixcoatl).[18] There is a scene in the Codex Borgia showing the black and the red Tezcatlipoca playing ball in the *tlachco*, which leads us to believe that the latter is indeed the former's opposite and thus represents a milder, diurnal divinity.

The Enemy

The Aztecs commonly knew Tezcatlipoca by the date-name of One Death. In a similar vein we find that one of his best-known transfigurations was that of Yaotl, the Enemy.[19] This form in fact makes quite clear to us that which was basic in his nature: his role as a sower of discord among men and cities. Whenever great men humiliated others in debate, scorned them in embassy, or demeaned them in anger, thus making war inevitable, Tezcatlipoca was responsible for the provocation. In further clarification of this role, we note that he was also called the Enemy of Both Sides, which stressed his single-minded concentration on discord itself, not on the victory of any one faction.[20] He consistently stirred up rancor so that peace should depart from cities and war should overrun the land. At such times blood flowed, prisoners were taken, and the gods feasted. Without the Enemy to induce men to engage in war the service of the gods might falter. A further extension of this transfiguration is Tezcatlipoca's occasional appearance as Itztli, the deified obsidian knife of sacrifice.[21]

The Enemy's part in war was more fundamental than the part played by Huitzilopochtli. This latter god was indeed a Mars, as we shall see in a later chapter. But he was a warrior god only because the people who considered him their tribal totem, the Mexica, were themselves warlike—his real role lay in representing the Mexica, not in representing war itself.

The Enemy did represent war itself. He was the tutelary god of the arsenal, which became his temple.[22] He was the lord of battles and had woven into his mantle an overall design of the skull and crossbones. He alone ruled the battlefield, for he decided who should live and who should die there. Warriors killed in the melee went to join the retinue of the sun, but it was the Enemy who dispatched them. He was said to adorn himself with flowers, a euphemism for the lives of fallen heroes. Sometimes his mirror is shown emitting not only smoke but also that complicated Aztec hieroglyph for war: *teoatl tlachinolli*, "divine liquid and burnt things."[23]

One of the most curious transfigurations of the Enemy is Ixquimilli, the Blindfolded One, always shown with a bandage over his eyes to emphasize his impartiality.[24] He had originally been a Toltec god and had been carried to far places by the warriors of Tula. The star assigned him in the heavens was supposed to be blindfolded, to walk backward, and to be, whenever it appeared, an omen of war. Thus was the berserker character of Tezcatlipoca emphasized. Ixquimilli probably also represented punishment as meted out by inscrutable power.

The Enemy's world as seen in his sunless mirror was thus a world of war, war brought into men's midst by him and under his aegis.

Ixquimilli censing a temple of night (Cospi)

To us today this is a bleak and morbid view of God, but we must grant its uncompromising quality and even, perhaps, its antique grandeur.

The Youth

Because Yaotl was a warrior, his youth was also stressed and in this transfiguration he becomes Telpochtli, the Young Male, conceived to be virgin.[25] He it was who presided as patron deity over the *telpoch-calli* or bachelor's hall, where boys were trained in the service of the state and the arts of war.[26] He was the youngest of the gods, never aging, and in fact he was thought to be reborn each year as a youth already adorned for war.[27] In this regard we recall *telpoch-tiliztli*, "the young," a special group of young people serving the god and wearing his livery.[28] After sunset in each of the city wards these boys and girls, richly clad, gathered to dance and sing in the deity's honor until midnight.

There were two centers for this young god's worship outside the Great Basin. One was in the valley of Toluca, where he was venerated as the god Tlamatzincatl, probably an Adonis-type god who was reborn every year.[29] The other was more famous and possessed a celebrated shrine on the outer slope of Mount Popocatepetl. Great numbers of the pious came to this site from as far away as Guatemala to celebrate the youthful god's festival. Here he was called the Virginal Youth; in the fashion of such godlings he was thought to live a chaste life in the forest, clad in deerskins and eating wild fruit and insects.[30]

Tezcatlipoca in Chalco

In Mexico there were two shrines to Nappateuctli, Four Times Lord, the patron deity of Chalco who was also classed as one of the Tla-loque.[31] In 1465, upon the defeat of the Chalca, the Mexica had seized that god and brought him back to install him in the great central temenos of their capital. The fact that Four Times Lord was known to be a transfiguration of Tezcatlipoca, and one particularly prone to produce drought, gives special significance to the few data we have on him.[32] The translation of the name fits in well with Tezcatlipoca, a god several times presented in quadruplicate. And like Tezcatlipoca, whose *ixiptla* wandered among the people during the whole year, the impersonator of Nappateuctli moved among the people of Chalco through the year, blessing them with drops of water shaken from a reed aspergillum.

Nappateuctli had led an Aztec people, the Tlacochcalca, out of the steppe and down into the Great Basin, where they had settled and erected a shrine for him at Tlapitzahuayan in Chalco.[33] The Tlacochcalca, however, soon ran into difficulties with hostile Chalca groups and were finally reduced to a state of abject terror. Their god was naturally also misprized and mocked. At last, when the pressure was no longer bearable, the Tlacochcalca nobles and priests took their god to the city of Coyohuacan, where they received asylum. With that exodus a terrible drought began in Chalco, affecting the whole land except that portion which had formerly belonged to the god— there rain fell. The drought called forth by the insulted god lasted long enough to seriously disrupt the Chalca state. Finally the Chalca rulers acknowledged their guilt and sent emissaries to Coyohuacan to offer Nappateuctli the first place in their pantheon and to plead with him to return. The god relented and, carried by his *teomama* or special priest, was escorted with great pomp back to the holy mountain of Chalco. The drought ended.[34] It may have been this famous episode which made Tlapitzahuayan the primary shrine of Tezcatlipoca in the whole of the Great Basin.

The Mocker

The Aztecs spoke of Tezcatlipoca with solemn conviction: "We men are your spectacle or show, at which you either jeer or rejoice."[35] They therefore called him Moquequeloa, the Mocker. Perhaps we can understand the quotation by attempting to grasp the role of sudden reversals in Aztec life. From its earliest appearance in history Aztec society had been warlike; it possessed a dynamic quality which has few peers. Cities in and around the Great Basin, which had formerly been Toltec, had been maintaining themselves only with difficulty when the proto-Aztec groups dispersed by the fall of Tula overran them. In a short time these cities had created that political culture which we now call Aztec. In this culture the city-state was conceived to be a kind of pantry for the god, providing him with his daily fare through the harsh harvests of war. Such a kinetic society was plentiful in suddenly wealthy men, frequent in the false appearance of friendships, and abundant in overthrows and surprising elevations of the humble to the seats of rule. Mutability was the rule.

Only a god like Tezcatlipoca could explain such an extreme situation. And only he could reward and punish its actors. In fact the reversals were his handiwork.

Tezcatlipoca does not have an inner law of his own; he is not, in other words, a nomistic god as is Jehovah in the late canonical prophets. In fact, Tezcatlipoca is *opoche*, "left-handed" or, as we might more figuratively translate it, sinister and not to be trusted. The pride of the mighty sometimes angers him so that he afflicts them with demotion or disease. On the other hand, with no motivation whatsoever, he raises up unknown men and casts them into the empty seats of the mighty. There was no way of being sure of his continuing favor. One simply granted that his will was capricious and that he could and would deliberately delude one.

One of the most interesting features of the mythology of Tezcatlipoca, and one which unequivocally points to his delight in hoodwinking men, is his appearance as a slave. In the Codex Borbonicus he is pictured as the black Tezcatlipoca wearing the starry crown of night.[36] Yet, paradoxically, he is simultaneously depicted with his neck caught in the wooden collar commonly worn by slaves, the symbol of baseness. Such mockery was peculiar to Tezcatlipoca. To celebrate his day-sign, rich men removed these restraining collars from their slaves and treated them as guests, flattering and feasting them until the god's day was over.[37] To have contravened this custom would have exposed them to the god's malice; they themselves might suddenly be reduced to slavery. Slaves were the *ixiptla* and the beloved sons of Tezcatlipoca—the living tokens of his power to reduce all men to misery.

But if he brought misery he also presided over plenty. In this transfiguration he was Omacatl, Two Reed, a god worshiped particularly in the Mexican ward of Huitznahuac.[38] Two Reed was the patron of invitations to feasts, these symbolizing the abundance Tezcatlipoca could dispense when so minded. It is supposed that to this transfiguration of Tezcatlipoca belongs the curious myth in which he persuades a follower of his to cross the eastern sea and bring back from the mansions of the sun the arts and instruments of music, both song and dance.[39] Nowhere else do we find Tezcatlipoca as a culture hero.

Tezcatlipoca is the only Aztec god known to have been abused by his devotees for his misdeeds. Disease was one of his gifts; often a person who was so afflicted, having petitioned the god in vain, ended up cursing him.

Tezcatlipoca and the State

Just as Tezcatlipoca laughs at the struggles of common men, so he laughs at the posturing of rulers. But his concern here has a different quality, for he was the patron of the state, being in this capacity sometimes called the Master of the Lords of the Earth.[40] A newly elected *tlatoani*, or ruler of an Aztec city, addressing the god, was careful to mention those former peers of his who had helped elevate him to power, men "who had been born and sanctified in signs and constellations under which lords are born, to be your instruments and images, to preside over your kingdoms, you being within them and speaking with their lips, they pronouncing your words."[41]

In this sense there was only one ruler of all the earthly states: Tezcatlipoca, the god of kings.[42] The *icpalli* or royal cushion was his. He was conceived to be the total ruler, so much so that he could be called Monenequi, a word that suggests his haughtiness and capriciousness of rule; it can be translated as He Who Pretends to Be What He Is Not.[43] In this regard we might mention that there is a possibility that the famous Aztec name of Moteuczoma, He Who Becomes Wrathful as Does a Lord, belongs to Tezcatlipoca in this transfiguration.[44] So closely were Aztec rulers identified in their prestige with Tezcatlipoca that, on their death, their faces were sometimes covered with the rich mask of that god.

Tezcatlipoca's relationship to the state is somewhat ambivalent. He was the source of all royal authority and by that very fact the office of the *tlatoani* possessed an enduring majesty. All victories were of his giving, yet the incumbent of any regal office had no assurance of security, for he could be unseated by the god in an instant and for no cause. "Sad stories of the deaths of kings" were a commonplace in Aztec history. Tezcatlipoca's mockery even mocked itself, and only the intensity of Aztec belief in him prevented this excess from degenerating into caricature and effrontery.

The Great God

Having offered these insights into the popular understanding of this god, we should say something about that side of him, undoubtedly of great antiquity, which had been formulated by his priesthood.

As the Great God he had several names or transfigurations which are significant. Perhaps the most revealing of these was Titlacahuan, which means We Are His Slaves. Under this appellation he was specific to Tula and had been formed in accordance with that city's imperial thinking–from which connection, no doubt, came his universalism. He had an avatar, Macuiltotec, whose name expresses this completeness: Our Lord Five shows him as the numen behind the number which summed up the totality of things.[45]

This god had no corporeal body; invisible as wind or darkness, he lived everywhere. Inasmuch as he was, according to one of our sources, the Soul of the World, it followed that men were never far from him at any instant.[46] He was revered at wayside shrines and every house, great or small, possessed an image of him. He was truly ubiquitous.

He was also unknowable. His words came to men like shadows passing, and of his great acts none was more astounding than his own self-creation, wherefore he was known as Moyocoyani. Not only did he make himself (thus being something of a god *ex nihilo*), but he was more vaguely the creator of all things and of all men. This creation he governed with constant surveillance, and no human heart could keep an ugly desire hidden from him. Yet out of this god's wrath against his creatures might sometimes come, interestingly enough, compassion; only he could grant mercy to men in their afflictions, and sometimes he did.

We stop here to point out one of the difficult problems in the study of Aztec religion which we have briefly touched on before–the determination of the identity of that god described by the divine epithets Tloque Nahuaque and Yohualli Ehecatl, Night and Wind. These designations are crucial in any attempt to understand Tezcatlipoca. In a previous chapter we have spoken of Tloque Nahuaque of Tezcoco as if he were a god wholly separate from all others, yet here we must identify him as one of Tezcatlipoca's transfigurations.

The fact is that the two divine epithets can be free-standing and can simply refer to God rather than to any particular god. However, only Tezcatlipoca can really carry the tremendous implications contained within the epithets. What we are saying is that, if an Aztec had been asked to identify the deity to whom these terms most aptly applied, he would unquestioningly have answered Tezcatlipoca. In the name Tloque Nahuaque there are strong overtones of ubiquity and immanence. This divine designation was apparently known to the Toltecs and was later, in Aztec times, used at all levels of society, from nobles and priests down to commoners. Its antiquity is undoubted. But, because the term implied a metaphysic as much as a religious certainty, Tloque Nahuaque was removed from the earthly habitat otherwise so congenial to Tezcatlipoca and placed in the topmost heaven, where he lived as an "only" god.[47] The Aztec city which most favored this transfiguration of Tezcatlipoca, and the only one as far as we know which erected a temple to him (thus beginning the process of separating him from Tezcatlipoca), was Tezcoco. The pyramid upon which this temple rested had exactly the number of stages as there were ascending levels in the heavens. The shrine, painted black on the outside with stars depicted on it, was provided with special musical instruments which periodically sounded. Nezahualcoyotl, the ruler who had this religious edifice constructed, broke with Aztec custom when he ordered that no image of the god was to be placed within the shrine. This was consonant, of course, with the connotation of the epithet applied to the god, Night and Wind, the double phrase stressing the god's impenetrability, invisibility, and untouchableness.

Tezcatlipoca in Myth—His Work in the Heavens

I have mentioned that in the priestly thought of the Aztecs Tezcatlipoca was a creator. In Aztec mythology he was also presented as a creator. An analysis of the myths explicating his creativity is therefore of importance in pinpointing his place in the more popular, as opposed to the priestly, understanding.

We know that, as a prime mover, Tezcatlipoca initiated the series of five aeons which determined once and for all the chronology of cosmos. He became the first of the suns, appropriately called Jaguar Sun, which was the darkest of them all. In his role as sinister demiurge he can be referred to as Left-Handed Jaguar.[48]

This original aeon was the age of the giants, the primordial race. All was on a brutal and colossal scale. The giants ate only acorns and pine nuts, and their strength was such that they could pull trees up. One version of their downfall says that the sky fell on them and crushed them. In a more orthodox tale, a horde of jaguars attacked them—alternatively it was said that it was Tezcatlipoca who became a jaguar and destroyed them. The aeon itself ended only with the extinguishing of Tezcatlipoca's sun. This feat was performed by the god Quetzalcoatl, who knocked Tezcatlipoca out of the sky, whence he tumbled into the dark waters that surrounded the earth. This is memorialized, one of our sources says, by Tezcatlipoca's constellation, the Great Bear, when it sinks under the horizon.[49]

What strikes us in the myth of the first sun is the importance of Tezcatlipoca's association with the jaguar, and we are probably justified in inferring that this animal aspect of his tale is very old, possibly older than the specific god himself, who may have been attracted into the animal role at a later time. At any rate in the myth the sun was a jaguar and was a peculiarly dark luminary associated with night and the night sky.

One would have expected this central myth to refer to the god's mirror foot, but such is not the case. We can only feel that this feature of his story has disappeared in the mists of time. We might look for the details of such a lost myth in several places. One is the great Codex Borgia, which contains one richly detailed plate which may be pertinent; this plate, however, cannot be interpreted with certainty, so we can only surmise that there is a connection.[50] In the picture we see the black Tezcatlipoca trapped in the nighttime within

The knife god Itztli with avatars of Tezcatlipoca (Borgia)

a great blood-red enclosure made of sacrificial knives. Tecpatl, the god of the knife, sits centrally within the enclosure and has caught Tezcatlipoca by the foot. In the persons of his four doubles the god seems to have wrenched himself free and to be fleeing, his foot then being replaced with the smoking mirror. If this scenario is indeed the skeleton of our hypothetical myth, no trace of it has survived anywhere in the literature. However, the battle between a young astral god and a primordial sea monster, in which the god loses his foot, is well known in Aztec iconography.

Then there is the myth of Tezcatlipoca's fall from heaven.[51] Here we are told that he had sinned and, like Lucifer, was hurled down from the ambrosial regions. It may well be that his foot was torn off in that cosmic episode. The sin for which he was exiled was lubricity, for it was he who had seduced the virgin goddess Xochiquetzal and, disguised as Xolotl, dragged her with him into the underworld.[52] A variant of his fall has it that he stealthily let himself down to earth on a single cobweb.

In itself this Aztec myth does not provide us with a satisfactory answer to our question, but an interesting Tarascan parallel may.[53] This is the tale of the great god Taras Upeme, who—in the course of a gargantuan drinking bout in the heavens—used violence and for it was hurled from the skies, which is why he is lame. From such a parallel we can guess that there may once have been a connection between Tezcatlipoca's fall from heaven and his loss of a foot and its replacement by a mirror. After a long series of adaptations and re-tellings this part of the myth might well have been lost. But all this is mere speculation and only serves to show that we are not able to be precise about this important feature of the god's appearance.

We have previously noticed the role played by Tezcatlipoca, along with his counterpart Quetzalcoatl, in the great act of lifting up the sky and setting it firmly above the earth. Therefore, we do not need to retell this creation myth.

We know that, in his embodiment as the Enemy, Tezcatlipoca was the instigator and patron of war. His mythology describes him in an even more intimate sense as one of its creators. Here it all came about as a result of the decision by the four creator gods—among whom Tezcatlipoca was first—to create war as a way of nourishing the new sun. Tezcatlipoca formed four hundred men and five women for this first exercise in armed conflict.[54] The war which resulted was of course on a stellar plane, for we already know that the four hundred warriors were conceived to be the stars in their courses. This served as a model for all earthly wars, the purpose of both modes of war, cosmic and earthly, being identical–the feeding of the gods.

This myth is practically identical with that of Mixcoatl and the Four Hundred Mimixcoa which will be told in chapter 6, a primitive myth describing the introduction of warfare among men. That the Aztecs themselves realized this identity between the two myths is apparent from their contention that at one point in his career Tezcatlipoca changed his name to Mixcoatl.[55] Thus as a god of war Mixcoatl is, in the teaching of the priesthood of Tezcatlipoca, simply another transfiguration of their own superior god.

The God in Tula

Tezcatlipoca had sinned in the heavens and had been cast down. When he came down from the empyrean, so ran the myth, he first showed himself to the Toltecs on the summit of the Mount of Mirrors, presumably near Tula. He appeared under the guise either of the god Titlacahuan or of Tlacahuepan, another transfiguration.[56]

This mythic datum initiates a cycle of tales concerning Tezcatlipoca in Tula that is of great importance for the study of Mesoamerican religion. Instead of treating him cosmically as the creation myths do, this cycle ties him narrowly to a definite geographical location, the Toltec capital. We realize that we are here confronted with a god whose cult centered in Tula, and we may consequently expect to find in some of the tales references to that cult and its vicissitudes. For instance, Tezcatlipoca's hostile relationship with Quetzalcoatl in Tula is narrated in two ways, though in both the victory of the former over the latter is consistently emphasized.

In the first myth Tezcatlipoca challenged Quetzalcoatl to a contest in the *tlachco* and as a winning stratagem changed himself into a jaguar.[57] This had the effect of so frightening Quetzalcoatl's supporters that his influence declined to the point where he was forced into exile. This tale was obviously patterned on a stellar myth: not the night sky swallowing the sun–for Quetzalcoatl never represented the sun–but perhaps the night defeating the Evening Star, the planet Venus. We know that both Tezcatlipoca and Quetzalcoatl were lords of the stars and that their street across the sky was the Milky Way.[58]

The second myth is more euhemeristic and casts Tezcatlipoca as the evil sorcerer in Tula equipped with all manner of cunning enchantments. Prominent among these were his famous distorting mirror, magic potions, shape shifting, and finally sexual suggestion. This was one of the most detailed and widely known of all the Aztec myths, and it will be fully analyzed in the next chapter. Only Tezcatlipoca's malevolent part in it is important to us here. This part of the myth tells how, after completely undermining the virtue and therefore the religious authority of Quetzalcoatl, Tezcatlipoca pursued him until he had forced him far beyond the confines of the Toltec empire. It needs little perception to see this as a cult conflict in Tula, with an older god being demoted and partially eclipsed by a more vigorous and younger god.

But Tezcatlipoca's Tula cycle of myths contains some curious tales altogether unrelated to Quetzalcoatl. In one of these Tezcatlipoca took the form of an ithyphallic foreigner who seduced the ruler's daughter and finally married her.[59] The foreigner was an embarrassment to the Toltec nobility, and they plotted to abandon him in a battle against Tula's enemies. But, even though betrayed in this fashion, the foreigner returned victoriously, to become highly respected and acceptable to all. This tale possibly points to the introduction of a foreign god who was then cast as a transfiguration of Tezcatlipoca.

In another tale Tezcatlipoca proclaimed a great celebration for the Toltecs, during which he sang and drummed for them.[60] The people, gathered together from all parts of the empire, were thus evilly enchanted and could not stop dancing until, in their frenzy, they fell from the high crags of Texcalpan and, tumbling to the bottom, were turned to stones.

Another time the god proclaimed a flower festival and, when the great ones of the empire had assembled in Xochitlan, he turned upon them and massacred them. Those who escaped trampled each other to death in their panic.

Again Tezcatlipoca disguised himself in the marketplace and set about performing magic. One of his sleights was to make a miniature man dance in the palm of his hand. Thousands pressing around him to see the amazing figure died in the fierce pressures of the crowd. This happened time and time again. Finally Tezcatlipoca incited the crowd to stone the dancing figure and kill him. The dead body, now become great in size, rotted before their eyes, the stench smothering thousands. The Toltecs attempted to drag the poisonous figure away, but he had become as heavy as a mountain. Many were crushed as the great figure rolled over them.[61]

Another time Tezcatlipoca, disguised as an old woman, sat in Tula and toasted maize. The delicious aroma spread throughout the kingdom and people from all over were drawn to the source. When he had thus trapped them Tezcatlipoca killed them.

In all these stories the element of sorcery is dominant. In the tale of the foreigner and the tale of the massacre at Xochitlan, however, Tezcatlipoca is also shown as a warrior. These are not surprising facts. What is of greater interest is that these tales, taken altogether, are presented as presaging the end of the Toltec empire. Numbers of vassals gather in Tula and are destroyed, great celebrations end in disaster, and Tezcatlipoca as the god Titlacahuan is always central, for it is he who wills the evil end. Omens predict the approaching doom; the mountain of Zacatepec is seen to be burning at night, and from that the Toltecs know their destruction is near.

As related by Sahagún, who is here our prime source, the Titlacahuan myths refer to the latter days of the Toltec capital, when it was subject to a drought of major proportions. The cult of Tezcatlipoca seems to have been pushing hard in those late days to attain dominance in Tula and was faced with competition from the older and undoubtedly more firmly established Quetzalcoatl cult. The tumults attendant upon Tezcatlipoca's victory quite possibly contributed to Tula's collapse—in which case it would have been a Pyrrhic victory for that god, for Quetzalcoatl by his very defeat was given a new and strangely effective mythology, as we shall see in the next chapter. But the Aztecs inherited Tezcatlipoca with all the attributes of a universal god, while Quetzalcoatl remained circumscribed. We can surmise that, as the centuries closed over Tula, Tezcatlipoca was the undisputed king of the gods, without rival and without peer.

Huemac

Besides his transfiguration as Titlacahuan, Tezcatlipoca was also known in Tula as Huemac, He Who Is in a Big Hand, though this title was apparently never used by the later Aztecs to refer to him. Huemac was a phantom or double of Tezcatlipoca.[62] Specifically he was that sorcerer god who had led the original Toltecs on the long wandering that had finally resulted in the founding of their great city.[63] From that time on Toltec rulers occasionally bore the god's name as their own.

It may be that this aspect of the god belonged to some semisavage Chichimec stratum of the early Toltec people. Indeed one source is quite certain that Huemac was a Chichimec chieftain who, at some point in the history of Tula, conquered it and later abandoned it. We might infer from this that that part of the Toltec people who claimed Chichimec origin considered their leader to be the personification of Huemac and therefore assigned him the god's name as a title. That there was a competing ruler among the Toltecs who bore Quetzal-coatl's name is also clear and will be discussed in the following chapter.

The final days of Tula are curiously tied to this ambivalent figure. The last Toltec ruler was named Huemac. As the empire thundered down about him and his supporters turned upon him, he fled south into the Great Basin, hoping to find refuge in some of the formerly Toltec cities there. But at the foot of the rock of Chapultepec he was overtaken and killed by his pursuers.

One can also tell this story in terms of myth. This myth states that at the very end of Tula's history Huemac played a game of *tlachtli* with the rain gods and lost.[64] As a result a devastating drought shri-veled the land for four years, destroying even the hardiest cactus. The drought was broken only when Huemac secured an oracle from the sacred spring of Chapultepec and made the required sacrifice, whereupon he disappeared into a cavern there. In that chthonian world he still rules as king, and he will not return. In this myth we clearly have a god who is connected with *tlachtli*, drought, darkness, and caves—all items that comport well with Tezcatlipoca. This can be true in spite of the fact that, as a mountain god in Chapultepec, Hue-mac must also be one of the Tlaloque.

Tezcatlipoca in Cult

In the varieties of his theophanies Tezcatlipoca was exceptional. In the expressiveness and somberness of his mythology he was out-standing. But it is in his cult presence that we see him as unique.

His great festival appropriately fell in the Aztec month of Toxcatl, roughly equivalent to our month of May, a time when severe drought sometimes occurs in Central Mexico, causing the newly planted crops to wither before they can establish themselves. But the festival on that occasion was far more than an appeal to a potentially evil god that he refrain from afflicting the land with drought and famine. It was also the ultimate confirmation of his continuing presence among the Aztecs—a statement of the inescapability of his presence. Inasmuch as it was sometimes said to be the most important festival in the Aztec calendar, a summary of it is in order.

As the month of Toxcatl closed, the *ixiptla* of Tezcatlipoca for the coming year was chosen. He had been selected by reason of his perfection of body and grace and for his general educability. In some Aztec cities he was selected from the slave class, in others from the prisoners of war. For a whole year he was the epiphany of Tezcatlipoca, the very person of the god walking among men, and to that end he was given the god's name, Titlacahuan. He was trained to some degree of sophistication in playing the flute, in dancing, and in dignified behavior. He was provided with a rotating guard of warriors who acted as his pages but who also saw to it that he did not escape. Like the god himself, he was housed during the day in the Tlacochcalco, his own temple. Come nighttime this Titlacahuan walked through the city, free to go where he wished though always accompanied by his guardians. Before he came down from the pyramid terrace in the darkness, he stood at the top of the steps and blew on his pipe to the four directions, alerting people everywhere so they might pray to him asking for their heart's desire. Then, accompanied by his guards with torches, he moved out into the sleeping city. As he walked among the houses he danced and jangled the rattles on his arms and legs and blew loudly on the flute. Awakened by these shrill sounds, the people knew them to be the authentic voice of the god. Women with sick children held them out to him and begged that he withdraw his evil from them; he was the god in whose providence were also all good things, fame and wealth, health and the esteem of others. Before the sun could rise above the horizon he was escorted back to his cage in the temple, where the lords could come to revere him during the day.

Thus it went for the course of a year till Toxcatl came round again. During this twenty-day period before his death, the young *ixiptla* was invested with the full regalia of the god, and it was the ruler himself who, now as a menial, attired him. In addition the *ixiptla* was ceremonially wedded to four great goddesses in the persons of four beautiful girls, and with them he took as much sexual pleasure as he desired.[65]

Five days before the end of the month, the ruler of the city went into retirement, thus permitting it to be seen that only Titlacahuan truly ruled over men. Then on the last day of the month, the *ixiptla*, accompanied by his wives, was taken across the lake to make a landing near the city of Ixtapalapa. At a designated spot his wives bade him good-bye, and he was led to his shrine near Tlapitzahuayan.[66] He was forced to ascend the steps leading to the top, turning and break-ing his flutes and other instruments at each step. At the top he was immediately seized by the waiting priests and sacrificed. His opened body was not tumbled down the steps, however, as was the custom among the Aztecs, but was reverently carried down in the arms of the officiants. At the bottom the cadaver was decapitated and defleshed. The pieces of flesh were taken back to the city, where they were in-corporated into a sacred meal given to the ruler and the princes of the state.

Before this cannibal meal was served, the new *ixiptla* for the coming year had been designated, and he also partook of the repast. On that last solemn day of the month of Toxcatl—again contrary to custom—no other person was sacrificed. However, every fourth year a departure was made from this concentration on the one victim: at those times others were sacrificed to serve as food for the departed Titlacahuan.[67]

This fourth-year celebration was penitential in purpose. The clair-voyant Tezcatlipoca was aware of every man's sins and, on his quad-rennial appearance, he granted plenary remission to those who sought it. Penitents whipped each other with knotted cords as they moved about the cities in procession. In Tenochtitlan they then bathed in what was called the blue and the yellow waters of Tezca-tlipoca to wash away the remnants of their evildoing. No other god had the power to offer such sweeping renewal.

Cult acknowledged Tezcatlipoca's omnipresence. Whereas Huit-zilopochtli's priesthood could come only from the pure-blooded Mex-ica, Tezcatlipoca's came from those who as children had been de-voted by their parents to the god—racial affiliation here made no difference, for Tezcatlipoca touched all men equally. He walked among the people all the days of the year in the cities, just as he re-vealed himself on the *momoztli* in the countryside. These were low, flattopped stone altars or seats, sometimes round, erected beside paths, in the markets, and at every crossroads. There were no con-structions on top, for the god had no home, only places where he rested. On the last five days of every month these stoops were dec-orated with fresh fir boughs. They were everywhere, so many that no one could ever ignore the god's presence.

An Assessment

How do we assess this god?

First it is important to note his protean characteristics. He is the symbol of total rule and majesty, an evil and destructive sorcerer, a warlord, a rain withholder, a virginal young man, a seducer, a creator, and a ghastly demon. He is secretive, whimsical, all-knowing, forgiving, absurd, and malicious. He is invisible and ubiquitous and final. He inhabits the night sky, caves, crossroads, reed beds, the countryside, and the city. Such variety might be expected to have diluted his omnipotence. Strangely enough it did not.

Historically he is a patchwork of transfigurations placed over a dimly perceived nucleus. We have stated our belief that the deepest layer of his being was that of the shaman and that the perverse quality inherent in the figure of the shaman was sufficiently strong to control the other characteristics as they were added. Tezcatlipoca is superior to the dual lord and lady gods because, in their late forms, they had become mere priestly abstractions, whereas Tezcatlipoca was always felt to be a living presence. Even when he is given such universal epithets as the Immanent One, He through Whom We Live, and the Self-Created, personality still inheres in him. Weird because of his unerring power to see and to know, the seer becomes the god of unimpeachable will, untrammeled, and therefore generally evil in men's minds—for men always wish to limit God. In their inscrutability and their holiness there are decided resemblances between Tezcatlipoca and the God of Job.

Inasmuch as he served as a template for the depiction of other important male gods, notably Mixcoatl and Huitzilopochtli, Tezcatlipoca is of true grandeur. Indeed in a sense we must think of these latter two as essentially avatars or reworkings of Tezcatlipoca. In this situation of close identity we can see how clearly he was the very model of sovereignty for the Aztecs.

But it is always the negative quality which is paramount in Tezcatlipoca. He has the power to forgive, but nothing in his nature compels him to forgive. He is above all earthly law, but he has established no law within himself. He sends disease, not always as punishment and sometimes without reason. His mastery of discord serves no eschatological purpose in human history but only the purpose of lesser gods who wish to drink and dine. He creates, but in his creation he is the grand exemplar of evil and deception. He does not love, he does not even hate—he is simply the sheer power and will of God without his law and without his love.

Thus, though indubitably majestic, Tezcatlipoca is truncated. He is indeed Jupiter, the king of the gods, but he has no kingdom, for such would imply a polity and a purposive order. And he has none.

5. Quetzalcoatl

How He Is Different

If there is any one Aztec god who is known to everyone it is certainly Quetzalcoatl, an enigmatic figure who has fascinated western man from Cortés and the early friars down to the present. There is an explanation for this interest: Quetzalcoatl is the only Aztec god human enough for us to idealize. The others are the very essence of godhead, awesome and often egregious in conception. But Quetzalcoatl is different. He has escaped from the cold ruins of Mexico to inhabit the aesthetic and imaginative world of today, in the process inspiring some of the world's novelists and painters. He is thus a controversial subject, lively and kaleidoscopic. The salient facts about his cult and mythology will be found in this chapter.

His Name and Appearance

There is luckily no difficulty in translating the name Quetzalcoatl; it means simply Plumed Serpent. The plumes referred to are the exquisite green tail feathers of the once common, now nearly extinct, quetzal found in Central America. These plumes were so prized that the world *quetzalli* came to mean "precious" or "treasure." Additionally, depending on the context, the Aztecs used the word *coatl*, "snake," to mean "dragon" as well as—somewhat amazingly—"twin" (pl. *cocoa*). Quetzalcoatl can thus mean with equal correctness either Plumed Serpent or Precious Twin. We are mentioning this latter translation because it specifies the relationship the god has with Xolotl, his most common transfiguration, whom we will consider later.

A large percentage of the gods depicted in Aztec art at first sight appear to us to be monuments of the uncouth, and certainly none more so than Quetzalcoatl. Here we come upon the first curious fact about him, namely that he very often does not appear as a plumed serpent at all but as a bearded man painted black and wearing a grotesque red buccal mask.[1] On his head is either a tall conical jaguar-skin bonnet, characteristic of the Huaxtec culture on the Gulf coast, or a smaller two-colored truncated cap. This headgear often includes a sharp bone from which flows the penitential blood presented as nourishing the god's *nahualli*, the lovely quetzal. There hangs around his neck a conch pectoral sectioned to reveal its graceful inner convolutions. This was the god's so-called wind jewel, supposedly symbolizing the swirling winds that precede the downpour.[2] He wears

The Plumed Serpent and his personification as Ehecatl (Laud)

jaguarskin cuffs around his ankles, and he carries a distinctive sinuous baton studded with jewels that represent stars. This was the *xonecuilli*, which may have symbolized the seven stars grouped in an S-curve in the constellation of the Little Bear.[3] The god occasionally carries a shield decorated with the feathers of marine birds, but he seldom brandishes darts and atlatl as do most of the other gods; rather he carries the sacred thorn of the penitential priest. The most striking and certainly the most significant item of these vestments is the buccal mask. In the hieroglyphic system used by the Aztecs this alone could serve to represent the god.

Quetzalcoatl is actually fourfold. He is originally a flying dragon called the Plumed Serpent. He is also Ehecatl, the Wind. He is the Morning Star, whose name is Ce Acatl, One Reed. And finally he is the Toltec priest-ruler, Topiltzin. One of the difficulties in analyzing the god is to separate these four impersonations. Their names sometimes interchange in a most disconcerting way.

Quetzalcoatl as the Celestial Dragon

The Mesoamerican dragon, patterned upon the rattlesnake, was a common and early mythical creature. From the La Venta culture (1250 B.C. to 600 B.C.) in southern Vera Cruz and Tabasco comes a well-known depiction of the dragon with a rattlesnake's tail and a plumed crest. He appears again out of the same culture on the rocks of Chalcatzinco, just to the south of Mount Popocatepetl, and several times in the caves of Guerrero.

From that stretch of the Gulf coast anciently called Xicalanco come references to plumed serpents—that area in fact is stated to have been the creature's native habitat[4]. On the Totonac coast he appears as a chimera equipped with rattles and able to fly about in a great rush of wind. Among the Maya the sky dragon was modeled on the iguana or the alligator as well as on the rattlesnake. In the central highlands of Mexico the sky dragon was known from early Teotihuacan times. This blue dragon pours great torrents of water from his mouth, and his body is covered with feathers. These ancient dragons were not forgotten easily. When the Spaniards entered the land they learned that the valley of Tehuacan near Puebla had been terrorized repeatedly by flying griffins, forcing many of the inhabitants to leave.

It is difficult to know with any accuracy what these early dragons symbolized. I suspect that they were built on a loose and all-inclusive pattern, that they had powers ranging from the atmospheric to the stellar, and that they represented "sky" in whatever sense was uppermost at the moment: tornadoes and waterspouts, the searing sun of a long drought, the rain, the faint light of dawn, the opacity of the night sky, the zodiacal wheel, and the stars – these might all fall under the rubric of the dragon in situations we can only dimly imagine. By the same token, the dragon might have been restricted in certain cultures to symbolizing simply the sky and the rains contained within it, or perhaps only the dawn, or the winds, etc. Certainly the sense of all that is overhead as a vast coiling or sleeping serpent armed with talons, his body sheathed in a hauberk of blue green feathers, is a powerful and vivid concept; once established in an early peasant population, it could have become both a canon in art and a dogma in belief. At least it seems to have done so in Mesoamerica from La Venta times on. Quetzalcoatl, the Plumed Serpent of the Aztecs, was the epitome of these celestial dragons.

His connection with the sky is well attested. Omeyocan, the heavenly residence of the high gods, was particularly associated with Quetzalcoatl. There he held converse with Star Skirt and other deities, and from there he was to be sent down to earth on his great mission. We are also informed that, in company with Tezcatlipoca, he heaved up the sky on his shoulders, and we have already noted that the two gods were sentinels along the Milky Way.

These are indications of a connection between Quetzalcoatl and the sky which we are unable to be precise about but which the traditional blackness of his color attests to, for black represented the impalpable to the Aztec mind.[5] The god's transfiguration as a genius of the night sky may have been reinforced in the first place by the Mesoamerican priests' (of whom he was the archetype) well-known predilection for nocturnal practices. We know that his *ixiptla* was always sacrificed at midnight. As the sky dragon he thus had jurisdiction in the night sky as well as in the sky of the day.

We have stated that Quetzalcoatl was a source of waters. An unequivocal statement to this effect comes from the time of the entry of the Spaniards. When Cortés was approaching Cholula, the holy city of Quetzalcoatl, the inhabitants believed that their god would infallibly protect them from any assault; they thought that, if the Spaniards should so much as chip off one piece of stucco from the god's temple base, rivers of water would gush forth and drown them. As a lord of celestial waters Quetzalcoatl could also, like Tlaloc, demand that children be sacrificed to him in times of drought,[6] and in the form in which he was known to the Maya his patronage of water was undisputed. By the Mexicans he could be referred to as "the father of the cloud children."[7] Even today in certain parts of the state of Puebla a cloudburst is called a *quetzalcoatl*.

Quetzalcoatl as the Wind

The above conception of the god as a celestial dragon may be considered primary, but he has one closely connected transfiguration which is much more determinate–Ehecatl, the Wind. It is this divinity who is commonly represented wearing a Huaxtec cap and the wind jewel.

High winds are known everywhere in the world, and everywhere people marvel at invisibility married to such great violence. When to this wonder are added early man's speculations on the equivalence of life and breath, he is apt to deify air as a demiurge and consider it far more subtle than fire or earth or water. Ehecatl as a god of wind is just such a deification.

What we know about Quetzalcoatl points to the fact that the Aztecs saw him as a being far apart from the other gods–the only one, that is, who was thought to have a special care for men and a special relationship to them. Known as Nine Wind and feathered with black instead of green plumes, he was credited with the creation of the first man and woman of the fifth sun.[8] As the god One Wind he was the patron of midnight thieves and sorcerers. We should point out here, however, that as wind he was generally part of the larger and less dynamic entity of air. The word for air or a barely perceptible breeze in Nahuatl is *ecatl*; simple reduplication produces the greater violence of wind, *ehecatl*. It is doubtless the former more refined, less tangible verbal background in the god's nature which allows for the statement in his mythology that he received his commission as a master of wisdom and subtlety up in that highest of the heavens, Omeyocan. Quetzalcoatl's attributes of wisdom will be commented on later; we mention them here simply to point out the conceptual affinity they bear to the intangibility of air, the whisper or clamor of its passage, its ubiquity, and above all its presence as the token distinguishing the quick from the dead. Classic Nahuatl had a number of words for the various states of the air and the types of wind.[9] It is interesting to find among these that the whirlwind or squall was called *ehecacoatl* or "wind snake," showing the ease with which the Aztec mind accepted

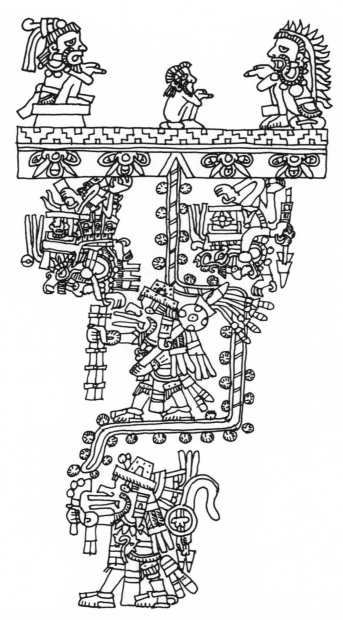

The god Nine Wind (Quetzalcoatl) descending from the heavens on his mission to man (Vindobonensis)

the reptilian nature of the wind.[10] Ehecacoatl was also one of the names of Quetzalcoatl; sometimes even *ecamalacatl*, the common word for whirlwind, was used to refer to him.

The Gulf coast of Mexico has always known violent winds, ranging from the furious winter *nortes* of the state of Vera Cruz to the destructive hurricanes of Yucatan. The old Huaxtec culture, long preceding the Aztec, was located in the northern coastal plains and its backcountry. Its most important port, Panuco, is said to have been the point where Quetzalcoatl first debarked to colonize Mesoamerica. This information supplements other evidence pointing to his coastal origin, such as his Huaxtec apparel and the sectioned seashell he wore. In a certain mythological depiction Ehecatl is shown emerging from a high wave of the sea, as if he were personifying the Gulf storm. Nearby (on the seashore?) stands the great goddess of the Huaxtecs in a combative pose, while behind her Ehecatl again appears as a flying serpent.[11] Whatever the meaning of this scene, it places Ehecatl without question in the Huaxtec lowlands, as do mural representations from certain temples in the area.

The Aztecs never confused Ehecatl with Tlaloc even though both had to do with rain.[12] The latter was always a deity resident in or on the mountain and thus was connected with the earth; rain was his sole dominion. As the Wind, Quetzalcoatl never loses his connection with the sky and he is never portrayed as an earth god; rain is only part of his dominion. This sharp differentiation is further evidenced in the description the Aztecs gave of Ehecatl as the forerunner or "ambassador" of Tlaloc.[13] Ehecatl came ahead of the rain god, sweeping his path before him, this identifying him especially with the darkness, the swirling dust, and the heightened winds that precede the storm.

Quetzalcoatl as the Morning Star

There can be no doubt that the Toltecs inherited Quetzalcoatl from precedent cultures. In the Teotihuacan culture Quetzalcoatl appears to have been the sky dragon, an aqueous being worshiped by a newly urbanized people. When the Toltecs took over this prestigious god they changed him into a patron of warriors, giving him the date-name of Ce Acatl and claiming that he had been the first ruler of Tula.[14] Wherever the Toltec knights went they took him with them. They portrayed him thrashing about in the heavens over their array,

The god of the Morning Star striking a goddess (Cospi)

his ardor and fury the model for theirs. The Aztecs borrowed this figuration. They too portrayed the god as if he were floating above the heads of their advancing warriors, and they specifically connected their nobility with him when they cast him as the patron god of the *calmecac*, the noblemen's school.

It is at this point in our analysis of Quetzalcoatl that our difficulties really begin. Why should the sky dragon have been equated with the god Ce Acatl, the Morning Star? It is certainly a far leap from a being who represents sky, its winds, waters, and myriads of stars, to one particular star whose bailiwick was combat and sacrifice and who had nothing to do with dragons or serpents in the mythology. We may extract a few answers to this question from the following data relating to the Morning Star.

Mesoamerica everywhere worshiped the Morning Star, seeing in him either a warrior or a hunter. Among the Tarascans, for instance, he was the harbinger of war.[15] The Aztecs described him as the Great Star and named him Tlahuizcalpanteuctli, Lord at the Time of Dawn; in fact, he was as much the dawn as he was that star which particularly distinguished it. Their date-name for him was Ce Acatl, One Reed. Being greatly feared, this deity had a most vivid mythology.

It was sometimes said that Ce Acatl was the one who first brought light, being therefore older than the sun, a preexistent power as it were.[16] Of all the celestial bodies he was second only to the sun in the honors accorded him. He was descended from a warlike woman created by Tezcatlipoca, and he was cast as the pious son of Mixcoatl, fighter and hunter. He would become the legendary first ruler of Tula. His unusual piety was attested by the seven-year fasting and penance he performed out in the steppe, praying to the gods that he might excel in war. Short-lived as he might be in the dawn, his prowess was known to all.

But his reputation was evil. In the splendor of his rising as a doomed star, he cast forth glittering rays which were his darts. His greatest duel had been with the new sun, the day star, wherein, acting in his capacity as the god of ice, he had attempted to prevent the sun's ascension.[17] His defeat at the hands of Tonatiuh made him the paragon of the captured and sacrificed warrior. Therefore, any person born on the day Ce Acatl was unlucky and could become either a thief or a sorcerer.

An interesting Aztec myth has come down to us which clearly casts Quetzalcoatl as the Morning Star. It has been rather generally slighted by mythographers up to now, so we present it here in some detail.[18]

Quetzalcoatl was the son of Camaxtli, an avatar of Mixcoatl, and Chimalma; he was born in Michatlauhco, Fish Deeps. His mother died giving birth to him, so he was raised by his grandfathers. Because his father favored him, his brothers hated him and plotted to kill him. They therefore sent him up to a height called Burned-Off Hill and set fires all around the base, confidently expecting him to perish. But he squeezed himself into a hole and escaped. On his way home he hunted and brought back some game to his father. Once again the brothers tried to kill him, this time by inducing him to climb into the topmost branches of a high tree. When he was thus exposed, they shot at him but he feigned death and dropped to the ground. After they had left, he again hunted and returned to his father with a rabbit. By now Camaxtli knew that his other sons were attempting to kill Quetzalcoatl, and he charged them with the fact. Because of this public censure, they turned on their father and destroyed him, taking his body far away and burying it in a mountain. They told Quetzalcoatl that their father had changed into a great mountain and needed wild game sacrificed to him. But Quetzalcoatl suspected a trick and escaped up onto that mountain, from which he rained arrows down upon them, killing them all. Out of their skulls drinking cups were made.

In this myth there is nothing of the celestial dragon vomiting waters or of Ehecatl the invisible traveler. If we remember that Camaxtli was that form of Mixcoatl identified as the red Tezcatlipoca, i.e., the diurnal sun, we can understand that Quetzalcoatl and his many brothers are here the stars, that in fact Quetzalcoatl is the Morning Star and his brothers are the Four Hundred Mimixcoa. The sun (here Camaxtli) is destroyed by the night and its hosts of stars, this being plainly stated in the myth. But a second contest, not otherwise noted in Aztec mythology, is then presented to us: the rivalry between Ce Acatl and all the other stars. Here again the myth states the natural fact that the Morning Star does outlast the other stars, though only for a short period, thus in a sense defeating them. The burial of Camaxtli in the mountain is the actual disappearance of the sun beneath the horizon. At nighttime the underground sun needs sacrifices in order to strengthen himself in the battle against the demons of darkness. When Ce Acatl leaps up into the sky (the high tree) or climbs the high mountain, this no doubt represents his victorious emergence above the horizon, just ahead of the sun. He is cast as an archer and a great hunter, well-known professions of the Morning Star. The burning hill is the pyre of dawn and, as all Mesoamerican peoples knew, the Morning Star was born out of the eastern ocean, here called Michatlauhco.

The significant twist in this myth is that, while it tells the old familiar astral tale, it does so from the viewpoint of the Morning Star and not that of the sun. The Morning Star is here the hero, the beloved of the sun, though the enemy is the same, night and the stars. Almost certainly this is a myth handed down from the Toltecs, whose warrior god was that particular Quetzalcoatl known as Ce Acatl.

To the Aztecs the rising of the Morning Star was in no sense the serene event it is to us; it was tense, dramatic, and ominous. The redness of dawn was the stain of blood in the sky and, as Hector fled before Achilles, so did this champion flee before the great one who had outmatched him: he falls, leaving the celestial battlefield in the possession of the sun.

The first heliacal rising of the planet Venus during the year was especially inauspicious. Depending on that day's sign Ce Acatl's rage directed itself against various categories of being, such as old people, infants, rulers, the rain, or youths.[19] If he attacked the rain the result was especially horrifying, for drought would set in and the people would weaken and die. When the young were menaced, careful parents closed their doors lest the uncanny shafts of Ce Acatl paralyze their children.

In their excessive fear of the Morning Star, the Aztecs sought to placate him with sacrifices. To this end they adopted his pillar cult, which had flourished in Mesoamerica in places as widely separated as Xochicalco and Teayo on the Gulf coast in Vera Cruz. In Tenochtitlan his free-standing pillar was known as In the Midst of the Heavens and, on the heliacal rising of the planet, the rites celebrated at the foot of that shaft were especially sanguinary.[20]

Of all the transfigurations of Quetzalcoatl, Ce Acatl is the easiest for us to keep separate. The Aztecs themselves never forgot that these two were distinct deities, bound together only by the one reference in the myth where Quetzalcoatl, in flight from Tezcatlipoca, immolated himself on the shores of the Gulf so that his burning heart should ascend like a spark into the heavens to become the Morning Star. A gloss on this episode said that Quetzalcoatl disappeared for a time into the underworld, where he provided himself with atlatl and darts and only then rose as the felonious Ce Acatl.[21] This is a companion tale to the story of the creation of the fifth sun. Just as the god Nanahuatl leaped into the pyre to become the sun, so did Quetzalcoatl voluntarily perish in the flames to become the Morning Star.

Their essential distinction is clearly seen in the confusion of date-names associated with them. The original date-name of Quetzalcoatl, the culture hero and god of the air, appears to have been Chiucnahui Ehecatl, Nine Wind. Ce Acatl or One Reed was the date-name of the war god of the Toltecs, who was the Morning Star. The myth of the translation of Quetzalcoatl's heart into the Morning Star logically connects the two, for it states that that divine event took place on the day (or in the year) 1 Reed. Thus the birthdate of the Morning Star is the same as the disappearance or death of the god of the air. Inasmuch as deathdates had no augural significance in Aztec lore and did not serve as posthumous names of either mortals or gods, it is evident that the two forms of Quetzalcoatl, Ce Acatl and Chiucnahui Ehecatl, were originally unconnected.[22] After the partial fusing did take place, it finally became inevitable that Quetzalcoatl would also be known as Ce Acatl.

The Aztecs never offered a reason why they held the two to be in reality one god. The myth we have cited is merely a statement that the heart of Quetzalcoatl, refined by a fire in the east, did become the god Ce Acatl. The only explanation I can summon up for the equation is that in the form of a celestial dragon, manifest in the winding course of the Milky Way, the night was extinguished by the burning of the dawn. The star which rose up from that fire must therefore be a manifestation of the dragon (i.e., his heart?). This is pure speculation and one can do what one wants with it. I feel the identification between the two gods, however, occurred early rather than late.

Quetzalcoatl as the Reforming Priest of Tula

So far we have been considering the lineaments of an ancient Mesoamerican god known to us as Quetzalcoatl, Ehecatl, and Ce Acatl, divine beings whose jurisdictions and capacities were not always consonant. As if this were not confusing enough, we are now introduced to an additional transfiguration who, however, was not fully divine but had once been a living man, a Toltec leader whose name or title was most probably Topiltzin.[23] In order to understand how this person melts into the conception of the divine Quetzalcoatl, we must summarize his story as it centers about the city of Tula.

First, before we relate the legend, let us state what we think happened historically.

The chronological setting of this fascinating tale is highly controversial, for there is the distinct possibility that Tula in the account refers not to the Toltec capital but to Teotihuacan, its predecessor, or to a conflation of the two. If so, then the expulsion of the great reformer we call Topiltzin would refer to the fall of Teotihuacan (ca. A.D. 700) and its attendant religious upheavals. For the ease of the argument, let us assume the more orthodox position here, namely that the scene of the action was the Toltec city.

Perhaps halfway through the Toltec period we find a certain Topiltzin as the high priest of Ce Acatl, in which capacity he was one of the magnates of Tula. This priest had been attracted to Tula from the outside, where he had acquired a formidable reputation for sanctity. We have mentioned that Ce Acatl was the Toltec war deity and that his cult concentrated on human sacrifice. This was now all imperiled, for the high priest came bringing a new gospel and a reformer's zeal. In fact we think we can see, behind the difficult sources covering that period, the introduction of a new and a revealed religion, the only one we know of in all Mesoamerica. The name given to the new avatar of Quetzalcoatl was probably Topiltzin, which we translate as Our Revered Prince, a name which would have been taken as a priestly title by our reformer as a matter of course. That the new religion was a proselytizing one we gather from the fact that the servitors of the god under the high priest were said to be noted travelers, going to far places and preaching from hilltops.[24]

The new high priest insisted that his god wanted only the mildest sacrifices, such as flowers and birds, and that he abhorred the effusion of human blood except in autosacrifice. His message was a penitential one, and he called for a new holiness on the part of all the Toltecs. This doctrine inevitably must have struck at the privileges and the way of life of the entire warrior class. Seeing their imperial god Ce Acatl as the captive of a lunatic whose preachings must surely sap the vitality of the state, they turned to the god Tezcatlipoca and his priesthood to aid them in defeating the new teaching. We do not know the details of the great religious struggle but we can see that it racked the state, soon reducing it to disorder, for the priest Topiltzin in his charismatic power had secured a large following by the time civil war broke out. In the end the Tezcatlipoca faction won, forcing the exile of Topiltzin along with a significant portion of Tula's population. This latter group moved southeast, passing through Cholula, until they came out on the Gulf coast. They were about to set forth in canoes on a journey to Acallan, an old Toltec staging point on the road east, when the great high priest died. Back in Tula the remaining inhabitants were unable to agree sufficiently to elect a leader, and some time passed before Tula rose again in a brief burst of glory.

With this as the skeleton of the story, admittedly reconstructed, let us turn back and tell the same story as the Aztecs recounted it in myth and in legend some centuries later.

Our hero was divine, being the son of Mixcoatl and the goddess Chimalma, and he was born in the province of Huitznahuac. When he was a youth being trained as a warrior, his father was treacherously killed by a brother-in-law, Apanecatl, and his remains hidden. With exemplary piety the young Quetzalcoatl sought the sacred bones and buried them in a temple, which he dedicated to his father. He then took vengeance upon his father's murderer.[25]

This opening is purely mythical, and we can see that the Quetzalcoatl being talked about is either the Plumed Serpent or Ce Acatl. The story continues, but it has now shifted to the figure of the holy man Topiltzin.

Quetzalcoatl had by now become a famous priest and was skilled in many arts. He had been sent down from heaven to reform men and turn them from their impious ways. To achieve his ends he formed a special group of priests with voices like trumpets, who called the people to penance and the new light. He first went to the city of Tulantzinco and for four years there practiced extreme abstinence.

By this time his fame and holiness were abroad in the land and he was treated as a god. The Toltecs petitioned him to come to Tula and establish his cult reforms. From the beginning Quetzalcoatl had been worshiped in Tula but always as Ce Acatl, the god of warriors. Under Topiltzin, Tula took on a new splendor, its god moved to higher harmonies, and there began a golden age of joy and plenty. This was because Topiltzin in his new service was pleasing to all the gods. Wisdom flowed from him. Arts, crafts, divination, the study of the sacred calendar, and such penitential practices as midnight bathing became the order of the day. Mankind's guilt was gradually being purged.

But sloth and envy crept in, and eventually gloom descended over the land.[26] Omens began to appear, presaging the fall of the city. Three sorcerers, all of them transfigurations of Tezcatlipoca, appeared in Tula and after some resistance secured an audience with Quetzalcoatl. Their object was to reinstitute the cult of human sacrifice. First they showed Topiltzin a mirror in which he beheld himself hideously deformed. Then he became, at their instigation, drunk on the juice of the maguey and thus broke his fast. Finally, responding to their blandishments, he performed the ultimate evil of fornication with his own sister. So ended his chastity and his holiness. And so ended the golden age.

Ruin closed in. The Toltec armies could no longer contain the pressures on the imperial borders and began to suffer defeats. Topiltzin hereupon buried his great treasures in his golden house and set all to the torch. The flowering trees in the environs of the city withered and turned into harsh mesquite, and the birds which had sung in their branches flew away into the east. On his departure Topiltzin's statue was thrown down and the temple of his god razed.[27] With a group of retainers, the exiled ruler took the road for the fabled land of Tlapallan, where he intended to consult the oracles. Along the way demons stripped him of all his arts: goldsmithing, woodworking, the composing and painting of books, feather working, etc. He finally arrived on the coast at Coatzacoalcos.

There are two statements in myth about what happened there. The first we have already mentioned as needed to explicate the connection between the celestial dragon and the Morning Star. According to that account Topiltzin threw himself into a pyre, from which his heart rose to become the Morning Star.[28]

The other version vividly contrasts with the first. In this version the god-man said farewell to his followers, prophesying that he would return on a year named as that one was, Ce Acatl, to reclaim his rule. He stepped onto a raft of serpents, of the sort reserved only for sorcerers and wise men, and floated away across the waves to Tlapallan. That was the last men ever saw of him.

From all this we see that Quetzalcoatl's most outstanding characteristic was his holiness, which in turn was derived from his priestly office. The Tula corpus of tales presents him almost as an anchorite, a man obsessed with personal purity and the leader of a commandery of priests vowed to observe an exacting religious rule. He was the one who first taught men to invoke the gods properly, to erect temples, and to institute rituals. Fasting, chastity, midnight bathing in icy water, and other penances were at the core of his teaching, for he saw that unless the priesthood, as a surrogate for all men, was penitentially involved at all times the gods would withhold abundance and leave men defenseless. His priesthood in fact was known for the special rigor of its practices—the famous four-year fast of the priests of Tehuacan, for instance, was made in imitation of the good works of Quetzalcoatl. It was said that his piety so impressed the gods that they once sent down a lizard which scratched in the earth as a sign that from that point forward harvests would be abundant—the lizard being the creature which symbolized male sexual activity and, by extension, plenty.[29]

It is difficult to reconstruct Topiltzin's new religion in any detail, but one guess is that it was a somewhat rarefied stellar religion stressing the divine authority of the gods who lived in the thirteenth heaven. Among the gods whom Topiltzin is said to have invoked were the ancient creator couple, Star Skirt and her consort, as well as the Tonaca gods who supplied men's sustenance.[30] From the little we can see, this religion seems to have been a throwback to the concepts of Teotihuacan, and in that sense perhaps the movement was a kind of Reformation. The most startling of Topiltzin's innovations was his retreat from the Toltec concept of human sacrifice and his return to an order of simple autosacrifice and the sacrifice of snakes, butterflies, birds, etc. His was a formidable and elitist piety and only the most sanctified could practice it. This new piety, as we know from the legend, was put to rout by the followers of Tezcatlipoca, and the time-honored human sacrifices were reinstituted. In Cholula itself, the center of the Quetzalcoatl cult, humans continued to be sacrificed to the celestial dragon and had their hearts torn out in the traditional manner. Topiltzin of Tula was ultimately forsaken.

Yet Topiltzin, the Toltec priest, was only a late graft on an old and sturdy plant. The god Quetzalcoatl, well before the Toltec period, had been conceived as a sacerdotal figure. The reforms no doubt belonged to the man Topiltzin, but the priestly complexion of the god Quetzalcoatl had been evident before him.

Tlapallan and the Myth of the Return

It is essential to say something about Tlapallan, the region of Topiltzin's reputed exile. In the first place it can be considered to be an actual geographical location somewhere to the east; from its name, Place of the Painted Things, we can learn little. Perhaps the painted things were books of wisdom. At the same time Tlapallan is also a never-never land, almost such an Eden as Tamoanchan. In one of the versions of the myth Quetzalcoatl is said to have passed eastward along the Gulf coast to the province of Acallan, in the present state of Campeche, and from there he traveled to Tlapallan. Tlapallan could therefore be the peninsula of Yucatan, site of the ruins of the Toltec city of Chichén Itzá.

We have tentatively placed the historic Topiltzin nearer to the end of Toltec history (traditionally A.D. 1168) than to its beginning (ca. A.D. 900). The reader must be warned, however, that Toltec chronology is a mass of contradictions and that few scholars agree on it.

Ever since the Toltecs had appeared they had been adventurers and travelers. They early sent strong parties down to the coastal route and into Yucatan, blazing the trail that Topiltzin was said to have taken later. They carried their god Ce Acatl, planting his worship in strategic sites along the way, such as Acallan and Champoton. It would be easy to understand this great eastward movement as a religious crusade, the insertion into foreign parts of a particularly bloody cult and its fire-breathing god. One of the Toltec groups took over the Mayan city of Chichén Itzá and made it into a place of architectural splendor. They had brought with them the Plumed Serpent and early translated his name into its Mayan equivalent, Kukulcan. There had accompanied him an entire cultus, a priesthood, and an orthodox high priest or *quetzalcoatl*. How this situation may have affected the later legend of Topiltzin's wandering we do not know, but it was certainly believed in Aztec days that Quetzalcoatl as Ce Acatl had anciently gone to Tlapallan and was worshiped there in several great centers.

Quetzalcoatl's predilection for wandering gave him an added name

or transfiguration: Nacxitl, the Traveler.[31] In fact the high priest Topiltzin–as he went into exile–could also be referred to under that
designation.[32] What is of interest is that this transfiguration of the
god was so firmly established in the Mayan areas that he became
Ah Nacxit Kukulcan, a great Carolingian figure who held court and
conferred legitimacy and kingdoms on Toltec and related groups
moving into the area. Clearly his warlike character was predominant
there.

All this makes it probable that Topiltzin, the reforming priest, did
not go to Tlapallan after leaving Tula, for the only transfigurations
of Quetzalcoatl whom we know there are the Plumed Serpent and
the Traveler, patrons of warriors and sacrifice. It is far more probable
that Topiltzin died on the coast, as the legend said.

It is not possible to doubt the objective existence of a remarkable
priestly figure whose piety and subsequent expulsion from an imperial city affected the imagination of later peoples. The Aztecs could
still lament his fate hundreds of years afterward, even though they
had not the slightest sympathy with his pacific teachings:

A great hall made of worked wood once stood in Tula:
Today only its serpent columns lie stretched out on the ground–
Nacxitl Topiltzin went away and suddenly left it all.[33]

But even more significant than the tale of Quetzalcoatl and Tlapallan was the prophecy of the return, widely spread throughout Mesoamerica.[34] This carried overtones of the return of the golden age on
the one hand and, on the other, Quetzalcoatl's reclamation of imperial power. The motif of the return of a folk hero to rectify evils
is of course common in history.

The year 1519 in the Christian calendar happened to correspond
roughly to the fateful year of the prophecy, 1 Reed (Ce Acatl), in
the Mexican calendar. In that year Hernando Cortés came out of the
Gulf of Mexico from the east to make his landfall in the Aztec empire.
Moteuczoma II understandably believed that the Spaniards were the
descendants of Quetzalcoatl and that Cortés was the spokesman of
the god himself. The god could only be that imperial figure far off
over the sea to the east to whom Cortés said he paid allegiance. This
astounding historic coincidence, purely fortuitous, deprived Moteuczoma of the will to resist–with consequences fatal to himself and his
people.

Long after the entry of the Spaniards the belief in the god's return
remained alive in various parts of Mesoamerica. In 1550 some of the

Zapotecs rose in rebellion, claiming that Quetzalcoatl had indeed redeemed his promise and had returned to lead them.[35] Nearer to Mexico City it was held as late as 1670 that the god's line survived and would soon return to reclaim his imperial privileges.[36] Meanwhile he was still thought to be living with the sun god in Tlapallan or to be asleep inside Mount Xicco.[37]

It is easy to distinguish the separate strands which make up this myth. Certainly the exile of the high priest Topiltzin and the wreckage of the state which followed were important. But there had been other divine disappearances into the east in Aztec lore, and these provided the mythic scenario upon which the Quetzalcoatl exile and return were modeled. Ehecatl once passed over the eastern sea to steal music from the sun, and again as Yohualli Ehecatl the god had led the first people out of the east to Mesoamerica, finally to disappear overseas with all his books and wisdom, promising to return and usher in the end of the world.[38] Again, just as Ce Acatl, the planet Venus, finally disappears over the oceanic waters in the east, so will he always return at the expiration of his synodic term. No doubt all these helped in forging the myth of the return and in giving it added vitality when it was retold about Topiltzin.

Xolotl as Twin to Quetzalcoatl

One of the problems relating to Quetzalcoatl involves his connections with the god called Xolotl.

Xolotl is a very ancient and complex god, certainly as old as Quetzalcoatl and possibly older.[39] Once, in fact, he is even referred to as Huehuexolotl, the Ancient Xolotl. The word *xolotl* probably originally meant "double," with the additional meanings of "servant" or "page" and probably "beast" or "monster."[40] We have already had occasion to note that the *coatl*, "serpent," in Quetzalcoatl's name can be equally well translated as "twin." It is certainly not a coincidence then that our two gods, Quetzalcoatl and Xolotl, were both considered to be counterparts of each other, the latter being the dark or demonic partner who operated in the underworld. We can clearly see Xolotl as binary in the myth where the fleeing god changes into a double-stalked maize plant and, then, into a double-stalked maguey.[41] In this respect he was Coaxolotl, Xolotl as Twin, presiding not only over the birth of twins but over all other monstrous births as well. When the two twin gods are juxtaposed they represent the planet Venus in its two phases, the Morning Star and the Evening Star.

Xolotl is generally painted as an animal with great claws and a stripe along the muzzle. It is difficult to identify the species intended but the badger, said by the Aztecs to have been born underground, is as likely a candidate as any.[42] Or, after all, he may have been a dog, as most scholars think. The iconography is remarkably consistent in showing Xolotl wearing the regalia of Quetzalcoatl, even to such items as his Huaxtec cap and the wind jewel. Occasionally in Mixtec paintings he is shown doubled, in other words as a set of twins modeled on himself, neither one being in the guise of Quetzalcoatl.

In myth he was one of the gods present at the creation of the sun, and it was he who, to compel the sun to move, sacrificed all the assisting gods and finally himself.[43] A variant myth showed Ehecatl– i.e., Quetzalcoatl–sacrificing Xolotl in Teotihuacan so the sun might emerge from the underworld;[44] Xolotl was additionally the god so familiar with the underworld that he was chosen to bring from there the bones from which the first men would be created, an act otherwise attributed to Quetzalcoatl.[45] And it was Xolotl who nourished these first men.

The sacrifice of the gods in Teotihuacan is symbolic of the erasing of the starry host from the heavens as the sun rises. Thus in the myth Xolotl, as the sacrificer, must represent Venus, though it is ambiguous whether he is the Morning Star or the Evening Star. In the Codex Borbonicus he is shown sacrificing the setting sun, a role certainly appropriate to Venus as the Evening Star.[46] What adds support to the identification is Xolotl's intimate association with the *nahuallachco*, the "wizard's ball court,"[47] which, as we have stated, is the night sky conceived as a field where celestial bodies, as godlike powers, struggle with each other and where capture and sacrifice must ensue. In one of the myths Xolotl plays in the *tlachco* against Piltzinteuctli, the chthonian sun.[48] We know that Xolotl was one of the gods whose image was set up by the Aztecs of Tenochtitlan in or near the ball court.

Thus it is clear that in most cases Quetzalcoatl is the Morning Star who has as his twin Xolotl, the Evening Star. But confusion is not dissipated with this assumption. In origin Xolotl might well have been an inclusive version of both phases of the planet Venus. At some later period–when Quetzalcoatl had already drawn the Morning Star into himself–Xolotl, as another and alien concept of the planet Venus with a different mythology and perhaps from an earlier culture, might have been promoted to become his twin. This twinning did not happen to Tlahuizcalpanteuctli, the pan-Mesoamerican version of the Morning Star, for that god's regalia and mythology were always kept quite separate from those of Quetzalcoatl. Thus of the three Mesoamerican gods of the planet Venus, no doubt each originally from a different culture, Ce Acatl was fused with the celestial dragon and Xolotl became his twin, but Tlahuizcalpanteuctli remained outside the circle of attraction.

The twinning we have mentioned adds a vague dualism to the concept of Quetzalcoatl for, while Xolotl is never presented as similar to Quetzalcoatl, who was revered as a culture hero, he is always presented as a chthonic being and therefore as something of an opposite. Their mythologies, however, show no hostility; in fact they have hardly any connection worth mentioning. Xolotl is affected by Quetzalcoatl to the extent of being identified by the wearing of his regalia. Quetzalcoatl has no similar need of his twin. In this case the mask can move in one direction only. Xolotl definitely belongs in the religion of Quetzalcoatl, but beyond structuring him as the dark twin in the underworld the priests made no attempt to enlarge his role.

Quetzalcoatl in Cholula

When the city of Teotihuacan collapsed in the eighth century, its halls, avenues, and temples were emptied and its cult observances ceased. A sister city, however, almost as old, continued the splendid urban tradition. This was Cholula at the eastern base of Mount Popocatepetl, a city reputedly founded by Quetzalcoatl.

While the Aztec cities always centered around their tutelary god, some were religiously eclectic and harbored a multiplicity of cults. Cholula was unique in concentrating so heavily on one god, Quetzalcoatl. The numerous other temples in the city were indeed devoted to other gods, but most of these were establishments brought in from the outside and supported by other rulers who wished to bathe their gods in the nimbus of Quetzalcoatl. In fact, if any city could claim to be the holy center of the Aztec world, that city would be Cholula.

The fact that Cholula was the focus of so much piety and the constant comings and goings of its people made it exceedingly rich. Generally wealth came to Aztec cities from conquests and tribute, but here was something significantly different. Cholula was a city of traffickers, not of warriors. Out of its gateways went caravans of porters bent under stupendous loads and led by the most astute of Mesoamerican merchants. It followed that Quetzalcoatl was a lord of riches and as such he could appear in a transfiguration as the god Yacateuctli, Lord of the Van, that special god of merchants who was immanent in their walking staves.[49] Because of the prominence of Cholula's merchants in Mesoamerican exchange, Quetzalcoatl thus early took on commercial coloration and, in the great banquets given by the merchants of that city to display their wealth, many tales were told of the god's buying and selling ventures and of his fabulous working of jade and turquoise.

Quetzalcoatl's pyramid temple in Cholula, the most massive structure ever built in the pre-Columbian world, was called Tlachiualtepec, the Mountain Made by Men.[50] In its pre-Aztec heyday it must have been of unsurpassed magnificence. Pilgrims visited it from more than three hundred miles away. It was an ancient foundation, its first or innermost terrace being dated to A.D. 100; it was contemporary, therefore, with early Teotihuacan. By A.D. 500 the great Cholula Altar II had been erected at the base of the pyramid, bearing a carved relief of two plumed serpents symmetrically opposed to each other. But as at Teotihuacan the sides of the pyramid, left without maintenance, finally crumbled and fell away. The stately house of Quetzalcoatl which had once capped the pyramid was then replaced by a smaller round temple on a pedestal just to the northwest. The renown of the site, however, did not diminish, whatever its ruinous state, and Quetzalcoatl continued to give out oracles there to those who sought them—either on the feast of his birthday, 7 Reed, or on the date of his death and transfiguration, 1 Reed.

Today, from the balustrade of the church of the Virgen de los Remedios which tops the artificial hill, one can glance from Tlascala in the north down the ancient road to the southeast which led from Tepeyacac to Tehuacan, and thence to Tochtepec. This was the country of Quetzalcoatl, an extensive portion of the area inhabited by the Aztecs, where he was especially revered. It is a more impressive site in many ways than Teotihuacan, for the greatest mountains of Mesoamerica stand on either horizon and in their season the rain clouds come and go over the landscape, preceded by gusts of wind and dust. If one were to worship a celestial dragon, one would certainly choose to do it here.

Quetzalcoatl as Demiurge and Culture Hero

The Aztecs never succeeded in wholly isolating the concept of original creation or in recognizing its essential singularity. They parceled it out in bits and pieces—the creation of men from rocks here, the creation of earth from water there, and so on. Therefore several gods are involved in the myths; their creative acts are sometimes identical but are always arranged in a descending hierarchy of authority. Demiurgic action, in other words, takes the place of true creation. Of the great demiurges Quetzalcoatl was the only one who might be considered close to the Aztecs for, though a god, he had had a mortal body and had died or slipped away. We shall excerpt here those mythological tales relating to his demiurgic actions.

In the empyrean the gods Two Lord and Two Lady sit in state with Quetzalcoatl between them. They determine or "affirm"[51] that a child shall come into being, whereat Quetzalcoatl "makes" the child. In this capacity, like Tezcatlipoca, Quetzalcoatl is called creator and maker, but we can see that he is more agent than principal. At least once, however, when the Aztec thinker was faced with the problem of ascertaining divine jurisdiction in this field, he made the statement that Quetzalcoatl created all men even though Tezcatlipoca remained their master. In other words there was a tendency among the Aztecs to tie a significant part of men's allegiance to Quetzalcoatl. Time and time again they iterated the fact that he had created the first human couple and that he continues to create each child as it is born. And his priesthood went even further: they sometimes claimed that he created the world and all things in it, an arrogation of supremacy more properly belonging to Tezcatlipoca.[52]

What we must understand is that those relations Quetzalcoatl has with men come not so much from any inherent primacy but, rather, from his priestly office and his ability to predict each person's fate from their birthdates. Outward appearances to the contrary, Quetzalcoatl is still the culture hero, not the creator, in these situations.

An Aztec myth we have already alluded to defines exactly how Quetzalcoatl is related to man.[53] When the fourth sun had ended, with the extinction of mankind, the gods stood deprived of their customary services. Accordingly they decided upon the re-creation of men, and they deputed Quetzalcoatl and his *nahualli* or double, who is here clearly Xolotl, to go into the underworld and cajole the Lord of the Dead into releasing the bones of those men. The Lord of the Dead imposed upon Quetzalcoatl, as a test of his worthiness,

the task of blowing notes on his conch trumpet–an impossibility because there was no hole bored through the end. However, with the
aid of worms which perforated it and the loud buzzing of wasps
which entered it, Quetzalcoatl fulfilled the terms laid upon him and
departed with the bones. After accidents which destroyed the perfection of the bones, he and his *nahualli* succeeded in bringing them
up to Tamoanchan, where the gods eagerly awaited the conclusion
of his mission. The Great Mother took the bones, ground them up,
and placed them in an earthen tub. Over this Quetzalcoatl drew
blood from his genitals, allowing the precious fluid to flow into the
dust. The other gods followed suit, and out of the paste came a man
and then a woman, the first created humans of the fifth sun.

Quetzalcoatl's role in this re-creation is modeled first on the culture
hero who goes in search of preexistent bones and second on the
fertility hero whose blood (qua semen) falls into the clay receptacle
(the womb of the Earth Mother) to engender sons. This is obvious
folklore, but it fails to tell us of a uniquely creative act, for Quetzalcoatl acts here only in cooperation with other gods.

In the myth of the finding of maize, Quetzalcoatl functions purely
as a discoverer.[54] In this myth the divine food, maize, was secreted
in a mountain called Tonacatepetl. Quetzalcoatl discovered the location of this mountain from an ant, whereupon he changed himself
into a replica of that insect in order to approach the site and yet
escape detection. After he brought away a sample of the maize, he
and the other gods tasted it and pronounced it good. Quetzalcoatl
then tried to bring the great pile away on his back but was unable to.
It was the diseased god Nanahuatl who finally threshed the mountain and separated it into vast piles of all the seeds and grains men
eat.

In another tale we have considered, the culture hero Quetzalcoatl
went to the cave of Xochicalco to aid his grandparents Oxomoco and
Cipactonal in designing the sacred almanac of 260 days; in fact in
some sources he is said to have alone invented this all-important
framework of time and destiny and to have passed on to men the art
of interpreting it. As the god Ehecatl he also brought the intoxicating
liquor of the maguey down to earth, at great peril to himself, so that
men might experience some relief from their toil.[55] In all these instances we see Quetzalcoatl standing midway between gods and men
but acting as a patron of the skills and needs of the latter.

Quetzalcoatl in Mexico-Tenochtitlan

In Tenochtitlan the god Quetzalcoatl held an important but not over-riding cultic position. Ceremonially speaking, the deities Tezcatli-poca, Huitzilopochtli, Cihuacoatl, and Tlaloc wielded more influence. Nevertheless the cultic sphere which did belong to Quetzalcoatl was centrally placed because of the historic implications attached to it. Moteuczoma II was a devotee of his and was constantly seeking oracles from the god's famous fasting priests in Tehuacan.

But Moteuczoma was not the first of the royal line of Mexico to feel a special relationship to Quetzalcoatl. According to one tradition the Mexican throne had belonged to Quetzalcoatl himself, who had been its legendary first incumbent.[56] This was simply another way of saying that all the Mexican rulers claimed a direct line of descent back to him as a god in Tula. And because the sons of Mexican nobles were trained in the *calmecac*, whose patron was the god Quetzalcoatl, it was believed that he had conferred their aristocratic privileges upon them also.[57] The corollary of these beliefs was that, when Quetzal-coatl returned as prophesied in the year 1 Reed, the Mexican ruler, whoever he might be, would be required to relinquish his powers and emoluments to the rightful ruler.[58]

The seeming actualization of the prophecy in 1519 swiftly under-mined the Mexican state. Moteuczoma felt himself especially threat-ened because it was he who sat on the *icpalli* that belonged to Que-tzalcoatl. That he yielded it to Cortés without contest should aston-ish no one.

It was customary in Tenochtitlan, Cholula, and no doubt other Aztec cities for the priests of Quetzalcoatl to sound his great drum at dawn and dusk. The hoarse reverberation of this instrument, heard for a great distance, was considered to be the very voice of the wind god.[59] Only after the god had thus spoken could merchants leave the city in the morning, taking up their staves and hitching on their backpacks. Only then could purveyors of food and sundries enter the city. In this way the god divided day from night, for his was a priest's knowledge of days and hours and all their distinctions. And at dusk when the voice spoke again from the templetop, a hush fell and people gathered up their belongings and whispered to each other, "Let us go home, for Ehecatl has spoken." And the city could then sleep.

If Tlaloc and the goddesses of maize and flowing water brought Tenochtitlan its very existence, Quetzalcoatl brought it a constitution and a way of life. His return to the seat of rule could only mean an entirely new dispensation. And at that time kings would step down and even the hours of day and night might be changed.

Concluding Remarks

The distinction between Quetzalcoatl's drum and the flute of Tezcatlipoca may serve to draw our attention to the relationship between the two deities. The drum rationally separated night from day and ordered the work of society. Though the voice was supposed to be that of the cyclonic wind, it was necessarily tied in with the rain clouds which would follow and with man's well-being. It was a voice congenial to social man. But the shrill and crazy flute came unexpectedly in the night and spoke not to social man but to the anxious individual: to his weakness and his consciousness of transgression. This in essence is the difference between the two Aztec gods.

But there is more to it than this. It is certainly not without meaning that, when the four sons of the Tonaca gods decided to delegate their powers of creation, they chose Tezcatlipoca and Quetzalcoatl. Additionally, when it was necessary to separate Cipactli into two parts and have the upper part raised to become the sky, Tezcatlipoca and Quetzalcoatl were chosen to perform that labor. Questions now arise. Are we dealing here with a manifestation of a basic dualism and, if so, why were these two gods chosen to illustrate the principle? Some scholars have in fact believed that the Mesoamerican religions were basically dualistic.[60] But there is an even more curious connection between the two deities: the name Huemac, which we have previously adjudged to Tezcatlipoca, was also used occasionally to identify Quetzalcoatl. This would imply some form of common identity.

A dualistic religion opposes life to death, light to darkness, infinity to finitude, good to evil, spirit to matter. Dualism involves a total illogic. In any thoroughgoing application of the principle there can be no resolution expressed in myth; neither death nor life, darkness nor light ever wins, and thus no tale can be told concerning it. Or, where it is asserted that one of the principles will prevail in the end, the dualism is thus dispersed and rendered meaningless. But Aztec religion makes no bones about its certainties; death prevails as does darkness, the truest worship is at night, the most potent gods are those of discord, the fifth and final aeon will come to an ineluctable end and there will be no more. One of our sources, as if to nail down this victory of nullity, goes so far as to state that Tezcatlipoca created Quetzalcoatl. In the Codex Borgia Tezcatlipoca is depicted as having possessed himself of all Quetzalcoatl's regalia, and we do not find the reverse. In the Toltec cycle it was Tezcatlipoca who finally subdued Quetzalcoatl, tempting him to his fall and subsequent exile. And once we even hear of a sacrifice to Ehecatl performed in Tezcatlipoca's temple.

The Aztec, then, did not believe that the cosmos was perfectly balanced between opposites—to him it was essentially dark and hostile. As for a balanced dichotomy between spirit and matter, he never made any distinction between them, believing them to be one thing.

But in the pairing of Tezcatlipoca and Quetzalcoatl it is obvious that the Aztec thinker was trying to express something of importance. He seemed to sense that the figure of the shaman, as represented by Tezcatlipoca, with his gusts of passion and his untrammeled will, was just as necessary to explain creation as was Quetzalcoatl the priest, with his penances and his wisdom. The divine was both vitality and form. Not that these two faces of God were coequal and opposite, fighting against each other for supremacy. Rather the Aztecs felt that the inexplicability of God exceeded his resources of justice. This why I do not believe that we are dealing here with dualism and, if dualism did not exist in the confrontation of Tezcatlipoca and Quetzalcoatl, it did not exist anywhere in Aztec religion. Tezcatlipoca and Quetzalcoatl in the myths are not quality opposites. They are simply different, one based on the shamanic, the other on the priestly tradition.

In the final analysis Quetzalcoatl is an imperfectly realized god. As the celestial dragon he is a whole being, but he is diffuse. The clearest definition the Aztecs gave of him was in his transfiguration as Ehecatl, the Wind. But even here there was an aborting. One might have expected, as happened to gods of air or wind in several religions, that Ehecatl would gradually refine into "breath," a concept which could finally come to signify "spirit." But there is no hint of this in our sources. Rather he remained the personification of violent wind and cloudburst and flooding rain, so a great possibility remained unfulfilled. As the subtle and indefinable air, however, he did find a pseudotheophany as "wisdom," and from this came the priest and the culture hero.

His connection with the Morning Star might have come about because of his profession as a priest, this including his arrangement of the *tonalpohualli* and his ability to gauge the stars in their courses.

But a priestly and an intellectual interpretation did not at all comport with the already established characterization of the Morning Star as a brutal warrior. Thus Ce Acatl the god was prevented from developing into an exponent of stellar or astrological order. And in the end the chaste and pious priest, Topiltzin, who might have crystallized into a god of purity, was tarnished by his misdeeds and shunted off into the realms of prophecy. Quetzalcoatl is a god hesitantly and unsurely put together. As developed over the centuries, insofar as we can see him, he showed a potential orientation which was never fully realized.

6. The Making of Huitzilopochtli

Chichimec Religion

When the Aztecs, late in their history, commented on their indebtedness to the peoples of the past, they mentioned the sinewy men of the Gran Chichimeca first:[1]

> Is it that perhaps we could betray the teaching of the ancestors, of the Chichimecs, Toltecs, Culhua and Tepaneca? No, our hearts have received life from them, were born, were nourished and strengthened through that great piety of others.[2]

The Chichimecs varied greatly in their cultures. The more northerly ones presumably were the most circumscribed in their beliefs, as would befit people whose relationship with the more isolated steppe was close. Those bordering on the urban centers of Mesoamerica had absorbed more complex beliefs and had begun to fix their gods in their times and places. They had added skirmish and warfare to their hunting and gathering and had adopted the matching custom of human sacrifice. Chichimec religion undoubtedly concentrated heavily on human sacrifice and cannibalism, and it may have been the Chichimec element which was translated into the special dynamic of the great Toltec armies.

It is not difficult to reconstruct the basic religious beliefs of the more primitive Chichimecs. In the austerity of life on the mountainside and the cactus flats they had no time to erect elaborate shrines. Where there was a god or a power whom they wished to signalize, they erected a small bark-paper banner and set it in the ground.³ Its fluttering in the wind was an earnest of the god's presence. If the band had a close rapport with some urban center and practiced some agriculture, more elaborate observances were needed. The band may then have been a tribe.

Designated members of the band carried fetishes of the gods on their backs, wrapped in ceremonial bundles. The god Mixcoatl, for instance, was represented by a sacred arrow or dart. When his *teomama* or "god bearer" rested with the band on bivouac, the arrow was brought out, stuck into a ball of wadded grass, and placed reverently on a rock ledge. The goddess Obsidian Knife Butterfly was likewise immanent in a fetish: the knife of sacrifice. She too was carried humbly about by her god bearer. Human captives were always hard to come by but, when they were taken, her knife was essential in the killing and the cannibal meal which followed.

We are fortunate that a number of narratives from Chichimec mythology dealing with the divine beings known as the Mimixcoa have survived. These were later incorporated by the Aztecs into their own corpus of divine tales. The Mimixcoa cycle of myths is in fact the richest to have come down to us from such early times.

There are at least ten tales in the cycle. Not all of them are known in detail, some being merely alluded to in our sources. They may be briefly listed as follows: (1) the story of the birth of the Four Hundred and of the Five Mimixcoa; the myths of Mixcoatl (2) as the ancestor of all the Mesoamerican peoples, (3) as the creator of the Chichimec people in particular, (4) as the first to make fire from the drillboard, (5) as the creator of war, (6) as the ravisher of the goddess Chimalma, and, consequently, (7) as the father of Ce Acatl, the pious youth who collected Mixcoatl's bones after his murder by his other sons; (8) the myth of the hunters Xiuhnel and Mimich and the two-headed deer; (9) the tale of the shooting of Itzpapalotl by the white Mixcoatl; and finally (10) the tale of the burning of Itzpapalotl and her transformation into the sacred knife carried by Mixcoatl.

The abundance and variety in this list tell us much about the power of the Chichimec tradition in Aztec religious culture.

Mixcoatl

The initial myth in the series is in a real sense the first charter of the Aztec people and the sacred writ of their way of life, revealing the

sun and the earth to have been the parents of gods and men.⁴ It needs
little imagination to see that the Mimixcoa, the protagonists in the
myth, are at one level the deified ancestors of the Aztecs.

Anciently in the north there was a place of origins called Chicomoztoc, the Seven Caves. Within these caverns lived the Four Hundred Mimixcoa, a turbulent group of titans born of the earth goddess.
Their father the sun taught them the use of weapons so they might
hunt and supply their divine parents with nourishment. But the Mimixcoa in their arrogance defied their parents, lived wantonly, and
drank a wine made from cactus. In response to the situation, which
became ever more unbearable, the Earth Mother bore five additional
Mimixcoa who were destined to avenge their father.⁵ The sun provided these lateborn children with sharper and more deadly weapons
and instructed them for the first time in the arts of war. Thus instructed, the five cunningly hid themselves on and under the earth and,
at a prearranged signal, burst out upon their four hundred brothers
and vanquished them. The blood of the Four Hundred served as
drink for the sun and the earth, and their hearts, torn out in the first
recorded act of sacrifice, were offered as choice food. The few survivors relinquished the ancestral Seven Caves to the victorious Five,
the heroic chief of whom was called Mixcoatl (the singular form of
the plural Mimixcoa).

The above is a straightforward, easily understood tale. It states a
belief that the ancestors came out of the earth somewhere in the north
but that their impiety brought upon them the punishment of war and
strife. The innocence of their lives as primitives was lost. The divine
command to make war is the controlling element in the myth.

But an even more radical view of the cosmos was achieved in the
myth by its contradictory attribution of virtue to the condition of
war: it was the duty of children to provide through warfare the sustenance required by their parents, i.e., hearts and blood. The parents
being divine, the filial virtue thus became an orthodoxy which served
to maintain the daily coursing of the sun and the fecundity of the
earth. We note that nothing is said about man as a farmer or about
the gods as bringers of rain. There is no Cain in this story; there is
only Esau.

We must now look more closely at the Mimixcoa. The name literally
translated means Cloud Serpents. However we are to interpret the
name, the Mimixcoa are to be identified as the stellar multitudes who
are also the souls of the ancestors, innumerable sparks of life, vaguely
hostile because nocturnal and remote. Indeed they are even said in

One of the Mimixcoa with his accouterments (Borbonicus)

literature to be demons who descend from the sky to terrify men.[6] In brief they represent the souls of those Chichimec ancestors who had been present at the beginning of all things. They indicate the great antiquity of the north as opposed to the other directions associated with man and they further underline its oppressive and deathly qualities. The number 400 has reference to their legions and is accordingly translated as "innumerable."

With the Five Mimixcoa we begin the story of that cultural reorientation which turned hunters into warriors. If the Four Hundred conjure up a life of hunting and gathering, the Five represent a subsequent and prolonged state of tutelage under the influence of great centers like Teotihuacan and Tula and their armies. The Five are individually named—unlike the anonymous Four Hundred—and clearly represent a collection of old Chichimec deities, a tiny pantheon of the steppes, as it were, imported into the ambience of civilization. No doubt they were also thought of as patrons of the five directions. The leader of the group is a synoptic figure and includes them all, hence his name Mixcoatl.[7]

In myth Tezcatlipoca is said to have changed himself into Mixcoatl in the second year after the great flood at the end of the fourth aeon, when the sky crashed down upon the earth. Acting then as Mixcoatl the divine one proceeded to create fire by drilling with a stick into a fireboard.[8] This was the first light, for the fifth sun had not yet been created. The myth is evidently at pains to point out a fundamental relationship between the supreme god Tezcatlipoca and Mixcoatl. In a sense we can therefore consider the latter to be a transfiguration of the former, roughly modeled along the same lines but stripped of his supremacy. This does not contradict the other, equally obvious connection of Mixcoatl with Tlahuizcalpanteuctli, the Morning Star. Mixcoatl in fact is almost a perfect replica of that god of the dawn in both his trappings (as depicted in the codices) and in his mythology, which makes him the father of Ce Acatl.

Mixcoatl was a Herculean figure, rude and virile. He was the central figure in the Chichimec pantheon, a hunter god, a Homeric wanderer, and an ancestral warrior. In Aztec iconography he can easily be distinguished by his war paint: he has a black mask smeared across the eyes and nose and his whitened body is lined with vertical red stripes. Two eagle feathers dangle from his hair, and he carries a bow and arrows and a net hunting basket. The arrow is that special fetish in which he becomes incarnate. The deer and the cactus were closely associated with him. He was widely honored in his time by such peoples as the Tarascans, the Otomí, the Toltecs, and the Chichimecs. His mythology is depicted in Mitla. The distant Nicarao people of Central America stressed his peripatetic propensities, worshiping him as a god of merchants.

An important tale depicts Mixcoatl as a conqueror.[9] With his sacred knife reverently bundled up and carried on his back, he left the steppe country and as he moved south engaged in battle. His objective was the land of Huitznahuac. There he encountered Chimalma, Shield Hand, the naked goddess of that land; after ravishing her women, he impregnated her. Their son was to become the famous Quetzalcoatl, who later ruled in Tula.

If the myth of the Four Hundred Mimixcoa depicts how and why the Aztec ancestors discovered war, this myth of Mixcoatl in the singular depicts them as already skilled in that art, advancing southward against strong nations and subduing them. It is the same in subject matter as the Aztecs' legend of their trek southward from Aztlan, only here it is told as a myth.

But one might properly ask here, If indeed the Mimixcoa were supposed to be the stars, why should Mixcoatl himself not be a stellar projection?

Mixcoatl may have been built upon one of two models: the sun or the planet Venus. A third possibility exists, which indeed may be logically preferable: with the passage of many centuries of myth telling and myth conflation, Mixcoatl could be understood in certain contexts as the sun and in others as Venus.

If Mixcoatl is basically the symbol of the planet Venus, we can understand why he (and his quadruplicate selves) can defeat the Four Hundred Mimixcoa—it is because as the Morning Star he outlasts his peers in the night sky and lives to challenge the sun. The one most impressive item of support for the contention that he is ultimately to be derived from the planet Venus is the myth which we introduced in the section on Quetzalcoatl as the Morning Star. Mixcoatl was killed by his children, the Mimixcoa, whereat Quetzalcoatl (Ce Acatl) decently buried his bones. That myth is best explained as referring to the Venus cycle, wherein the Evening Star (Mixcoatl?) disappears from the skies to reappear after an absence as the Morning Star (i.e., as his son Ce Acatl). This would explain the equivalence, in a star seen separately in its two phases, as a father/son relationship. In all the myths concerning him Quetzalcoatl is assigned only one named father: Mixcoatl. On the other hand, if Mixcoatl is the sun, we must believe that Ce Acatl, the Morning Star, is the son of the solar deity, a statement made nowhere in Aztec mythology. But, if Mixcoatl is that phase of the planet Venus known as the Evening Star, an important myth becomes consistent in its parts.

But the tentative reading of one myth alone is a slender prop for a definitive finding, and it is probably best to recognize Mixcoatl only as a heavily overlaid stellar hero. The important thing to the Aztecs was that he was the epitome of the hunter and the warrior and that he was the most authentically Chichimec of all their gods.

The Sacred Journey of the Mexica

The best known of the Aztec people, the Mexica, have left us a tale of their early wanderings wherein we can trace the historical evolution of their focal god, Huitzilopochtli, a luxury not usually given to students of religions.

Huitzilopochtli begins in the ancestral homeland of Aztlan as a minor transfiguration of Mixcoatl known first as Tetzauhteotl, the Omen.[10] Traditionally the Mexica left Aztlan, their homeland in the northern steppe, along with other Aztec groups in the year 1 Knife (A.D. 1168). Soon after they had started, a crucial command from the god gave them a destiny and enjoined their obedience. The divine voice issued from a tree under which they were camped; it commanded them to split off from the other Aztec groups and take a new name: Mecitin, which in time became Mexitin and then Mexica. After giving this oracle, the tree broke in two and toppled down. One of our sources here adds, "With this incident of the Broken Tree begins the book of the history of the Aztecs."[11]

It does not take much imagination to see the above episode as a Mexican story accounting for the fact that, while claiming to be Aztecs (i.e., heirs of the Toltecs), the Mexica also insisted on their own special status. This special status was made patent by their assumption of a new name. The name is important.

We do not know what they were called before this—if indeed they even existed as a recognizable group—but we can state with fair accuracy that the deity who gave the oracle from the Broken Tree was called Mecitli. This deity insisted that they be known as her people and bear her name.

The problem is to discover who this deity was. A number of our sources insist that Mecitli was simply another name for Huitzilopochtli. The name Mecitli (less frequently Mexitli) may mean Maguey

Grandmother, which would identify the deity as a goddess.[12] This goddess had a *teomama* who translated her oracles and in fact later advised the Mexica, soon after their release from Culhua domination, to take to themselves a king. She is elsewhere identified in myth as the Earth Mother who had suckled the famous Five Mimixcoa, one of whom, as we know, was Mixcoatl himself.[13] It would appear from this that the goddess from Aztlan, called Shield Hand by the other Aztecs, was called Maguey Grandmother by the Mexica. Thus the probability that the Mexica began their wandering with two deities—female and male, Mecitli and a form of Mixcoatl—is strongly reinforced by the mother/son relationship mentioned in the myth.

The goddess was in many ways the more impressive of the two deities. The Mexica, when they were servants of the people of Culhuacan, were settled in a nearby place which became known as Mexicaltzinco, the Little House of Mecitli. When they fled out into the lake soon after that to found their city, they gave the name Mexico-Tenochtitlan to the spot among the reeds to which the omen had led them. Mexico means quite simply Mecitli's Place;[14] Tenochtitlan merely describes it as "near the nopal cactus." It was this early preeminence of Mecitli which caused some of the later Mexica, in reply to Spanish questions, to substitute Huitzilopochtli for her, thereby confusing both her sex and her identity.

The Broken Tree thus represents in legend the formation of a tribe under divine auspices. We may be sure that the episode was inserted in the legend at a much later period, when Huitzilopochtli had become the commanding god of the Mexica. It was only natural that he should appear to be the source of the crucial oracle.

Following the Broken Tree episode the Mexica moved to Coatepec. This mountain, close to Tula, was of special holiness because it was there, according to the myth of the gigantomachy, that Huitzilopochtli was born from the Earth Mother Coatlicue, and it was there that he defeated the evil Huitznahua, thus asserting his sovereignty. At the god's command the Mexica dammed a nearby river and flooded the surrounding countryside. This created a vast lake from which rose Mount Coatepec. Here, in an island paradise, the Mexica performed the New Fire ceremony which ushered in a new age of fifty-two years. But, because they became contented and forgot their destiny, the god broke the dam and drained the lake.

Sadly the Mexica resumed their journey, passing through the ruined city of Tula to finally arrive in the Basin of Mexico. They were the last tribe to enter that lacustrine world, for all the other Aztec groups were already settled there in cities. The Mexica made their first home on the shores of Lake Tezcoco under the great rock of Chapultepec. Here they became known as fierce warriors; in fact they so often offended their neighbors, the Tepaneca and the Culhua, that a coalition was formed to oust them. They were defeated and scattered, the survivors being taken to the city of Culhuacan. But the Mexica endured even that servitude; they married Culhua women and again rose to become a warrior class. They built a temple to Huitzilopochtli in the area and, to dedicate it, asked the lord of Culhuacan for one of his daughters. The Culhua thought that a marriage was intended and were thoroughly shocked to discover that the girl had been sacrificed in the cult of Huitzilopochtli's mother, Coatlicue. In the upheaval which followed, the Mexica fled out into the lake, taking their god with them.

Their destiny was fulfilled when various signs were miraculously displayed in the reedbeds of the lake. The Mexica knew that their god had at last unequivocally spoken when he commanded them to found their city of Mexico-Tenochtitlan where an eagle was seen perched on a cactus.

Thus was the sacred journey completed. Huitzilopochtli had brought them at last to the appointed place. The novitiate of the Mexica was completed and they could now, from their newly founded capital, look ahead to the acquisition of vast domains.

The Gigantomachy at Coatepec

We must now return to the sojourn of the Mexica at Coatepec, near Tula.

Whether or not the Mexica actually did pass through the site of Tula, the legend had to state that they did. In legend Tula was as Edenic as Aztlan itself. Contact with Tula gave a tribe prestige it could not otherwise have acquired.

What we need to consider here is the god who forced the Mexica on by breaking the dam and drying up the waters. Up to now we have identified him as a form of Mixcoatl and have called him the Omen. At this point in the legend of the sacred journey of the Mexica, are we to begin calling him Huitzilopochtli, the famous hero of the myth of the gigantomachy? To answer this we must first consider that Mexican myth.[15]

In the myth Coatepec is the world mountain, that piece of land which was first upthrust at the world's beginning. The aboriginal quality of this mountain is confirmed when we learn that the Mexica celebrated the New Fire ceremony on its summit, thus initiating a new age.

The Earth Mother lived in Coatepec, and there she had born the Huitznahua, the Four Hundred Southerners—early titans who, like the Mimixcoa, could be thought of as the stars rising out of the earth's body at nightfall. The leader of these titans was Coyolxauhqui, literally She Is Decorated with Tinkling Bells, a goddess who in the pre-Aztec level of the myth must certainly have been the moon.[16]

As the story begins we see the Earth Mother engaged in sweeping, when a tuft of white feathers fell from the heavens. This she inserted under her skirt for safekeeping and soon thereafter found herself to be pregnant. When her children heard of this inexplicable pregnancy they were filled with shame, and at the urging of Coyolxauhqui they decided to destroy their mother. Aware of these terrible intentions, the Great Mother became frightened but was reassured by the unborn child speaking from within her womb. Meanwhile the Four Hundred Southerners, arrayed as fierce warriors, gathered in their rows and columns and moved out to the assault of the primordial mountain. As the attack came on, Huitzilopochtli sprang from the womb fully accoutered and painted for war. He carried a death-dealing weapon, the fire dragon wrapped in flames, with which he killed Coyolxauhqui. He decapitated her and rolled her body down the mountain so that she broke in many pieces. Her head remained on the mountaintop. Huitzilopochtli then hurled himself on the Four Hundred, destroying many and scattering the rest into the far south. He stripped their bodies and assumed their devices and regalia, thus giving himself a new name, the Southern or Huitznahua Warrior. Another version of the myth has Huitzilopochtli defeating Coyolxauhqui and the Southerners in a midnight game in the *tlachco*, sacrificing them there and eating their hearts.[17] So ended a tale that originally told how the sun scattered the stars, while the moon waned and paled as a severed head might do.

The vitality of this myth for the Mexica has long been acknowledged, but it has received increased recognition because of the recent discovery in the Zocalo of the beautifully preserved stone disk displaying the dismembered body of Coyolxauhqui. She is here thought of as a demon of the nighttime, as well as the moon. She is embellished with belt, bangles, and anklets of serpents and wears a serpent on her forehead like the Egyptian uraeus. In other words, she is an avatar of the Earth Mother.

Laid over this antique astral myth are the late and easily identified glosses of a people accustomed to war. The diurnal rising of the sun was interpreted by them as the result of a collision of hostile forces, a contest between the solitary hero of Mexico and his circumambient enemies. We recall that his only father had been a handful of feathers, such as all warriors displayed in their topknots or pasted onto their bodies. That bunch of feathers thus represented war as an obligation sent down from a heavenly authority.

This gigantic birth and the ensuing cosmic battle were mimed every year in Mexico in the god's festival of the Raising of the Banners.[18] In this performance, outstanding for its drama, an idol of Huitzilopoch-tli called Painal, the Runner, traced the historic journey of the Mexica around the lake from Chapultepec to Culhuacan, Mexicaltzinco, and back to Tenochtitlan over the causeway. By the same token, insofar as Huitzilopochtli was modeled on the sun, the circuit could also stand for the sun's orbital journey. This ritual will be considered at length later.

The adaptation of an old myth to a people's later national uses is here clearly displayed. We can guess that the gigantomachy had been a tale inherited from the Toltecs and that it was introduced into the later Aztec world by the Culhua. It is also a fair guess that the Mexica acquired it during their stay in Culhuacan and there substituted Hui-tzilopochtli for its original hero, whatever his name may have been.

Yet, while Huitzilopochtli stood in the place of the sun god and while he could even be vaguely thought of as the sun, his basically ethnic character was never submerged. He was *the* Mexican and he accurately reflected the obsessive interest in war of Mexico's knightly class. We already know that his priests could come only from those wards of the city known to be purely Mexican in origin. In one of the god's feasts all Mexican children born during the preceding year were scarified on the chest as a sign of their cult affiliation. In ritual Hui-tzilopochtli's great deeds were borne before him painted in a holy book, which deeds of course were the mighty works of the Mexican armies. Thus in Huitzilopochtli the highest aspirations of the Mexica were spelled out. The guardian deities of the other Aztec peoples resembled him to an extent, but his festival was the most splendidly developed of them all.

Chapultepec and Tlaloc

The rock of Chapultepec which stood on the shores of Lake Tezcoco overlooked that site which would one day be Mexico. Some of the early chieftains of the Mexica were buried under the rock, and on its steep face the later rulers of Mexico had their figures carved along with the glyphs giving their names. The legend of the sacred journey reveals the importance of the rock in the founding of Tenochtitlan.

Long before the Mexica took up their residence there, Chapultepec had been a famous Toltec site. A sacred spring gushed out from under the rock. People who bathed in it found renewal and healing from the contagions of sin. From the earliest days a priest of Tlaloc had been stationed there. Near the summit was a fissure called Tlachtonco, the Small Ball Court, a hellmouth which led one mysteriously into inner caverns. This hidden paradise was Cincalco, and its particular lord was Huemac.

We have already mentioned how drought afflicted the Toltec empire and how Huemac, the last ruler, played a game of ball with the rain gods and lost. In the end Huemac was obliged to send down to the sacred spring of Chapultepec for an oracle which he hoped would turn aside the divine wrath. Thus consulted, Tlaloc demanded a young Mexican maiden, and only after she had been sacrificed and thrown down into a hellmouth in the lake did he countermand the drought.[19]

The whole point of this tale was to magnify the presence of Tlaloc at Chapultepec. All our sources seem to suggest that Tlaloc was the god of the lake and, just as he rested on the summit of the great mountain on the Basin's east side, so on this western side he resided in the rock of Chapultepec, holding sway over all the mud flats out in the water—one of which was to become the site of Tenochtitlan. Huitzilopochtli himself is never mentioned as being present at the rock. When the inhabitants of Mexico erected their focal pyramid, they placed two shrines of equal size on the summit: one for Huitzilopochtli and one for Tlaloc. Tlaloc, however, was the elder god at that site and surely its territorial patron. Huitzilopochtli was a latecomer; Tlaloc is even said to have addressed Huitzilopochtli as his son. And we know that the Aztecs thought Tlaloc himself to have been involved to some extent in the actual founding of Tenochtitlan. In the minds of the Mexica, Tlaloc and Huitzilopochtli were almost like companion gods, though their jurisdictions differed. Certainly Tlaloc's sovereignty at Chapultepec (the prior home of the Mexica and the source of their later capital's potable water) was a sign of his immense importance to those on the lake. The city of Mexico was inconceivable without that rock looming up some two and a half miles away.

Culhuacan and Opochtli

From Aztlan on through their residence in Chapultepec the Mexica had worshiped a form of Mixcoatl, a deity whom we have not yet given any certain name. After the disaster at the rock they were widely dispersed and suffered disruptions in all aspects of their life, including their cult. A number of them were thrown under the jurisdiction of the city of Culhuacan on the south shore of the lake. The Culhua, a Toltec tribe, had long preceded the Mexica into the Basin and were in the process of rebuilding Toltec prestige; in fact they counted their royal lineage from Tula. From them the Tenochca Mexica were to derive many things: a house of strong rulers, claims to be heirs of Toltec legitimacy, and the worship of certain gods—among whom was, as we hope to make clear, Huitzilopochtli himself. The evidence for this last statement is complicated, so we must go into it at some length.

By the time the Mexica settled near Culhuacan they had become a true marsh people, trained to live off the produce of the lake. The land the Culhua allotted them was worthless for agriculture, so their real homes were their canoes. They lived in depressed circumstances and paid a heavy tribute to their masters. More important, their god had been either kidnaped or demoted; at the very least he had been immunized. Certainly he had failed his people in the recent battle. One source says that he had been seized by the Culhua when the Mexica entered their territory and that he was held hostage for their good behavior. Another source says that, to protect him from just this fate, the Mexica hid him underground.[20] At any rate their god needed reformulation.

It is difficult to say just what was happening to the Mexica during this period of their servitude, but we can be sure that the difficulties involved their god—which of course meant their own identity. The city of Culhuacan itself had been frequently involved in religious controversies and was generally hostile to the intrusive Mexican cult, which it tried in every way to cheapen.

It was during these approximately twenty years under their Culhua masters that the Mexica either took a new god, refurbished their old god, or amalgamated him with another. I opt for the third possibility. At any rate from this point on we can talk with confidence about Huitzilopochtli as the tribal deity of the Mexica. On occasions the earlier denomination of the god, the Omen, was added to the name Huitzilopochtli as a modifier.

At this point we have to consider the name Huitzilopochtli to see whether it throws any light on the new god's identity.

It may or may not be significant that the Mexican ruler who had been captured at Chapultepec and hauled away to Culhuacan, to be sacrificed in a memorable ceremony, was named Huitzilihuitl, Hummingbird Feather, or that that was also the name given to the first legitimate ruler of the Tenochca Mexica. Certainly it happened that the *huitzilin* or hummingbird at this late stage suddenly became of religious importance to the Mexica. We suspect that the hummingbird's supposed powers of resuscitation in the springtime, following a winter of hibernation, may have had something to do with it.[21] In fact when we recall that in Mayan lore the sun can disguise himself as a hummingbird and that Huitzilopochtli in the myth of the gigantomachy plays the role of the sun, we can theorize that the solstitial renewal of the sun is implied.

But the completion of Huitzilopochtli did not occur until he had met a god named Opochtli, the Left-Handed One. Opochtli was worshiped in Cuitlahuac, Huitzilopochco, and probably Culhuacan, Aztec communities in the southern part of the Basin. He was known as the leading Chichimec god of the marsh folk of the south, and he was certainly older than Huitzilopochtli. As a hunter he had two important transfigurations, Amimitl and Atlahua. The former, whose name means Harpoon, was also a transfiguration of Mixcoatl, being in fact the personification of that deity's arrow.[22] He had been venerated in a temple on the legendary island of Aztlan.[23] The name of the latter means Lord of the Atlatl. Particularly formidable because of his left-handedness, Opochtli thus had as his two transfigurations deifications of the weapons for which he was famous.

Opochtli could also be classed as a member of the Tlaloque because of his intimate association with water and fishermen.[24] He was described as He Who Divides the Waters.[25] He had invented such implements as the atlatl, the net, the fishing trident, the canoe pole, and the bird snare.[26] His impersonator was annually sacrificed in Mexico at the Feast of the Mountains, a ceremony in which all the Tlaloque were venerated. As the god of Huitzilopochco he had jurisdiction over its famous waters, Hummingbird Spring.[27] And when the Mexica moved to that city during their residence in the greater domain of Culhuacan, it was the god Opochtli who welcomed them.

Thus the Mexica came upon Opochtli at a low ebb in the fortunes of their own god. There seems little doubt that their life as a water folk impelled them to an accommodation with Opochtli and that they subsequently remodeled their tribal god in his image. At that time, they probably bestowed upon him the name he thenceforth bore: Huitzilopochtli, the God Opochtli as a Hummingbird. One source remembers with great specificity this crucial point in Mexican religious history:

> And that water god [Opochtli] came upon the Indian who carried the breechclout and mantle of Huitzilopochtli and at the meeting gave him some arms which are those with which they kill ducks and an atlatl. Because Huitzilopochtli was left-handed like him, this water god said that he should be his son. And they were very close. And the name of the place where they met was changed; it had been called Huitzilatl [Hummingbird Water], but thenceforth was called Huitzilopochco [Where Huitzilopochtli Resides].[28]

There was a natural reluctance on the part of the later Mexica to display this redesigning of their national god, for it had been done when they were in a state of near slavery and when their early god was subject to the humiliation of imprisonment. In order to change its focus, the story was therefore deliberately disguised.[29] The account was changed to state that when the Tenochca finally decided that they must have a king, as did the other peoples of the Basin, they secured an oracle from the deity Mecitli that they should accept Acamapichtli, the son of a great Mexican nobleman and warrior named Opochtli, whom they had left behind in Culhuacan. The wife of this lord was named Iztahuatzin, Mistress of Salt. It needs little perspicacity to see in that nobleman and his wife the southern god Opochtli and his consort, the well-known goddess of salt.

The religious situation in Culhuacan in those days was precarious. We can consider two examples of the mutual aversion felt by Mexica and Culhua. In the first incident we can see that the Mexica had finally agreed upon the lineaments of their new god, now named Huitzilopochtli.[30] Because they wished to dedicate a suitable shrine to him and increase his prestige, they appealed to their masters for a dedicatory gift. Feelings were running so high at the time that the Culhua sent a canoe full of human excrement, dead birds, and other rubbish. All this was cast on the shrine, which was so befouled that the Mexica were forced to ceremonially cleanse the whole precinct.

In the second incident, which we have already mentioned, we see the Mexica building a companion temple to Toci, Our Grandmother, the great goddess of Culhuacan who was to be thought of as Huitzilopochtli's mother.[31] The Mexica applied to the ruler of Culhuacan for one of his daughters, who would act as surrogate for the goddess. Culhuacan was religiously split at the time, and the ruler happened to favor the Mexica and their religious expansion. He sent them one of his daughters, understanding of course that she was to be appropriately honored. The Mexica, however, sacrificed her, skinned her, and dressed a priest in her skin. The royal father was invited to a follow-up ceremony and witnessed the priest dancing about in his daughter's skin. The furor caused by this shocking action led to the expulsion of the Mexica from Culhua territory and their flight out into the lake. Culhuacan itself began to break up as a result of these and other religious upheavals.

We may or may not wish to believe these two stories. Certain things about them are obvious exaggerations, but they do point to an all-important shift of the Mexica from their traditional worship of Mecitli and Tetzauhteotl to Toci and Huitzilopochtli. That realignment must have been drastic, as we can gather from the historic events which followed.

The Founding of Mexico-Tenochtitlan

The attempt to dignify the new god, so incongruously patterned on Mixcoatl and Tlaloc, thus failed suddenly and disastrously as a result of the expulsion of the Tenochca. The refugees, carrying their revitalized tribal mascot, moved north through a series of mud flats in the lake until they entered Tepaneca territory. They settled on a shoal in the lake just south of the island of Tlatilulco, where the other half of their tribe, the Tlatilulca, had been installed for several years. The place where they set up their first shrine on the mud flats became Mexico-Tenochtitlan, Mecitli's Place near the Nopal Cactus.

The Mexica later gave two contrasting versions of the omens connected with the founding of Tenochtitlan: the omen of the heart of Copil and that of the drowning of Axolohua. These throw considerable light on the final meaning that was to be attached to the god Huitzilopochtli.

The first version refers back to the residence of the Mexica on the rock of Chapultepec.[32] We are told that at that time a renegade Mexican named Copil, a sorcerer, stirred up the other nations against the Mexica. Before a league could be formed, he appeared at Chapultepec and met the *teomama* of the Mexican god in a frightening shamanic contest. Copil's god could not withstand the Mexican god, however, and the defeated Copil was seized and sacrificed. His head was buried in the rock, but his heart was taken out into the lake and hurled into the reeds. There it took root and grew to be the famous nopal cactus that marked the site of Tenochtitlan. This version of the founding legend obviously attempted to incorporate a specific historical datum, and we may well believe that the Mexica were active on the island of Tenochtitlan long before its traditional founding. The shamanic contest was inserted to keep Huitzilopochtli in the center of the event.

The second legend is even more revealing.[33] It begins with the expulsion from Culhuacan. Floundering in the reedy parts of the lake, the fleeing Mexica sent ahead two of their holy men, Axolohua and another, to find and consecrate a spot which they might call their own. In their search these two came upon a rock barely rising above the surface of the lake, whereon grew a nopal with an eagle perched on its top. In order that he might make contact with Tlaloc, the great lord of the place, Axolohua was accordingly drowned there. The following day he rose from the lake to announce that he had met Tlaloc, who had confirmed that that spot was the one where they should build a permanent altar to Huitzilopochtli. The altar was subsequently built at the foot of the nopal and marked the center out of which the city of Mexico was to grow.

What is of interest here is that the possessor of the site was Tlaloc and that only he could grant permission to "his son" Huitzilopochtli to settle there. It is indeed possible, though we are not told this, that the Tlaloc acting there was specifically his avatar Opochtli. The oracle-priest Axolohua, from his name as well as his actions, was certainly concerned with the cult of Tlaloc, not with that of Huitzilopochtli.[34] At any rate the intimate association of Tlaloc with Huitzilopochtli in their adjoining temples on top of the great pyramid is hereby explained.

An eagle on a nopal which grows out of the prone Earth Mother (Borgia)

The Cult of Huitzilopochtli

We have noted that the great temple in Mexico-Tenochtitlan could be thought of as Coatepec, the sacred mountain where Huitzilopochtli had achieved his victory over the Huitznahua gods. The temples of both Huitzilopochtli and Tlaloc stood on the pyramid's summit, so close together as to be almost joined. Both faced west and were approached by adjacent stairways. Placed on Huitzilopochtli's half of the terrace was a huge stone head of Coyolxauhqui, her eyes closed in death to recall her decapitation.[35] The pillars in Huitzilopochtli's temple are said to have represented the *tzitzimime*, who held up the sky. Architecturally everything was designed to elevate the temple into the empyrean, to announce it as the height of sovereignty. Its political implications, in fact, cannot be mistaken: it was the congelation of the Mexican insistence that they were the true masters of the Aztec world.

Huitzilopochtli's priesthood, of whom there were some five thousand, was unique. The other gods received as neophytes the children of any peoples, but Huitzilopochtli restricted his neophytes to those born in the six wards of the city considered to be purely Mexican. In fact one of the designations for this body of priests was simply "the Mexica." This exclusivity was relaxed at only two points. Huitzilopochtli's priesthood was shared with his mother, the great goddess, as well as with Tlaloc. This inner priesthood was thus an institutional embodiment of the divine sanction behind the state.

During the year Huitzilopochtli was honored in three festivals, but only the last–Panquetzaliztli, the Raising of the Banners–was exclusively his.[36] At that time of the year all the harvests were in and the Aztec world was ready for war. It was thus the appropriate time for Mexico to honor and invoke its Martian overlord as it turned outward to seek the enemy. But the other Aztec states had also put themselves under arms and were honoring their own gods of war. Thus arose another designation for the great feast–Coailhuitl, the Feast Common to All; captives taken in previous battles were hoarded against the festival day so there might be a plethora of sacrifices.

In the ceremony which reenacted the myth of the gigantomachy Huitzilopochtli appeared in his transfiguration as Painal, the Runner, an idol (probably a bundle) carried about whenever a procession was necessary. If Huitzilopochtli was considered to be the god of formal and organized warfare, the Runner was the god of sudden raids and ambushes. Appropriately, he wore the smoking mirror of Tezcatlipoca in his hair, and it was his image which was brought down from the templetop on the day of the Panquetzaliztli to perform the running of Huitzilopochtli. This was a circuit of some twenty miles made during the day by a priest carrying the image of the god on his back. It began at the templetop and ended there. The entire Mexican nation, both Tenochca and Tlatilulca, turned out for this all-important tribal rite, and as the *teomama* raced around the lake some of the people ran after him to demonstrate their identity with the god.

The route and its stations are of some interest. Having descended from his shrine, the Runner went first to the nearby Ball Court of the Gods. Four victims were sacrificed here and their corpses dragged about to bloody the entire area. This squares with the version of the myth which has Huitzilopochtli playing a game of *tlachtli* with Coyolxauhqui, defeating her and then cutting off her head in the center of the court. We understand that this quadruple sacrifice ritually summarized the defeat of the astral titans by the sun.

Meanwhile the god on the back of his *teomama* sped on up through Tlatilulco, the sister city, and over the causeway to the island of Nonohualco. Here the Runner was greeted by an image of that titan who, in the myth, had gone over to Huitzilopochtli and kept him informed of the movements of the forces under Coyolxauhqui. Then, at Popotlan, the Runner left the causeway and moved down the lakeside past Chapultepec to the holy site of Huitzilopocho, whence he finally regained Mexico via the southern causeway. This running over the early tribal route represented Huitzilopochtli's speedy reconnoitering of the enemy forces, just as it can probably represent the coursing of the sun.

While the god was on his circuit, other participants were miming the events recounted in the myth. Two parties of those destined for sacrifice had been assembled and armed at the foot of the temple. One group was composed of slaves bought by rich merchants as offerings in this ceremony; the other consisted of captives taken in war, here identified with the titanic Southerners. Whereas the scene in the *tlachco* was a reenactment of the great battle in conceptual terms, this rite was a simulacrum of the full reality of the battle, for both parties fought with real weapons, and deaths and captures eventuated. The Runner's return brought this ritual conflict to an end.

Upon the Runner's return the *xiuhcoatl*, the turquoise dragon made up as a great fire-breathing mask followed by an undulating paper tail, was brought down the temple steps to represent the weapon Huitzilopochtli hurled upon the Southerners from the top of the world mountain. At the foot of the pyramid had been placed a sacrificial bowl containing bits of paper taken from the victims-to-be, each piece representing a particular captive or slave.

As the dragon reached the foot of the pyramid it was set on fire and flung down upon the bowl of papers—they were all consumed, just as in the myth Huitzilopochtli hurled his thunderbolt down to reduce his enemy to ashes.

But the myth had a sequel: Huitzilopochtli rounded up those of the titans he had captured, sacrificed them to himself, and thus, at the beginning of things, taught the Mexica the uses of human sacrifice. The Panquetzaliztli ended with a well-nigh interminable slaughter of victims.

We have noticed only the most salient acts in this tribal ritual of the Mexica. There are many fascinating details, but a consideration of these here would lead us away from our main point, which is Huitzilopochtli as the symbol of the Mexican cycle of life: warfare, heroism, sacrifice, and cannibalism.

The Completed Huitzilopochtli

Huitzilopochtli is the only Aztec god whose historical evolution we can discern, however dimly. By the same token he is the only major Aztec deity not represented in the *tonalamatl*, the book of augural days. These two facts are opposite faces of the same coin. Huitzilopochtli was the talismanic god of a recently formed nation whose people had had to gain distinction by feats of fortitude and valor; they certainly carried no glory down from their past, which had been meager at best. Their rise to greatness had come suddenly, after trials that would have crushed a lesser people. So, in the final crisis of that history which led up to the founding of Tenochtitlan, Huitzilopochtli had been hastily thrown together out of the odds and ends of di-

Huitzilopochtli before his shrine (Borbonicus)

vinities. But, while he contained shreds of the earth goddess, of Mix-coatl, of Tezcatlipoca, and of a Culhua lord of waters, he was recognizably the historical experience and the historical destiny of one single tribe.

Huitzilopochtli was not a god with a homogeneous nature, as was Tlaloc. He clearly did not represent any generic experience, as did Chalchiuhtlicue (water), or Tlazolteotl (sex), or Xipe (spring). He was built on quite a different model, having been produced out of a mixture of both natural and historical elements. None of the other great gods could boast the latter. Thus only the ancient gods, fully understood as spirits of nature, could be found in the *tonalamatl*, for only they were applicable everywhere.

Of all the great deities we suppose that Huitzilopochtli most vividly resembles Tezcatlipoca, one of whose most prominent transfigurations was the Enemy. It is indeed a fair statement to make, namely that Huitzilopochtli himself was a transfiguration, through Mixcoatl, of Tezcatlipoca. In support of this there is plenty of textual and plastic evidence. For instance, in the famous bewitching of Quetzalcoatl in Tula, Tezcatlipoca appears to him in four guises: himself, Tlacahuepan, Titlacahuan, and Huitzilopochtli.[37] Again this appears in the myth where Tezcatlipoca is driving the Toltec people insane with curiosity as they watch the tiny homunculus dancing in his hand. That tiny figure is identified as Huitzilopochtli. Yet, though he may be considered a transfiguration of Tezcatlipoca, our god had finally been painted over with purely Mexican colors. He no longer belongs to the Aztec world at large but only to one among its many tribes. Thus the resemblance to Tezcatlipoca remains generic only.

Blue was the color of Huitzilopochtli. His face was painted with horizontal stripes of alternating blue and yellow. His helmet represented his *nahualli*, the hummingbird, its beak acting as a visor over his forehead. On his back he bore that curious feather and paper construction called the *anecuyotl*, the device of the titans which he had appropriated as a sign of his victory over them. His left leg was thought to be withered and was pasted all over with feathers, a variation on the Tezcatlipoca motif.[38]

As the matchless warrior he carried a special shield, the *tehuehuelli*. He brandished two incomparable darts such as no mortal or deity dared face, the *xiuhcoatl* and the *mamalhuaztli*. In iconography the former appears as a serpent-headed boomerang encrusted with turquoise mosaic. In battle this instrument took on life to become the fire-breathing sky dragon which, when hurled, acted as a thunderbolt—blasting and incinerating all it fell upon. It was in fact a well-known chimeralike beast and was common even outside Huitzilopochtli's mythology. But here we see it used as the weapon of victory over the Southerners. The *mamalhuaztli* was the drilling stick and board with which fire was made. The power inherent in the production of fire was spectacular, and this power too had been appropriated by Huitzilopochtli. As the god of victory on the battlefield, Huitzilopochtli was thus perfectly endowed.

We have already discussed his transfiguration as the Runner. Besides this god he appeared in Tlatilulco as Tlacahuepan, whose statue was often called Blue Sky.[39] Tlacahuepan, whose name means Man Beam or Man Post, was a Toltec god who had been taken over by the Tlatilulca as their transfiguration of Huitzilopochtli, specifically as his younger brother. Tlacahuepan was patterned on Tezcatlipoca and in fact was even called the Demon. In Tenochtitlan he appears as Tlacahuepan-Cuexcoch, which refers to the fact that he wears on the back of his head, or *cuexcochtli*, the face mask of a skull.

There was another transfiguration of Huitzilopochtli which has not been sufficiently studied. As the god Huitznahuatl he personified the Four Hundred Southerners who had been overcome by him. When we recall that Huitzilopochtli was their brother we can see why he could be referred to as the Huitznahuatl par excellence or even as Huitznahuatl Yaotl, the Huitznahua Enemy. The concept of the close identity of captor with captive is well established in Aztec thought, no doubt coming from the custom of eating the captive to acquire his courage. At any rate we know that Tlacahuepan was worshiped in the temple of Huitznahuac in Mexico, as were the titanic Four Hundred and their synoptic god Huitznahuatl Yaotl. The equation of Tlacahuepan and Huitznahuatl is thus made—along with the corollary that the latter must also be seen as an avatar of Huitzilopochtli. We are therefore not surprised to learn that on the feast day of the god Huitznahuatl all the magnates of Mexico played a sacred game in the Ball Court of the Mirrors, this being a variant reenactment of the cosmic myth of the Toltecs.[40]

When they were putting the finishing touches on their national deity, the Mexica could have had no problem defining his standing in relation to Tezcatlipoca, the greatest god of the Aztec pantheon: Huitzilopochtli was a lesser god in every way. In the annual feast of Toxcatl, as we have learned, the *ixiptla* of Tezcatlipoca was selected to act as the god's surrogate for the year. In that same festival Huitzilopochtli's *ixiptla* was also selected to go through the same year and to be sacrificed at the same time. This impersonator was called the Younger Brother; he wandered about the streets with Tezcatlipoca's *ixiptla*, but he was considered far less sacred and indeed was hardly noticed.[41] In the end he was sacrificed in a different and less ceremonial manner. Even in the minds of the Mexica there was no doubt that, by reason of his cosmic character, Tezcatlipoca was superior to Huitzilopochtli.

The narrowly defined historic role played by Huitzilopochtli prevented him from filling the role of a nature god. Yet we have seen that he was built from pieces of nature gods: he harks back to an ominous voice from the cave; his myth is a mixture of astral elements and the mythologies of two northern gods, Mixcoatl and Tezcatlipoca; his left-handedness was derived from Opochtli. But he was never recognizably the sun, nor was he the mighty hunter of the steppe, nor a perverse lord of darkness, nor a master of waters. These had simply provided elements for the framework upon which he was built. He was a more original deity than any of the above, however greater they may have been. His uniqueness was in his narrowness. He was not even Aztec–he represented only the Mexica as they mated war with human sacrifice in a divinely sanctioned history.

7. The Goddesses

Preliminary Remarks

Earlier in this work I have set down categories under which we could conveniently position the various Aztec divinities. These four categories were the explanatory, the affective, the providential, and the focal. Only the second and the third are useful when we are considering the goddesses. This is only to say that the Aztecs did not conceive of the female deity as providing a springboard for intellectual speculation, nor did they see her as at all interested in social arrangements or folk identification. The reason for this is that as Earth and as Woman her appearances and her effects were excessively concrete and simple. She did not invite thought or tease the creative fancy. She was the epitome of both terror and bounty and her worshipers experienced her as a whole being, one basically beyond definition. It is true that, because she included so many aspects of the divine, she could and did evolve a multitude of epithetical variations and transfigurations. But she easily resumed her unique identity and was always all-inclusive.

The goddess had many attributes designated by appropriate names, as we shall see in the sections which follow. Here we must point out her most material reduction and ultimate presence. She was Tlalteuctli, Earth Lady, the palpable rock and soil and slime upon which men moved and into which they were lowered at death. Tlalteuctli is not a goddess as such, a being anthropomorphically conceived about whom myths were told. She was the compendious numen of the earth, even more uncompromisingly so than Tonatiuh was the numen of the sky. In the speculative thought of the Aztecs she could be referred to as the mother of all men, even as Tonatiuh was their father. But her impact upon the Aztecs was a religious seizure and a terror which had nothing intellectual about it. Unlike the deities to whom she gave rise and who were always conceived in female shape, she was depicted as a gargantuan toad slavering blood, with clashing jaws at every joint. She represented chaos.

Tonan, the Mother

We may group a constellation of the many names applied to the goddess around that of Tonantzin, literally Our Holy Mother. Cihuatzin, Revered Lady; Toci, Our Grandmother; Ilama, Old Woman; Tocennan, All Mother; and Teteoinnan, Mother of the Gods—all speak to the same effect. As Tonan the goddess was simply the Mother. To each of her apotheoses were ascribed a flavor and sometimes a very definite geographical provenience and a characteristic cult, but they were all the same divinity underneath; their names shift like quicksilver, and one is often identified with another. We are here assuming that this group of titles, arbitrarily subsumed under our rubric Tonan, represents the basic conception of her as a divinity who received worship.

Tonan was a name given in Nahuatl to several mountains, these being the congelations of the Earth Mother at spots convenient for her worship.[1] Especially revered among these mountains was the headland jutting out into Lake Tezcoco and pointing southward toward the island cities of Mexico.[2] Its primacy among the Aztecs can be grasped by the fact that even the coming of the Spaniards could not eradicate its cult of Tonan, for almost overnight she became the Virgin of Guadalupe, Catholic and dressed as a lady of Spain. The ancient pilgrimages that formerly drew Indians to her pagan festival still draw them to her church on the same spot. The Virgin today is called Tonantzin, and she is known to have brown skin, though she has exchanged her stern pagan motherhood for a Christian tenderness and a solicitude not stressed by the Aztecs.

Very specifically, Tonan was the earth. The Mexica revered her as the goddess who was present at their own inception as a people, for she is once depicted on the mountain of Aztlan, the well-known homeland of the Aztec tribes. Beside her is the inscription "Our

Mother stood here."[3] As Cihuatzintli she was honored by the erection of a temple in Tenochtitlan during the perilous days of the Tepaneca War.[4] In this transfiguration her title was She Who Surrounds Us, possibly a reference to the wide world and its encompassing hills.

With Toci an equally impressive Earth Mother was brought into the Mexican pantheon from outside. Toci was a goddess with the usual assortment of female and telluric qualities. She could be called Tlalliiyollo, Heart of the Earth, and as such was thought to upheave the land and tumble down the crags in her mighty tremors.[5] She was the patroness of weaving, spinning, and curing. It was said that she had two divine sons—maize and the nemesis of maize, frost.

The Mexica worshiped this Great Mother when they were a defeated and enslaved people in Culhuacan. As the Culhua Our Grandmother (Toci) she was identical with the Mother of the Gods (Teteoinnan). She had been introduced into Tenochtitlan and attached to the state cult, but in a fashion which clearly reflected the past hostility between the Mexica and the Culhua. She was allowed no temple or priesthood of her own in the ceremonial center. Instead her worshipers built a high, inaccessible wooden platform on the south edge of the city for her image, which sat unattended all the days of the year. Canonically she was added to the Mexican collection of gods as Huitzilopochtli's grandmother or mother, depending on the needs of the moment. The relationship between the two deities, male and female, was easy to grasp inasmuch as Toci, the Culhua goddess, had as her most common epiphany a goddess of war: Yaocihuatl, Enemy Woman. In iconography Toci held a shield in one hand and a broom, representing her domestic side, in the other. There is the possibility that she had been carried down into the Basin of Mexico by the Culhua following the breakup of the Toltec empire. In Culhuacan Toci became one of the foremost Aztec goddesses,[6] worshiped by Aztec tribes other than the Culhua and the Mexica, notably by the Tlascalans. Everywhere her rites were of peculiar solemnity.

Her primacy is understood by her appearance as Teteoinnan. Here she was raised to the highest level of divinity and played an almost gynarchic role. She wore as her exclusive garment the so-called star skirt, a belted skirt of leather straps to which was sewn a profusion of seashells, whose dry rattling in the dance was an earnest of her holy presence.

In another transfiguration the Mother appears as Ilamateuctli or Leading Old Woman. She wore a Janus mask, one face in front and one behind, both with gaping mouths and popping eyes signifying, no doubt, her dual role as the giver of life and death.[7]

The remarks we have made about Tonan and her several transfigurations have almost surely given a false impression of logic and neatness. The facts are otherwise. Those early Spaniards who discussed Aztec religion never tell us how we may distinguish among the goddesses, which were the Mother's titles and which were, more properly, conceptualizations of her. Here, for the sake of clarity, we have arbitrarily placed Tonan as the archetypal goddess, and we have treated Toci, Teteoinnan, Ilamateuctli, and others as epithetical variations of her. All are based on the same two concepts, motherhood and earth, but the divinizations are not necessarily interchangeable, for their respective rites could differ and their respective temples could be the homes of unique rites. In any case the archetypal goddess is the Great Mother, who appears in some form or other among most of the peoples of the globe.

As we move farther away from this core image of the goddess, we begin to come upon aspects of her wherein she is no longer only a general principle or power but is also a patroness of a specific aspect of the universe. As a nurse and nourisher, for example, she appears as a set of providential goddesses; for the rest, as patroness of sexual desire, as goddess of death and demonry, and as instigator of war, she is fragmented into an imposing array of affective deities.

The Goddess as Nurse and Nourisher

As Yohualticitl, Midwife of the Night, the goddess directed the events connected with birth. She had especial jurisdiction over that ancient Mesoamerican institution of curing, the sweatbath, whose dark interior was symbolic of the primeval womb.[8] At various times before her delivery a pregnant woman might receive treatment within the sweathouse, and often it was utilized as an aid in the actual parturition. A return into the body of the Great Mother always conferred power.

In Aztec lore the goddess appears in a trifold fashion, providing man with food, water, and salt–the three necessities for daily living. In that order the goddesses are Chicomecoatl, Seven Snake; Chalchiuhtlicue, Jade Skirt; and Huixtocihuatl, the goddess of salt, the derivation of whose name is uncertain. In a sense the members of this group are the Three Graces of Aztec mythology, more benevolent than most of the other deities. All three were said to be sisters or companions of the Tlaloque, the rain gods and therefore the original purveyors of man's daily requirements.

Like the Roman Ceres, Seven Snake was the personification not only of corn but of harvested grains and fruit in general.[9] She could be thought of as the Great Mother living in the blissful land of Tlalocan, either dispensing or withholding her gifts. Cinteotl, the god of maize, was said to be her son, but he easily interchanges with Xilonen, the personification of the fresh maize as a virginal young girl. Thus Chicomecoatl herself is threefold: she is mother, virgin, and child. Sexual ambivalence, so frequent in Aztec mythology, thus plays a role here in the Aztec concept of the deity resident in maize.

When treated mythically by the Aztecs, maize is a male god. Young and resplendent, he is Tlazopilli, the Beloved Prince.[10] His birth was the result of a union in a sacred cave between the sun god and the Mother or, according to another account, it occurred in Tamoanchan. When treated conceptually, however, the young deity was Xilonen, a name which means something like Fresh Maize-Ear Girl. The milky sweetness of the new maize and its early harvest were commemorated in her. She was conceived as a maiden dancing joyously with outspread arms and a double ear of maize in each hand. She wore her hair loosened like the corn silk of the new maize. She is one of the few completely joyous and innocent figures in the Aztec pantheon.

A more popular level of the numen behind the great staple is represented by the Cicinteteo, the maize gods, associated not with myth or state cult but with the fields and the bins where the dried kernels were stored. These fragmentary deities became tangible to the Aztec farmer in an abundance of homemade fetishes and dolls made of corncobs.

Chalchiuhtlicue or Jade Skirt is a rather more complex goddess than her cereal sister. She represents water, but only a special aspect of it. If Tlaloc is the storm god who pours fertilizing rain over the earth, Jade Skirt is the earthly containment of these waters as they are collected into pools, springs, oceans, ditches, and coursing rivers. Nor was she always placid, as we know from a series of epithets referring to her as the Foaming One, the Tidal One, the Agitated One, etc. Among the Tlascalans she was worshiped as Matlalcueye, Blue Skirt, who presided over their extended lands as the majestic and isolated mountain today called Malinche.[11]

All rivers belonged to Jade Skirt by right. They were thought to flow out of Tlalocan. So close was the identification of this goddess with the water contained within the rocky shell of the mountain that, as was the case with Blue Skirt, she was often seen as the mountain itself. Mount Iztaccihuatl, White Woman, on the east side of the Great Basin was considered by the Mexica to be one of her trans-figurations. And, in the myth of Mixcoatl, the goddess Iztac (White) Chalchiuhtlicue bears the Four Hundred Mimixcoa in the interior of a mountain filled with deep waters.[12]

About Huixtocihuatl, the salt goddess, little is known beyond her close connection with water.

There is another goddess of importance who must also be classed as a provider. This is Mayahuel, the personification of the maguey, which produced *octli*, the intoxicating drink of the Aztecs. Because of her lavishness this goddess was thought of as many-breasted; as the earth goddess Mecitli, Maguey Grandmother, she suckled the Five Mimixcoa, thus duplicating the maternal duties of Iztac Chal-chiuhtlicue. It should be noted that the leaves of the maguey were likened to breasts, while the darker spines at the ends were nipples.[13] So central was this manifestation of the goddess that, as we have already noted, the Mexica adopted her as their mentor and took her name as their tribal patronymic.

A story was told about Mayahuel.[14] As a carefully guarded and desirable virgin she had been secluded in the recesses of the sky by her monstrous duenna, Tzitzimitl. In his transfiguration as the Wind Quetzalcoatl went on a mission to steal the young girl so that, through knowing her secret, men might overcome their sadness and, drinking *octli*, learn to dance and sing. With great cunning Quetzal-coatl seized her and fled down to earth, pursued by Tzitzimitl and her demonic cohorts. In desperation Quetzalcoatl changed himself and his female charge into trees. He was successful in his deception, but the demons succeeded in tearing the virgin tree apart. Later, from the ruined branches which Quetzalcoatl planted, came the maguey, one of the most important items in Aztec culture. *Octli*, today called pulque, is still drunk by the Mexican people.

Mayahuel is remarkable among the goddesses because of her en-tourage. Around her was stationed a cluster of at least fifteen well-known *octli* gods commonly referred to as the Four Hundred Rab-bits, all of them patrons of drunkenness.[15] Though they were all male gods and many of them were focal gods, we may consider them here as emanations of Mayahuel.

It is not surprising that so many Mesoamerican states should honor the Bacchic presence or that the abundance of bibulous gods should

have invited the Aztec mythmakers to organize them into a college—
even as the many mountain gods were brought together as the Tlaloque. Several of the Four Hundred Rabbits were simultaneously
members of their own college and of the Tlaloque as well; in other
words they were mountain spirits singled out as Corybantic masters
of revelry, attendants upon the great Earth Mother. But the Four
Hundred Rabbits generally differed from the Tlaloque, who were
gods resident in nature, by being strictly attached to the human community and to the strong drink that was so important a part of its
festivities. Some of this group of gods were demonic, such as the
Drowner, or the Strangler; all of them could topple their drunk devotees over precipices or otherwise destroy them.

The Four Hundred Rabbits were united by their patronage of the
orgiastic, and they could be worshiped together at one shrine. The
only one whose home temple has survived is Tepoztecatl, the patron
deity of the people of Tepoztlan on the southern face of the great
volcanic escarpment in Morelos. This temple—with its mysterious
and awesome approach and its view into the cleft in the mountain,
out of which protrudes a gigantic phallic rock—emphasizes the Dionysian nature of the god. A more interesting member of the Four
Hundred Rabbits, however, is Patecatl, said to have been Mayahuel's
particular consort. He was equated with the root which was ground
up and allowed to steep in the fermenting brew to lend it strength
and savor. Patecatl stands out from all the other *octli* gods as the only
one connected through his regalia with Quetzalcoatl. Myth derives
him from the Gulf coastlands, where *octli* was said to have been first
processed. In Mexico he was generally considered to be the greatest
of the Four Hundred Rabbits.

The Goddess as Springtime and Sexual Desire

Xochiquetzal is an Aztec goddess of love, differing from the Greek
Aphrodite only in her close and more obvious identification with
the basic Earth Mother. Her name means Precious Flower or, more
literally, Flower Feather.

Few peoples have equaled the Aztecs and their modern descendants in the love of flowers, and none have surpassed them in creating vast floral displays featuring strong color contrasts. On her feast
day Precious Flower, in the person of her *ixiptla*, was shown seated
in a veritable arbor of flowers.[16] In the courtyard of the temple boys

clad as butterflies and birds sat in the branches of a flowering tree, pretending to suck nectar, while below priests garbed as the various gods shot at them with dummy blowguns–the scene thus re-created being an evocation of the lost land of Tamoanchan and the pleasant life lived there under the world tree. All the while people were dancing about the goddess, wearing garlands on their heads and heavy collars of flowers around their necks.

Precious Flower was conceived as a supremely beautiful maiden, and she could be referred to as the Virgin. Her cult was probably derived from the Toltecs and planted among the Aztecs through the mediation of the city of Culhuacan. Among the Aztec tribe known to us as the Tlalhuica, who had their capital in Cuernavaca, her festival was annually used to introduce the young to drink and to sex in a ceremonial and therefore a controlled way.[17] We cannot doubt that she corresponds in every way to our conception of primavera.

Her mythology is of interest.[18] She inhabited the paradise of Tamoanchan either as a matron or as a virgin, depending on whether fruitfulness or the promise of joy were of the moment. As matron she is said to have been variously the spouse of Piltzinteuctli, Lord of Princes, of Tlaloc, of the maize god, or of the Lord of Sustenance. As the first she is equated with the earth as the bride of the sky; as the second she is identified with fertility in general; as the last two she is the mother of corn. In any case, when conceived as a matron she is the Great Mother, the source of nourishment for men and beasts.

Her other role is that of the goddess of love and springtime, and as such she provides us with her most colorful myths. In those tales of other and golden years she always inhabits Tamoanchan, where she is surrounded by nymphs and jesters and courtly entertainers. She and her women spin and weave textiles of supernal beauty.

Flowers, conceived as the symbols of her virginity, were her particular gifts to mankind. A crude myth explicates this.[19] Quetzalcoatl once masturbated. His semen fell upon a great rock, out of which there flew a bat. At this time the gods had been planning the appearance of flowers which should spring out of the surface of the earth, so they commissioned the bat to bring back a piece of Precious Flower's vulva. While the goddess was sleeping the bat performed his charge and returned with a part of her virginity. From the washings of this came flowers that were beautiful but had no odor. The bat then flew with a piece of her vulva down into the underworld, where again it was washed. From this came all wondrously fragrant flowers.

It would appear that this tale is a floral variation of the Proserpine/ Hades myth.

Precious Flower's connection with flowers and fruit is even more curiously set forth in the myth of the world tree. There once grew in Tamoanchan a tree covered with blooms and all manner of fruit.[20] This tree could perform wonders. Whoever picked even one of its flowers would always be lucky in love. Succumbing to temptation, Precious Flower ate some of the fruit—whereupon the tree shuddered, broke in two, and bled as if wounded, thus revealing to all the other gods her defiance of the taboo. What is of interest in this story is that the sacred tree, which blossomed in Tamoanchan, was rooted far below in the earth—thus it had to rise through several layers of heaven in order to thrust its crown into the topmost one. In this fashion Precious Flower is brought into connection with the world tree, which bore flowers on its boughs in each heaven through which it rose. The eating of the fruit is probably what the myth refers to when it states that Precious Flower was the first female to sin, a reference to the fact that her patronage extended to illicit as well as to socially acceptable love.

As the deity who lost paradise through her willfulness she is transfigured as Ixnextli, Ashes in Eyes, a metaphor for a woman blinded by weeping.[21] Precious Flower thus pays for her sin by being unable to look full into the open skies of daytime, that region which she once so splendidly inhabited. So today men can never look directly at the sun.

We move to a matter of some importance: the question whether Precious Flower in myth repeats the seasonal story of the Hellenic Proserpine, as has been claimed by some scholars. We know that, when she was Tlaloc's wife, the god Tezcatlipoca seduced her. It was he who stole her and finally installed her amidst the delights of Tamoanchan. This, on first viewing, does not appear to be the carrying off of a virgin into the underworld, whence she returns with the recurrent spring. But a variant shows the above telling to have been garbled. In this variant Tezcatlipoca explicitly carries the goddess off from Tamoanchan down into the depths of the underworld. He does this by assuming many disguises, all of them repulsive and evil. No reason, however, is given for the rape itself, and nothing is said about the goddess' stay in the underworld. Inasmuch as Tezcatlipoca was a notorious seducer and Precious Flower was the personification of love, one's immediate reaction is to see nothing particularly seasonal in the myth.

There is a certain archaic text, however, which seems to corroborate the theory that Precious Flower can indeed act as a Proserpine figure.[22] In this myth we find Xolotl (here identified as one of Tezcatlipoca's disguises) further explicated as the Cave Dweller, a reference to the god's nocturnal or underworld connections. In the tale Xolotl is seen carrying Precious Flower off on his back. What is of interest is that the text mentions the maize god in a closely related but difficult context, as if Precious Flower were indeed interpreted there as the buried seed corn stored in the earth until the return of seed-planting time. In short I believe that the goddess can in fact be seen as a type of Proserpine, though her connection with delight and sexual passion is always most prominent and her identity as the Mother is never lost.

A passage in her cult seems to validate this interpretation.[23] Two girls were annually selected from an old Aztec lineage to ceremonially preside over the sowing of maize in the four world directions. They were finally sacrificed with their legs crossed to show that they were virgins—their bodies being dumped into a subterranean cellar which was then sealed, seemingly to represent their departure into the underworld or, in other words, the storage of the seed corn underground. Precious Flower's connection with the underworld therefore cannot be doubted.

There also existed a few narratives about Tezcatlipoca and the amours of Precious Flower. One of them is a typical folktale. The handsome youth Yappan, in order to preserve his chastity, commonly hid under a rock. He was guarded in this sequestration by Tezcatlipoca as the Enemy. Three goddesses, Star Skirt, Jade Skirt, and Precious Flower, each made attempts on the young man's virtue. The first two failed, and it was the third goddess who finally seduced him. In anger the Enemy struck off the young man's head, whereat he became a scorpion—whose custom, as we all know, is to live under rocks. This Aztec Judgment of Paris is told with more forthrightness than the Hellenic myth.

From the Gulf area there came into the Aztec pantheon another form of the goddess of love, far more important to individual Aztecs than was Precious Flower. Her name was Tlazolteotl, which literally means filth goddess but should be understood as sex goddess. There can be no doubt of her Huaxtec origin, for her male devotees in Tenochtitlan were called Huaxtecs and in her various ceremonies they went about naked, as was the Huaxtec custom. Down on the coast she was the Great Mother presiding over the moon and could be referred to as Totzin, Our Beginnings, or Tzinteotl, the goddess of the rump, a name which carried the explicit statement not only of dirt and sex but also of primacy, for *tzintli* (literally "anus") can also mean base, beginning, or first principle.[24] Her cult on the Gulf coast was certainly widespread from very early times; she was worshiped not only by the Huaxtecs but also by the Totonacs and very possibly the Maya. Fertility and sex were perhaps the most obvious emphases in her cult. She was generally depicted with bared breasts and was frequently connected in the codices with the coral snake, which symbolized lust. Phallic rites were performed in her religion. Prostitutes and nymphomaniacs could be known as "women of the sex goddess."[25]

Because of her patronage of adultery and sexual passion, Tlazolteotl became a mighty force in the personal lives of some members of Aztec society. She had the power not only to stir up passion but also to pardon sexual transgressions; for this latter purpose her cult provided the services of a special priest, who heard confessions and cleansed the person involved of the impurity caused by whatever sexual offense had been committed. In a transfiguration related to this confessional act the goddess was known as Tlaelcuani, Filth Eater.

The sex goddess was thus a transfiguration of either Toci or Xochiquetzal, depending on the emphasis one wished to give. The differ-

Ehecatl as a hurricane threatening Tlazolteotl (Laud)

ence between Tlazolteotl and Xochiquetzal, however, is quite clear. The latter's cult stressed gaiety and beauty, while the former accented the guilt attached to illicit sex and its disruptive and sometimes fatal consequences.

We are already aware of the Aztec propensity to quadruplicate divine beings. This had also taken place with the sex goddess at some stage of her religion, certainly long before her adoption by the Aztecs, though perhaps it may be closer to the truth to see the process as reversed and to say that from the many finally came the one. These four females appear simply as the sex goddesses or specifically as the Ixcuiname, a word of doubtful meaning.[26] We are told that the Ixcuiname in early times came up from the Gulf coast to Tula, bringing a cult act wherein Huaxtec warriors who had been captured were shot to death with arrows. The Ixcuiname were looked upon as the wives of those who were about to be sacrificed in that fashion. These four sisters were individually named the Oldest, the Younger, the Middle One, and the Youngest, names which easily became appended to women who were prone to sexual excesses. When merged into one, the four sisters became Ixcuina, patroness of prostitutes and loose women and also wife of the Lord of the Dead. Adulterous women and prostitutes who wished to cleanse themselves of the stain attached to their improprieties could go at midnight to crossroads (the particular haunt of the Ixcuiname), disrobe, and depart naked—thus leaving their sins behind them.

Nevertheless these four stand for more than mere sexual desire, for their mythology states that they were present as a sisterhood in the darkness which preceded the first rising of the fifth sun and that they, along with the Mimixcoa, represent the stars.[27] We might assume that the four sisters once represented the moon in its phases.

The Role of the Sidereal Goddess

The Aztec myth of the five ages of the world describes four abortive attempts to create a viable world order. Each of the four early suns finally weakened and fell from its station in the heavens, the disaster in each case being accompanied by a cosmic holocaust.

The myth of the creation of gods and men by Citlalinicue, Star Skirt, is essentially disassociated from this orthodox scheme of creation and exists as an explanation by itself alone. It refers only to the present age and therefore competes with and even contradicts the myth of the creation of the sun and the moon in Teotihuacan, which was the standard version of the origin of the fifth or present age. The two tales indeed differ greatly. While the Teotihuacan myth presents creation as the result of the collegial action of the gods, the version we are considering here revolves solely around one deity, Star Skirt, a ghostly and astral form of the Mother.

She and her consort Citlallatonac are the female and male forms of that principle from which all the stars were produced, and occasionally they are equated with Two Lord and Two Lady, who inhabit the highest heaven. The male principle, however, has nothing at all to do in the myth, being there simply to satisfy the logical need for a fertilizing presence—it is the goddess who originates all things.

We have previously seen that Star Skirt was understood as a personification of the Milky Way, though she could also be identified as a specific star or constellation. But she was also conceived as an abstract power and, as far as I know, she had no cult. I suspect that she was quite ancient and came from the Chichimec level of Aztec religion. Certainly she was devoid of any connections with agriculture or atmospheric effects. Her mythology is uncontaminated and straightforward.

Her power was limited to astral creation, and in Chalco it was taught that she had made the sun, the moon, and all the stars.[28] This, however, was merely one concrete way of stating her primacy. The full myth—one of the most interesting to come to us from the Aztec sources—was widely shared in Mesoamerica.[29] We have briefly considered it before, but we need to analyze it in greater depth. It ran as follows.

Originally the night sky was inhabited only by the wise old goddess and her consort. Then the goddess gave birth to the *tecpatl*, the flint knife, which fell down out of the sky and landed in Chicomoztoc. From it came the 1,600 heroes under their leader Xolotl. This host we can think of either as the full muster of the gods or as their visible counterparts, the stars in the night sky. But this divine host needed beings to serve them, so they petitioned their mother to provide them with such. She replied that they should ask the Lord of the Dead for the bones of the men destroyed in the previous age, and they should then revive them. The gods thereupon sent Xolotl on that mission which, after certain misadventures, he successfully completed. After the gods performed autosacrifice, man came into existence.

The myth therefore records the full gamut of creation, of both gods and men, and is plainly a priestly document. It treats authority as being ultimately celestial, and it dispenses with the concept of the Mother as tellurian and conditioned by the earthly element. What is created is a first principle–the knife–symbolizing the central role of sacrifice in the ongoing of the cosmos. The divine beings are all celestially connected but only with reference to the night sky and darkness, as is shown by the fact that Xolotl was their leader. The creation of men had little meaning for those who made this myth; the act signified merely the stabilizing of the society of the divine beings, in other words, the final organization of the cosmos. Star Skirt is the arbiter of that cosmos.

The Role of the Tellurian Goddess Coatlicue

There is a group of goddesses bound together by their common hideousness and thirst for blood. One might call them the Medusa group. Each is sufficiently distinguished from her sisters, but all participate in the Mixcoatl or Huitzilopochtli mythologies associated with the north. The semicivilized cultures of the northern steppe delineated these goddesses with truly monumental power. The later Aztecs were to refine upon these attributes but they did not substantially change them. These goddesses are Coatlicue, Serpent Skirt; Cihuacoatl, Snake Woman; and Itzpapalotl, Obsidian Knife Butterfly.

Serpent Skirt's myth takes one back to the beginning of the Aztec world and places her in the magic mountain of Culhuacan far to the north, a place of origin.[30] The goddess is described as black, dirty, disheveled, and of shocking ugliness, as befits a creature of the underground. She appears prominently in the myth of the gigantomachy, which we have already considered, though in that myth Coatepec substitutes for the mountain of Culhuacan. We have already told this story as it centers around the heroic Huitzilopochtli. Here we need only note in more detail the role of the goddess. In the myth she is the mountain itself, the Earth Mother who conceives all the celestial beings out of her cavernous womb: Huitzilopochtli, the sun; Coyolxauhqui, the moon; and the Huitznahua, the host of stars. We conclude that in the myth Serpent Skirt is a locus rather than a power, being the dark world from which all beings spring and within whose body the terrible conflict takes place.

Serpent Skirt is even more closely associated with Tula (and thus with Toltec religious concepts) in a garbled folktale that casts her as a diabolical queen of vast bulk who in some way is brought into connection with the fateful confrontation there between Tezcatlipoca and Quetzalcoatl.[31] The fact that her consort is once said to be the young fertility god Tlamatzincatl (a form of Tezcatlipoca) strengthens this connection.[32]

She had as an important transfiguration Chimalma, Shield Hand, the goddess of the Huitznahua.[33] Shield Hand was a naked cave goddess who was present at Aztlan as the Aztecs sallied from that point of origin, and she was also a war goddess.[34] We have alluded to her myth before. Moving south Mixcoatl came to the land of the Huitznahua, symbolized by the naked goddess and her nymphs. He shot four arrows at her (the usual Chichimec symbol for taking possession of a new land) but without success. She retired into the Red Caves but was forced out after Mixcoatl had raped her nymphs. Again she successfully avoided the arrows, whereupon the two copulated to produce the Morning Star.

In the late historic period Coatlicue was one of those goddesses identified by the Mexica with Iztaccihuatl, the snowy mountain which formed the eastern rampart of the Great Basin. There she was visibly the earth. In the city of Tenochtitlan she was worshiped as Our Mother of Coatlan (a city ward) and associated with spring flowers.[35]

There remains one more piece of evidence: that statue of Coatlicue which is so justly famous, one of the most splendid pieces in the National Museum in Mexico City. Without a doubt it originally stood in the temple built for Coatlicue by Moteuczoma II. This massive block of stone, looming and powerful, is truly repulsive; it is surely one of the most direct and most unequivocal pieces in art history—nothing can mitigate its horror. The skirt of writhing snakes and the necklace of hands and hearts from which dangles the skull pendant—these form the goddess' accouterments and strike the viewer first. But even more uncompromising is her form, the bared and flaccid breasts, the clutched hands that are really serpent heads, and the great taloned feet whose thumping tread we can almost hear. Above it all, she is decapitated: what appears to be her leering and idiotic face is a fantasy formed by two symmetrical spurts of blood that have been transfigured as they gush forth into the protruding heads of rattlesnakes.

On the underside of the monstrous feet, the Aztec sculptor has carved the year-date 1 Rabbit, the year of the creation of the earth and therefore the goddess' calendric name. This was also a most ominous year, for the goddess was accustomed to celebrate her birth-day with famines, destroying men by the thousands.

Cihuacoatl, a Statist Conception of the Goddess

Snake Woman has some claim to be considered the most feared and effective of all the goddesses. In the sequence in the Codex Borboni-cus depicting the rituals of the eighteen months, she is shown at the beginning and the end of the year, and she appears in the other months with a frequency almost matching that of all the other god-desses combined. We can understand this when we note that, before she was taken over by the Mexica, she had been the great goddess of Culhuacan, a city with clear Toltec antecedents.[36] Snake Woman was prestigious enough to dignify any Aztec city, no matter how im-perial its ambitions.

The powerful city of Xochimilco, in the southern part of the Basin, was also devoted to her cult. Two years after Mexico-Tenochtitlan had gained its independence in 1428, it attacked Xochimilco and sub-dued it. The Mexican war leader Itzcoatl thereupon ordered that a shrine be erected for Cihuacoatl in Tenochtitlan. Her statue was prob-ably taken from Xochimilco and permanently installed in the new shrine. It was in the following year that the Mexican ruler also vastly enlarged the temple of Huitzilopochtli. The two edifices and their cults were intimately related. In myth Snake Woman was the war god's mother; the two shrines were therefore properly adjoining and shared the same priesthood. This close connection between the cults gives us the key we need to interpret her role in the Aztec pantheon. She was there to trigger those wars over which her son, as the god of war, presided. He was the doer and the victory bringer, she the inciter.

This goddess is presented to us as a being almost as horrifying as her alter ego, Coatlicue. The lower part of her face is shown as a crude bare jawbone, and the grisly mouth is stretched wide to indi-cate her hunger for victims. Her hair is long and stringy, and two knives form a kind of diadem on her forehead. She is clothed and painted in chalky white. She was referred to as a horror and a de-vourer: she brought nothing but misery and toil and death.

In popular lore she was to become a night-walking bogey, braying and screaming as if demented: "And as she appeared before men, she was covered with chalk, like a court lady. She wore ear-plugs, obsidian ear-plugs. She appeared in white, garbed in white, standing white, pure white.'³⁷

On her back she carried the knife of sacrifice, swaddled as if it were her child. Among her many guiles was the ability to change herself into a serpent or into a lovely young woman who could entice young men who, after intercourse with her, withered away and died.³⁸

Her cult shows interesting features. For example, her shrine was not placed on the usual pyramid pedestal with stairs ascending to the top. It was rather low, as befitted a representation of the earth, and because of the blackness of its interior it was known as the Tlillan, the Place of Blackness.³⁹ The entrance was blocked not by the customary curtain but by a heavy portal or plug, as a cave might be.

Because Cihuacoatl represented the earth and its labyrinthine mysteries, her statue was of exceptional holiness and, unlike other idols, was never brought out where light or the gaze of men might demean it. Even her priests did not dare touch her statue; otherwise they held a privileged status before all other priestly colleges, for they were also Huitzilopochtli's servants.

In the sooty interior of the Tlillan, grouped around the goddess, were the images of the deities of the lands or great mountains in and surrounding Anahuac. They formed a kind of chthonic court of stone idols, the Tecuacuiltin, a name which was also carried by their priests. Whenever circumstances demanded that some particular land or mountain be honored, its idol would be taken out and carried back to its original shrine, perhaps several hundred miles away. After an appropriate service, it would be returned to the artificial cave presided over by Snake Woman, where it would resume its former subservience. Such centralization of the scattered cults of the sacred mountains of Mesoamerica gave the Mexica a greater measure of control over the land. The earth was indeed one in the Tlillan.

That the Tlillan was intended to represent the interior of the earth is made fully evident by the fact that a replica of the fire god's sacred hearth stood immediately in front of its portal. Victims destined for the goddess in her annual feast were cast into this ever burning fire, as was her own beautifully clothed image made of torch pine. Xiuhteuctli's fire was known to be located in the center of the earth.

In what we have said so far the goddess differs hardly at all from Serpent Skirt. In one respect, however, they diverge greatly. Serpent Skirt was represented as intimately related to the Aztecs in all the events of their legendary past. Cihuacoatl, on the contrary, was preempted by the Mexica to preside over and personify the collective hunger of the gods for human victims. Her cult in fact was an active part of the state apparatus in Tenochtitlan. Every eight days her priests went to the palace and formally complained that Cihuacoatl was starving. The ruler would release one or more of the prisoners taken in some recent foray, who would then be sacrificed.[40] Also, at unscheduled times, the priests would insert one of their sacrificial knives in a bundle intended to represent a papoose and surreptitiously send it off to the marketplace. There it would be left in the custody of some unsuspecting female vendor, who was asked to tend it until it was called for. It was, of course, not called for. Eventually, before the day was over, the bundle would be unwrapped and the grisly secret would come out: the goddess had been among the people and had left her thirsty offspring as a sign that the lords were not feeding her properly. Thus was pressure constantly exerted upon the state to seek further wars so that Snake Woman need not lack sustenance. In fact, more victims were offered to her than to any other goddess.

Cihuacoatl's high priest, who bore her name as the name of his office, was the most distinguished religious functionary in the Mexican state. Not only did he preside over her cult and wear her eagle clothes, as his official garb was called, but he was an official of the state second only to the *tlatoani*, with important duties as vicar, president, and supreme judge. His authority was plenary. Only a *tlatoani* could seat a *cihuacoatl*. Moteuczoma II, for instance, always issued his orders through this minister. Outside of Tenochtitlan only very important cities like Tezcoco or Culhuacan could support the office. The incumbents of the state's two superior offices thus functioned as *ixiptla* of the two deities whose importance to the Mexican state was paramount: Huitzilopochtli and Snake Woman.

So important, in fact, had the cult of this goddess become to the state, explicating the motivation behind its aggressive policies, that her original patronage of birth and verdure, natural to any Magna Mater, was either muted or assigned to her avatar Quilaztli.

Quilaztli is that common transfiguration of Snake Woman who was said to preside over birth.[41] Her name appears to mean Instrument That Generates Plants and as such she would be a form of Mother Earth.[42] She is, however, not to be confused with the goddess Seven Snake, who presided over corn and vegetables and was derived from a farming level of society; rather, Quilaztli went far back in the Chichimec past and presided over all edible things that grew wild in the steppe country. In fact her mythology is centered in the steppe and is closely connected with the Mixcoatl cycle. One source has it that the bones of Mixcoatl were interred in her temple. She was known as a witch and a shape shifter, but she was also a warrior of a renown equal to that of Mixcoatl himself. In Xochimilco, where we naturally expect to find her, she was worshiped as the two-headed deer of Mixcoatl.[43]

Itzpapalotl, the Chichimec Mother

Obsidian Knife Butterfly represents an Aztec form of the goddess whom we must definitely derive from a Chichimec past. A difficult and fascinating myth is concerned with this goddess.[44]

Two of the Mimixcoa–Xiuhnel, True Turquoise, and Mimich, Arrow Fish–were hunting in the steppe country when a pair of two-headed deer descended from the skies. The two hunters gave chase but finally had to desist and make camp. But the deer had changed into two women, one of whom enticed True Turquoise to drink some blood. He did so, immediately copulated with her, and then–turning on her–devoured her. The other woman, who was Obsidian Knife Butterfly, tried to entice Arrow Fish to eat something, but instead he made a fire with his fire drill and threw himself into it, being quickly followed by Obsidian Knife Butterfly. In this world of fire she pursued Arrow Fish without success. A giant barrel cactus had fallen down from the skies; in her haste she collided with it and was held. One of the demons dwelling in the sky saw this and thought to cast a dart at her, but she escaped and wandered off–combing her hair, painting her face, and lamenting the loss of Arrow Fish. This information came to the ears of the fire gods, who made off with her and cast her into a fire in the presence of Arrow Fish. In the great heat she burst into five stone fragments, each colored differently. The white sliver of stone, acutely sharp, was retrieved by Mixcoatl, who wrapped it up in a bundle and thenceforth carried it on his back as a god in all his conquests. This was the knife of sacrifice.

Nothing in this tale gives us the right to understand Obsidian Knife Butterfly as an earth goddess, yet we know she was so identified. We are in the presence here of the tendency of the Aztecs to see the Great Mother primarily as darkness and underearth, whence comes the secondary conceptualization of her as the night skies (which come flooding up from under the earth with every sunset); by extension, this inserts maternal creativity as well as demonism into the heavens.

A winged Itzpapalotl wearing a skirt fringed with knives (Borbonicus)

With this in mind as a principle of interpretation, we can attempt the following explanation of the myth.

The myth begins with Obsidian Knife Butterfly as a chimeralike creature with celestial associations and ends with her being identified as the sacred knife. The two-headed deer is known to be associated with Mixcoatl, and the knife is said to be his oracular fetish on the warpath. This certifies that the goddess is fully contained within Mixcoatl's mythology and that we need not look elsewhere to unravel her meaning.

The central part of the myth tells of the fire sacrifice in which the Mimixcoa are involved. Appended to this is the etiological tale giving the explanation of the fact that the white knife is the goddess herself.

We know that Obsidian Knife Butterfly was a kind of female counterpart of Mixcoatl—in addition to being the spirit of the earth—for she was closely associated with war and hunting. Her *nahualli*, in fact, was the deer. In the myth she is seen as an adversary of the Mimixcoa and kills one of them. This is consistent with the role of the Mother mentioned previously, who was outraged at the riotous activities of her titanic children. In fact in one version of the myth she kills all four hundred of the Mimixcoa. Arrow Fish in our myth is thus merely a representative of the group at large. Her killing of him, however, leads directly to her own death at the hands of the surviving member of the Mimixcoa, generally Mixcoatl himself. Sacrifice by fire is a common way to destroy the *ixiptla* of the Earth Mother, as we have seen, and this must be what is intended here.

Thus what we have is again the dreadful Earth Mother destroying her children, the ancestral spirits conceived as stars or titans, but being herself overpowered by her heroic son Mixcoatl. Because fire is at home in the earth's center, death by burning is appropriate to her case. Her wrath and her hunger, however, cannot be quenched by death, so she survives cultically as the sacrificial knife.

The tale has a brutal and primitive cast. Obsidian Knife Butterfly is a wholly Chichimec goddess and her only office was war. She is depicted with a defleshed face and talons for hands and feet; she is winged and is often shown swooping down from the heavens like a ghastly *tzitzimitl*. We are not surprised to see her in this form, but it comes as something of a shock to see her also cast in mythology as a double of Precious Flower, the lovely goddess who lost paradise.[45] Depictions of Obsidian Knife Butterfly in the codices show her regularly associated with the broken and bleeding tree of paradise. This is an outstanding example of the interpenetrability of the forms of the Great Mother.[46]

The Five

The Aztecs particularly liked to sum up the demonic propensities of the Magna Mater in colleges of five. For this purpose she was simply Cihuateotl, the Goddess, while the five were Cihuateteo, the Goddesses, or Cihuapipiltin, the Princesses.

These five were recruited from mortal women who had died in childbirth and who, by that manner of death, were divinized and ascended into the heavens. Though five was the model and the canonical number–one for each of the five directions–the Goddesses were also thought of as a swarm. Petitions were made to them at the numerous shrines dedicated to them along paths or at crossroads.[47] They were also honored in the city of Tenochtitlan in certain annual festivals. They were greatly feared because it was they who brought many of men's more hideous and painful ills: palsy, harelip, club-foot, strokes, spasms, etc. They were particularly vengeful toward children.

As mortal women who had died in childbirth, these divine beings were likened to warriors who had captured an enemy; in warrior fashion, the Goddess had struggled with the child and had succeeded in holding it fast until both died in the duel. This young woman after death became *mocihuaquetzqui*, "one [here the warrior] who has stood up like a woman," and required special obsequies. She was thought to live in the west and, because of her warlike skills, to form part of the entourage of the sun as he descended into the earth.

Both early and late levels of Mesoamerican religion have been combined in the conceptualization of these Goddesses. In their patronage of physical misfortune, they hark back to very early times. Here their female nature is simply a reflection of the fact that, insofar as women occasionally produced deformed children, they were cast into the very effigy of those spirits who had caused the calamities. At a much later time, when extraordinary conflict occasions and state armies had been called into being, death in childbirth was then–and only then–conceived as an analogue to the duel of one warrior with another. In that conflict the victor was the heroic young woman who maintained her grasp on the antagonist. Only this class of women could take their places beside males whose heroic deaths had translated them into the heavens.

The Goddess Summarized

It is difficult to know whether the Aztecs saw motherhood or death as the primary characteristic of the goddess. My impression is that in cult they leaned slightly toward the latter: there are several figurations built on the model of Serpent Skirt (Yaocihuatl, Cihuacoatl, Itzpapalotl, etc.), but there is only one Precious Flower. Both the codices and archaeology will bear out this proclivity. The repulsive and the lethal are displayed in many depictions of the goddess. It was as if, through her, the Aztecs spoke in the deepest tones of their pessimism. Sacrificial death, symbolized by the knife, was her issue—not the issue of some god of war, as we might logically have expected.

As if to nail this down with finality, when the Aztecs told the story of a once perfect happiness, it was the goddess, not the male god and deceiver Tezcatlipoca, who lost paradise. And in her role as Tlazolteotl she became outright carnality with all its attendant disasters. No male god, not even Tezcatlipoca, stood for the sensual with such an emphasis.

This bias in the Aztecs' understanding of the Great Mother was not at variance, however, with their understanding of her as a totality, an integrity. Certainly no peoples have so richly elaborated the culture of death as have the Aztecs and, if death held such an influence over their creative efforts, who else but the Mother should patronize that point of view? The male gods represent fairly well demarcated aspects of reality: war, the state, intoxicating drink, hunting, the Morning Star, and the like. The Mother may also appear as partial and narrow, as a goddess of salt or the tender maize or the moon, but with this difference: she never loses her first identity as a summation of man's experience. No corresponding concept of the father on the male side of the Aztec pantheon existed, not even Xiuhteuctli. Thus, while the various male gods remained disparate, the goddess, however many her transfigurations, was always one.

The above may appear incongruous, for it looks as if the female element had been allotted mythic centrality or, at the very least, primacy in a very masculine society. I can speak to this problem only by assuming that the Mother and her many forms derived from an early level of Mesoamerican religion, whereas the rise of such male gods as Huitzilopochtli or Ce Acatl had to wait on the formation of more complex social and political bonds and thus tended to occur later. The masculine orientation of later and more warlike societies may then have gone on to elaborate the deathly qualities of the goddess and generally to embellish her ghastliness, perhaps because of an unconscious hostility toward her—perhaps also because of a failing allegiance. No one really knows.

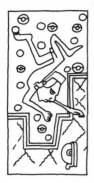

8. Man

The Creation of Man

Because the religion of the Aztecs was an accumulation from the past as much as it was a creation of their own warlike times, it was rich in contradictions. In one very sensitive area, however–that concerning the origin of man–it was remarkably consistent. Almost all sources agreed that men had been produced by the gods only after several attempts; once produced, they were allotted only an imputed merit and a menial rank.

The myths in which these concepts are enshrined are of varying quality, and only one provides informative detail. Most are set against the vast backdrop of the making and the unmaking of the successive aeons. In their attempts to create men the gods repeatedly failed in each of the aeons–except the present one. In the first four attempts men did not have maize to eat and they therefore had to subsist mainly on wild and almost inedible plants and nuts; death from hunger was thus their lot. So they were not complete men. At the extinction of each sun these defective men were turned into fish, monkeys, dogs, or birds, or they were said to have been killed by jaguars or giants. These early men were experimental and really belonged to a lower order of life.

An interesting tale was told about the earlier race of men who were changed into dogs.[1]

The god Tezcatlipoca, who had become aware that the world was going to be destroyed in a cataclysmic deluge, gave a certain man and woman the charge to chop down a giant fir tree and make a coffer or box in which to hide. Within this temporary refuge they were each to have one ear of maize, and they could eat only one kernel a day until the time came for their release. Their names were Tata and Nene, which are to be translated into something like our nursery names Daddy and Dolly.² A variant has it that they were instructed to escape the waters of the flood by climbing into the top of the tree. When the waters finally receded, the two mortals emerged and prepared for their new life—or clambered down from the tree, if the second version is preferred. Fish abounded in the slowly receding waters, so they gathered some of them to eat. It was apparently at this instant that fire was carelessly dropped from heaven. The two people put this sacred fire to the wood of the tree and were enabled to cook their fish.

The myth implies that theirs was an illicit action; fire belonged to the gods alone. Looking down from the heavens the two high gods, Star Skirt and her consort, cried out in anger at the sacrilege and sent Tezcatlipoca down to punish the two mortals for their presumption. Tezcatlipoca did this by decapitating them and attaching the heads to their posteriors, so that they ceased to be human and became dogs.

While this is in part an etiological tale to account for a dog's familiarity and intelligence, it also insists on the fact that men are the result of trials and errors performed by the divine beings. Perfection is no part of their being. Nor do the nursery names given to the two mortals in the myth lend them dignity. The point of the tale, however, turns on man's conquest of fire and on the price he paid for it. This myth was certainly not intended to be a standard account of the origin of men; the only point it really emphasizes is the treachery of Tezcatlipoca.

The myth of man's origins that was considered standard by all the Aztecs is found in the Quetzalcoatl cycle. And here we should recall that, while Tezcatlipoca was acknowledged everywhere to be man's master, the making of man was more often attributed to Quetzalcoatl, a distinction of great pathos when we consider the characters of the two gods. We have already alluded to this myth where Quetzalcoatl and his double enter the underworld to retrieve the bones of men, later revived by sprinkling them with blood taken from the gods. Men owe their being to the sacrificial action of the gods. Their lives are a clear debt.

It should be noted that in Aztec mythology Quetzalcoatl does not stand as a savior over or against man, for the life man receives is menial and harsh at best and, once Quetzalcoatl has performed his intrepid journey into the underworld and has formed the several aspects of human culture, he no longer interests himself greatly in man. In fact he tends to disappear, leaving the field to Tezcatlipoca–the one, therefore, who presents man with an immediate and indeed a suffocating sense of the divine.

One implication of the myth is that, had Quetzalcoatl not stumbled on his way up from the dead and shattered the bones, men would have been re-created on a larger and nobler scale. Thus was a happier fate for man lost. In brief, even with a miraculous and god-attended origin, man as depicted in the myth is not perfect and is presented as having at best a broken nature.

It is difficult for us to comprehend that a god who was himself only one step away from being compassionate should not have been understood as taking that step and offering mankind more than initiation into life. There was a tendency in Aztec thought to see Quetzalcoatl as the creator of all things, and certainly, of all the gods, he most resembled a compassionate being. The fact that this suggestion was not worked out in their mythology can be laid to the amazing power which cult held over the lives of the Aztecs. A heavy incidence of cult will almost always impede the growth of its opposite, which is a recognition of the dilemma of morality in human life and a statement of that tension in some appropriate myth.

The Quality of Man's Life

After having washed and bundled up the newborn baby, the midwife, speaking as the embodiment of the community, addressed him as follows, "You have come to reach the earth, the place of torment, the place of pain, where it is hot, where it is cold, where the wind blows. It is a place of one's affliction, of one's weariness, a place of thirst, a place of hunger, a place where one freezes, a place of weeping."[3] And, as if in ultimate repudiation of any possible contradictory view, she would add, "It is not true that it is a good place; it is a place of weeping, a place of sorrow, a place where one suffers."

Some years later the father, referring to the earth as man's abode, still insisted to his adolescent son: "Certainly it is a dangerous place, a revolting place, and a painful and afflicting place."[4]

Nuptial bathing and consummation of a marriage (Nuttall)

This view of the quality of man's years on earth lay at the bottom of almost all Aztec speculations. It was an apprehension of life which all peoples of the earth have shared, whether mutely or vocally, but which the Aztecs seem to have turned into an exclusive and all-embracing principle. They stated life's harshness in terms which, in their extremes, have not been equaled in any other culture with which I am familiar. It was in fact a distinct tour de force that the Aztecs could ever have elaborated such a rigid dogma and that they could have maintained it unchanged right down to the coming of the Spaniards. With artistic iteration and rhetorical embellishments they developed it far beyond what their culture or any culture demanded.

The extremism of the Aztec view of life had some curious consequences, two of which may be noted. On the one hand, the Aztec set out in a quite utilitarian way to connect his prior beliefs with the cosmos–thus he elaborated and carried to its logical conclusion the sacrificial cult (to be considered later). On the other hand he cried out in poetic passion, protesting at the inhumanity of such a view, wishing that he had never been born.

The brevity and impermanence of life for the Aztec contrasted sharply with its color and excitement.[5] He addressed the god Ipalnemohuani, Who Sustained One (here an avatar of Tezcatlipoca) accusingly:

> Only as painted figures in your book
> Have we lived here on earth.
>
> .   .   .   .
>
> We were no more than pictures
> Rubbed out, erased.[6]

But, beyond its evanescence, life presented such a situation of caprice, of sudden reversals, that the whim of Tezcatlipoca seemed indeed to be life's true constitution. Inequalities in rank and the sudden overthrow of wealth could only be explained in that fashion, and it was partially in response to this constant uncertainty that individual households possessed small images of Tezcatlipoca to placate the god. The Aztecs were vividly aware of the astounding and unforeseen turns of fate. A particularly haunting vision comes down to us of the crumbling and deserted house of an Aztec magnate:

> There all would answer the calls of nature–would urinate and
> defecate–and rubbish would be cast. Salts would lie evaporated;

and the earth would lie smoldering. Then it would be said, so that all might marvel: "Once, in this place, here, was the house of one who came commanding reverence. Here came a house-holder enjoying fame; there was always honor, and the house was swept clean. At least the rubbish was cast aside somewhere. And none might urinate on his walls or he would chide them. But now in his very place only the walls remain standing."[7]

This philosophical appreciation of the ubiquity of chance in life went hand in hand with the combativeness of Aztec society. Severe tensions were common, and violence and vindictiveness slept uneasily below the surface of everyday intercourse. The peacemaker was correspondingly valued. Ambition, drunkenness, and lust consumed many persons, and the noble was motivated almost solely by the possibility of achieving personal renown, holding distinguished offices, wearing brilliant garb, and founding a family. Once such good things had been acquired, an extreme touchiness characterized him; he feared public shame beyond anything and insisted on being honored according to his deserts. Even the diligent man who was in the process of acquiring wealth was constantly apprehensive lest he be brought down by gossip, intrigue, or illness. In honor of the god Drum Coyote, the Aztecs in fact celebrated a unique festival of discord,[8] thereby recognizing its ineradicable presence—conflict was the very stuff of their social lives.

Man and His Fate

For the Aztecs fate was not, as it is to us, an impersonal cosmic force, relentless and uninterested. It was a predisposition which acted upon individuals; it did not act upon mankind at large. An individual's *tonalli* predetermined his destiny.

Fate operated on a man, however, in less than a total way. Fundamental to his essence was, of course, his *tonalli*—the day he had been born—but this had to be interpreted by a priest skilled in the matter, one whose learning had come down to him from Quetzalcoatl.[9] Thus every child came into the world with a ready-made destiny which was then culturally interpreted to him. But one's fortune, no matter how clearly stated in the *tonalamatl*, might still be altered.[10] It could weaken or slip away, especially in the case of a very young child, and adjustments could then be attempted to recover or restore it. Or man could—by his own willful negligence—forsake his *tonalli* even if it were 1 Alligator, the most fortunate of all the 260 *tonalli*. Thus, by denying his fortune a man might effectively change it for the worse.

Tezcatlipoca, as the perfect autarch, stood alone outside of fate. "All our ways and works are not so much ours as in the hands of Him who moves us," the newly seated ruler was wont to say, thereby expressing the customary modified fatalism.[11] Tezcatlipoca could be petitioned–even by a man whose *tonalli* was hopeless–to the end that some mitigation of the misery attached to his particular fate might be granted or that, at least, the sins which were so inexorably committed because of it might be pardoned.[12] A person born on one of the five unspeakable *nemontemi* days, who later sickened and then survived contrary to all prophecy, was known to have been reprieved by Tezcatlipoca; he continued, however, to be thought of as only artificially alive.[13] In short, the Aztecs did not adopt a wholly rigorous determinism. Greater perhaps than the *tonalpohualli* were the power and the whim of Tezcatlipoca.

The net result of divine superiority over fate was thus not necessarily advantageous for Aztec man. In fact the larger meaning for the Aztec of Tezcatlipoca's sovereignty was an increase in tension and pessimism, for the only god who could nullify the *tonalli*, even if only partially, was himself a barbarian, without an inner law and wholly without an exterior policy.

The Nahualli

The concept of the *nahualli* is peripheral to the Aztec's concept of his fate. In addition to his soul a man could possess, as part of the power of his personality, a special affinity for an animal or some other aspect of nature. When considered in this fashion a man was a *nahualli*, a transcorporate being. The etymology of the Nahuatl word is uncertain, but it meant two rather different things to the Aztecs.[14]

In the first instance it meant a person who could magically transform himself into some other being or object, generally for nefarious purposes. He usually transformed himself into a beast such as a jaguar, a coyote, a dog, a snake, an eagle, or an owl. This power was not restricted to men: even a god could be a *nahualli*. Quetzalcoatl was naturally one; he could change himself, as we have seen in the myth of the creation of man, into the monster Xolotl. Huitzilopochtli was a *nahualli*, as was Tezcatlipoca, who could appear in the form of a coyote. Mictlanteuctli certainly appears as the owl. The exterior soul or alter ego was a very old Mesoamerican concept.

The belief goes back to the most ancient levels of shamanism, but in the Aztec period it was the professional sorcerer (the shaman's successor) who particularly cultivated this aspect of his calling. Even before he was born, a sorcerer could be detected by signs accompanying his mother's pregnancy, and his powers were correspondingly uncanny. But rulers and other unusual individuals endowed with charisma might also possess the power. In any case, it was always a highly charged and dangerous potential.

There was a related concept which was democratic in the sense that it was not restricted to the rare individual but applied to every individual in the society. This could take concrete form in the baptism of the newborn child in the family fire four days after birth; in this ceremony, the child might be dedicated to an animal appropriate to his birthdate.[15] Supposedly this closed a magic circle whereby that child when adult would suffer all the dangers and vicissitudes suffered by his individual animal or by his particular species of animals (our sources are often unclear as to which is implied). The animal thus became the personification of that man's fate, and in some readings of the concept the animal's death caused – indeed *was* – the simultaneous death of the person. An invisible and indestructible bond thus might unite a man with his animal partner – the two could exist simultaneously or the *nahualli* could become his animal counterpart while temporarily giving up his own being. If wounded in his animal form he carried the same wound in his human body. Such a belief still persists in Mexico today.[16] This concept of animal metempsychosis is directly tied into the *tonalpohualli* and thus takes on overtones of fate. It can be easily seen that the identification of an animal's fate and an individual man's fate turns out to have the same results as did the operations of a person's *tonalli*. It was an added way, though more primitive, for a man to understand what happened to him.

In the first meaning of the word *nahualli*, which implies the sorcerer or some other exceptional man, fate is in no sense involved. All that is implied is that the person is a shape shifter and has a preferred animal or object into which he can change. This is the hoary and shamanic level of the concept, and it harks back to such barbaric groups as believed that only the shaman possessed the power to change shape and become an animal and that he did so in quest of certain supernatural ends. In a later and urban context and under the influence of priests every man could be assigned to an animal depicted in the *tonalamatl* – an animal which was then a visible form of the fate already given him by his birthdate.

Thus the two systems are basically different, though inevitably some of the exoticism of the shamanic system sloughed off in the later period on the individual with his animal *tonalli*. The average individual's *tonalli* was never anything other than his fate. He probably could not use his animal association to consciously achieve a purpose, as the sorcerer could use his. Nor did the possession of such a *tonalli* enhance the power of a man's soul – it only enriched the lore connected with himself.

Hallucinogens and the Quality of Vision

In our discussion of the various gods we purposely omitted a group which the Aztecs differentiated from the others. These were the hallucinatory gods. We have seen that the many gods of drink were also placed in a separate category, but with the difference that they presided over the festive joys of the community. The hallucinatory gods, on the contrary, entered into an individual man, each with a strange and often dreadful message destined for him alone. They were vegetable gods whose ministrations enabled a man to multiply a thousandfold the power of his inner sight. There were a number of these hallucinogens, the most common being *yetl*, tobacco; *teonanacatl*, the narcotic mushroom; *ololiuhqui*, morning-glory seeds; and *peyotl*, peyote. The first was said to be the very body of the goddess Snake Woman, the name of the second means "flesh of the gods," the third was depicted in Teotihuacan sprouting from the body of a goddess of fecundity, and the last could appear as a small black being.[17] Thus were these substances deified.

These peculiar gods gave a person a supernaturally keen and chromatic vision. They led him into a part of his life which was otherwise completely unknown to him. When, in the company of his peers at specific rituals, a person drank the god, crushed in water or mixed with *octli*, he was able to command visions of his own destiny. At such surrealistic banquets a man might see anything:

> One sees that he is going to die; he begins to weep. Another
> sees that he will die in battle, another that he will be eaten by
> animals. Another sees himself captured in war. Another sees
> himself rich and happy. . . . Another sees that he will be an
> adulterer and that he will have his head crushed with stones.

. . . Another sees that he will fall from his housetop and die from the fall.[18]

Such foreknowledge could turn into visions so stupendous and horrifying that all control was lost by the *paini*, "the drinker of the concoction":

He who eats many of them sees many things which make him afraid, or make him laugh. He flees, hangs himself, hurls himself from a cliff, cries out, takes fright.[19]

The anxiety so central in the psyche of the Aztec (and correspondingly in all his religious concepts) seemed to him to be validated by visions received in gatherings where he indulged in *ololiuhqui* or *teonanacatl*. There is a scene in one of the codices which depicts just such a collation among the gods.[20] Quetzalcoatl, bearing on his back the divine mushroom, introduces the substance to a synod of eight gods, one of whom is shown weeping. While they eat the mushroom, Quetzalcoatl makes music with a bone rasp on a skull.

The use of these hallucinogens was of remarkable antiquity in Mesoamerica. The goddess of fecundity in one of the Teotihuacan murals can well be that deity called Green Snake by the Aztecs centuries later, a reference to the twining tendrils of the morning-glory vine and, indeed, the Aztecs' specific name for this plant.[21] She is shown with this plant sprouting from her body and dripping dew and seeds. Narcotic seeds were known and were articles of traffic among the Chichimecs in the northern steppe going back to early levels of shamanic practices. The *ololiuhqui* was commonly used in Morelos and neighboring regions, while *peyotl* was a cactus native to the arid parts of the north, the stamping grounds of the most primitive Chichimecs. *Teonanacatl* was widely known and used everywhere. Hallucinogens had early been adjuncts of shamanism, and it was from these lowly religious levels that the four vegetable gods above mentioned were ultimately produced.

Whereas in later priestly times a person's future was divined through the *tonalamatl*, in the antecedent shamanic religion it was through the hallucinogens or through trance that a person's fate was divined. This early auspicial system, however, was not abandoned when urbanization and the priestly class later appeared. It continued to exist side by side with the intricate and sophisticated *tonalpohualli*.[22] Both systems under the Aztecs had special roles to play in the life of the individual.

This leads us to the observation that the vividness and the nightmare quality so characteristic of Aztec religion were the result of millennia that had gone before, ages wherein early American man experienced the supernatural world in part through the hallucinogens. To go through the Codex Borgia slowly is to receive an indelible impression of supernatural clarity, high color, and eerie convulsions of meaning. There the Aztec imagination is shown stretched to its uttermost limit. Aztec cult as a whole appears under a similar compulsion. One of its qualities was a trancelike immediacy and sometimes a supernal horror. Surely this quality of Aztec religion is rooted in the hallucinatory cult. Indeed, Aztec cult as a whole can be thought of, not erroneously, as a staged hallucination.

The Cleansing of Sin

The Aztec midwife, as she was washing the newborn child, addressed him as follows:

> Perhaps he comes laden with evil; who knows the manner in which he comes laden with the evil burdens of his mother, his father? With what blotch, what filth, what evil of the mother, of the father, does the baby come laden?[23]

The Aztec was acutely aware of man's compromised condition, that at best he was a weak reed whipped about in a torrent of the divine. He knew how he was determined. But he could also feel guilt, which springs not from an ineluctable fate but from a sense of voluntary participation in evil. The sense of sin went deep in Aztec life. Guilt and penance were salient facts in their culture and were constantly portrayed in art. Sin is generally depicted as excrement, and the sinner suffering the consequences of his sin is likened to one who has to consume his own excrement or is shown afflicted with dysentery. Suicide, if we may judge from the abundance of depictions in the codices of persons strangling themselves, was common. Impelled by a deep religious sensitivity, the Aztecs had to create elaborate forms of cleansing and of penance, both public and private. Two deities—Tezcatlipoca and Tlazolteotl—are centrally connected with these rituals, though each for a different reason.

Tezcatlipoca was the very fountain of man's waywardness:

> He is arbitrary, he is capricious, he mocks. He wills in the
> manner he desires. He is placing us in the palm of his hand;
> he is making us round. We roll; we become as pellets. He is cast-

ing us from side to side. We make him laugh; he is making a mockery of us.[24]

As for Tlazolteotl, it was said: "evil and perverseness, debauched living—these Tlazolteotl offered one, cast upon one, inspired in one."[25]

Given the inevitability, indeed the seeming automatism, of sin, we might wonder why the Aztec worried at all about his own accountability. Yet he did. Theories and beliefs can be totally encompassing, but men's reactions are never total. Men act as if many worlds were true at once, and their spiritual lives are capable of entertaining impossibilities which their intellectual selves discard. So the Aztec sought to be forgiven for that sin which Tezcatlipoca or the goddess of sex had encouraged or even forced him to commit. The former deity, with the insouciance of the tyrant, might not even allow the individual in question knowledge of what his sin had been, but with the latter it was always evident that his sin had emerged from upheavals of sexual passion.

Confession was generally performed in the presence of a priest skilled in augural matters.[26] No contrition was expected of the sinner, only a dutiful counting or listing of all his infractions. A penance would be imposed, after which the deity would absorb the "filth" of the sins or, in another understanding of the economy of guilt, would wash the person clean. Even a cursory reading of the pertinent texts in Spanish and Nahuatl reveals the terrible anguish suffered by individuals as a result of sin. This was a quite different matter from the public ceremonies where an entire populace went to nearby rivers to wash and thus cleanse themselves communally of sins.[27]

As a surrogate for the whole community the priesthood was constantly engaged in penitential exercises. In the cult of Tlaloc, for instance, that god's priests bathed in the freezing lake waters at midnight, imitating the cries and the thrashings of water birds and expending themselves to the point of exhaustion. One of the most common practices was the journey alone by night up onto the chilly heights of the mountains.[28] This appears to have been done by the priests, not so much to purify themselves as to accrue merit and placate the gods. The priest chosen went out naked and painted black, carrying only his censer, his votive fir boughs, and a conch trumpet. Stumbling along through the night, he chewed powdered tobacco and blew blasts on his trumpet in response to the midnight trumpets sounded in the city far below him. Having pierced his ears and thighs with thorns and offered the blood to the god, he retraced his steps, shivering and dizzy from nicotine. Bogeys and fiends followed him and every sound and shape in the forest were surreal. The merit gained from these exercises was great.

Death, the Soul, and the Underworld

The idea of the soul was not especially promoted by the Aztecs, and this is probably consonant with their pessimism. A whole person could be referred to as *in ixtli in yollotl*, literally "face and heart" or, more figuratively, "outward appearance and inner being."[29] But what we commonly refer to as the soul was called *toyolia*, based on the verb *yoli*, "to live, to become alive." This may be the entity to which Clavigero refers when he states that the Aztecs, unlike the Otomí, believed the soul to be immortal. We know little about this soul or its relationship to the *tonalli* (also translated at times as "soul"), the destiny with which one is born.[30] There is no attempt in any of our sources to elucidate the *toyolia*. Presumably it was simply the life force. Among the Nicarao, a Nahua people, the *toyolia* was the breath of a person which left through his mouth when he died.

It was this soul, however, which—in the case of ancient and distinguished leaders, warriors, or great nobles—was called forth from the dead body to become part of the sun's entourage; sometimes it was said that such a person had become a god, even though his funerary cult would lapse at the expiration of the prescribed four years.[31] On the death of a great noble, his soul was thought of as taking flight like a bird or a butterfly. At such a time he was addressed by those attending:

> Awaken, it has reddened, dawn has set in. Already the flame-colored cock has sung, the flame-colored swallow; already the flame-colored butterfly flies.[32]

Specifically, the concept of the annihilation of the soul was rejected by the great man's mourners:

> When we die, it is not that we die, for still we live, we are resurrected. We still live, we awaken. Do you likewise.[33]

Statements like these were attributed by the Aztecs to their predecessors, the ancient people who had constructed the great pyramids of Teotihuacan, but they certainly formed part of their own beliefs as well. In fact exalted Aztec personages and rulers who had died were masked and attired as specific gods and might, by this mimicry, be supposed to fend off annihilation after death–though in many cases the divine regalia in which the corpse was clothed represented only that god who had sent the dead man the special illness which had destroyed him.[34] An exception to the rule of personal extinction, however, could be made in the case of certain national heroes, such as Topiltzin, Nezahualcoyotl, Nezahualpilli, and Moquiuix, leaders whose people had fallen on evil days after their demise.[35] These great men were supposed to have gone not to Mictlan but to Mount Xicco, whence at an appointed time they would return and restore the political glories of their nations.

When not contemplating the soul of a heroic warrior or a charismatic person, however, the Aztecs quickly fell back upon a view of the soul as inconsequential and meager. In a certain address to Tezcatlipoca they made this clear: "Our souls in your eyes are but as wisps of smoke or cloud rising out of the earth." This was the persistent undercurrent in their thinking.

Death was an overmastering horror constantly in their thoughts. So prominent was it in their every speculation that at the moment of birth a child was ceremoniously reminded of his impending death. At royal installations the new ruler and his four great princes all wore mantles with the skull and crossbones depicted on them as reminders of reality. Even kings, in one bleak view, went to Mictlan.

Mictlan, as might be expected, had many descriptions: the Land of the Unfleshed, the Place of Our Common Sleep, Our Universal Home, Where There Is No Way Out, Land of the Dumb, the Extensive Land, and others.[36] "It is where in the water or in the mud it is very deep: an abyss. It is dark, dark as night, a fearful place, a terrifying place. It is agitating–a frightful thing, a place of ill fortune, without end."[37]

The Aztecs elaborated the conception of Mictlan as a descending series of levels or possibly as concentric countries in the underearth, each distinguished by a unique torment or obstacle. While this is quite similar to the folklore of other peoples of the world at this stage of development, nevertheless among the Aztecs it is outlined in surprising detail.

If we count the surface of the earth as one, there were eight inferior regions through which the frail soul had to progress. A hellmouth or cave in the mountain allowed entry into this underworld, whose first marvel was the abyssal waters stored in the earth. The soul was carried across this by a red dog which had been sacrificed at his obsequies and which was to act as his guide on his journey.[38] Then, as two great cliffs were clashing together with the roar of a hundred earthquakes, the soul had to seize the appropriate moment and rush between them before they crushed him. Other threats followed, deserts and high mountains and dragons. The worst of these torments was encountered in that land across which moved a wind of hurricane force, the freezing air being filled with obsidian knives spinning and twisting every which way. The arduous journey through these purlieus of Mictlan lasted four years. When the soul had met each one of these dangers, he finally arrived in the presence of the Lord of the Dead. Here he was stripped of clothing and of all else and was destroyed.

There were of course other versions of Mictlan. The concept of the underground waters was sometimes expanded to replace the nine regions with nine rivers, or with three houses of fire, or occasionally each region was assigned the souls of people who had died of certain designated diseases.[39] The geography of hell has always been fascinating.

We note that the extinction of the soul on its arrival in the lowest region of Mictlan is at variance with the concept of a continuing cloud of undifferentiated ancestral spirits located in the far north. This latter, communal concept answered tribal needs; Mictlan, on the contrary, was applicable only to the individual. Neither concept, of course, had anything in common with the sophisticated speculation indulged in by the knightly class that life was, in any case, an unreal dream.

The Aztecs evinced no extraordinary fear of the dead, and funerary rites were less elaborate than one might expect in such a richly endowed society. Because the dead man's journey through Mictlan took four years, the site of his burial was visited and offerings were made during that period. But at the end of those four years all rites were decisively ended. To those living he was no more.

Ancestor worship did not arise among the Aztecs for the reason that they did not believe in the soul's ability to outlast the magical number of four years. After four years the soul entered a democracy of the extinct. However much their memories may have been honored, even the most resplendent rulers were not divinized after death. Death was a four-year journey in the underworld, that and nothing more. A man's grave site, even if in the patio of the house of the deceased or in the field which had belonged to him, was unmarked. Deceased Aztec rulers inhabited no monumental tombs. The charisma they had once had did not become a taboo at their place of burial.

With such a disparaging view of themselves, it is worth mentioning that the Aztecs created no compensatory cults of redemption. The reason must lie in the fact that they did not conceive man's essence to be the *imago dei* and therefore redeemable: rather, he was of such servile making and destiny that he was not worth saving.

Funeral Rites

In Aztec culture we are not surprised to find variety and contradiction. Uniformity is not to be expected from a civilization that admits that it is a patchwork made from bits and pieces out of the past. Nevertheless the variety in the Aztec funeral cult is exceptional. One might think that this speaks of a society that is either in transition or is still not a well-articulated whole. I think, rather, that the diversity accurately reflects the several stages in the history of the Aztec tribes, none of which were ever given up.

The Aztecs attributed the institution of funeral rites to Quetzalcoatl, whose wisdom had determined so many other cultural forms.[40] Nevertheless what they meant by that attribution was simply that his own self-immolation had provided the model of cremation for all rulers thereafter. Burial had been the practice of the Chichimecs, and it was not, for instance, until the Culhua introduced into Tezcoco the Toltec rites of cremation that the old Chichimec custom there gave way.

The burning of the dead was a usage of those Toltec warriors who were organized in lodges and believed that a dead hero entered the entourage of the sun. Only through the medium of fire could he be released from his body to aspire upward. Cremation among the Aztecs was therefore elitist, and its adoption marked their full conversion to the Toltec ideal. Commoners and young men who had not become successful warriors were buried, an earnest of the fact that their destiny was not in the heavens but in the underworld.

The last rites for a ruler, while sometimes of barbaric splendor, were not greatly different from those found elsewhere in the world at a similar level of culture. The obsequies of Axayacatl, for instance, began with the royal corpse dressed in the mantles and regalia of four gods: Huitzilopochtli, Tlaloc, Yohuallahuan (Xipe), and Quetzalcoatl.[41] Rulers from all the great Aztec cities came to greet the dead *tlatoani* for the last time as he sat in state, still ruling, for the required four days. They presented him with gifts to take into the other world. Among the most precious of these gifts were beautifully dressed slaves. Such slaves plus the dead ruler's favorites, his jesters, concubines, and other servitors were sacrificed over a *teponaztli* drum (instead of the usual stone of sacrifice), and their hearts were immolated along with their master. There might be as many as two hundred destroyed in such a suttee. There then followed a mourning period of eighty days during which additional human sacrifices were made to strengthen the dead man on his journey.

The ruler's survival after death was fortuitous at best. We have noted that among the Aztecs there did not exist an ancestor cult and the dead man had no marked grave site. During the appointed four years following his death, a box containing the dead man's relics with an image of him on top served as a focus of attention and was that which was finally buried.

There can be no doubt that the Aztec funerary ritual for rulers evinces an ideological confusion. The farewells addressed to the corpse were intended to dispatch him to Ximouayan and the other melancholy places of the underworld; in this respect his ending was no different from that of a commoner. Yet his court favorites and his personal paraphernalia were sent with him, ideally to serve him in some royal court in the world beyond. But again he was cremated, which assumes that his soul mounted into the heavens to join the sun as a single warrior. We must not expect logic from the Aztecs in religious matters; nevertheless the funeral cult for the dead Aztec ruler has indiscriminately gathered totally opposing ideas regarding the destiny of the deceased, namely the commoner's death, the death of the warrior, and the nondeath of the magnate. Aztec society was too young to have a single understanding of how cult should explicate belief in these matters.

The rites practiced for the dead warrior, on the contrary, are all of a piece, being undoubtedly derived from the Toltecs.[42] After a battle an army that was able to rescue the bodies of its fallen cremated them on the field but commonly brought each warrior's bereaved family one of his darts. For all warriors lost, whether killed or captured, wooden or reed images were made and equipped with the dead warrior's shield and weapons. These images were ceremoniously lamented and entertained by the widows with keening and dances. The images were then placed in the *tlacochcalli*, which was both the temple of Tezcatlipoca and an armory; there they were feasted for the last time, after which they were burned. The ashes were taken down to a certain hill in the area where the Mexica had lived when they were under the Culhua. No doubt in those far-off days they had used the summit of that hill as the burial ground for the ashes of their dead heroes and had continued the custom even after they had settled in Mexico.

In this short description of Aztec funeral rites, we have found no hint of ancestor worship. There is evident, of course, the need felt by all peoples to properly acknowledge the new state in which the deceased has found himself and to aid him in accommodating to it, but after that the Aztec dead merge into obscure and constantly attenuating legions. Even great leaders like Nezahualcoyotl, Tezozomoc, Xolotl, or Moteuczoma I were not thought to exist as spirits or presences to whom appeal could be made. Having no place for their mortal remains, they could exist only as figures in history or legend. In sum, they were memories only, not powers. I believe the reason for this must be sought in Aztec cult. So imperious, so overmastering were the demands of the gods for hearts and blood that the cult which developed to answer those demands ended by absorbing all the spiritual energies of the Aztecs. To have made much of their dead, to have ascribed godhead to them, or to have seen their charisma as demiurgic would certainly have been congenial to their thinking, but it would have been impossible to reproduce in cult, for it would have been inconsistent with the full service they owed to the gods.

The Aztec Individual

We have used the word "pessimism" to characterize Aztec man's attitude toward life. Like all highly colored words from one language applied to another culture, it does not fit well—and the expert knows it. Without backing off from anything of substance we have said in this chapter, we still wish to rectify any impression that Aztec life was one of unmitigated gloom and that the people moved about in it like zombies.

The Aztec was an active and vigorous person, certainly of no mean intellectual capacity. Yet his speculative life was restricted and the molds into which his thought could be poured were few. Such a stimulating tension as existed in the Hebrew world between the priest and the prophet did not exist in Anahuac. The Book of Job, which stated man's dependence upon the Divine as necessary and good and his hostility to it as his only present fate, would have been unthinkable in Anahuac. No model was set before the Aztec individual of another powerful, possible, and valid way of thought.

He continued to suffer, as all men do, but without an understanding of the good as an absolute commandment required by the Divine. Quetzalcoatl might here have served as an axial figure in Aztec religion, but his figure had been too quickly tarnished in legend, and his real role was projected into the future.

In fact the world the priest kept before Aztec eyes was so convincingly presented that it would have been something of a miracle had the solitary individual achieved a critique of it. The only relief that individual had was to compose songs of lament, over and over iterating that life after all was only a dream and of no real substance—but that was poetic license and did not really disturb the priesthood or the rulers. Indeed the great Nezahualcoyotl himself, of the imperial city of Tezcoco, seems to have been a ringleader in these feeble spiritual rebellions.

From this Aztec's point of view, how else could the cosmos be viewed except as an arena wherein two great and related principles seemed to operate side by side: the principle of human reversals and the principle of divine hunger, the first emanating from Tezcatlipoca, the second from Snake Woman. The cruel kinesis inserted into the cosmos by those two was the ultimate mode of being for the Aztec.

When he turned his eyes upward, this individual beheld the astral powers, glittering figures who came and went, rose and fell, and did battle with each other. Day and night were their clothes, and he watched their consecutions in awe and trepidation. But the cosmic commotion was far above his head. He did not understand it as having significance for him. The Lord of Sustenance and Quetzalcoatl might provide his nourishment and school him in wisdom, but they gave him no armor against anxiety or death. Fear and the defiance of fear were therefore exceedingly important parts of his life.

This is what I mean when I insist on the fact that pessimism was the hallmark of the Aztec individual. Under the system, he carried out his duties manfully, but the system in the final analysis deprecated his humanity. He was aware of this, but he had no alternative to an inherited style of thought. He therefore steeled himself and continued, in the process producing prodigies of action and creating one of mankind's unique cultures.

9. The Nuclear Cult: War, Sacrifice, and Cannibalism

The Nuclear Cult

> No slaves were taken in the wars of these natives, nor did they
> ransom any who were captured but kept them all for sacrifice,
> and such formed the majority of those sacrificed in the land.
> Few except those taken in war were sacrificed, for which rea-
> son wars were continuous.[1]

So wrote the Franciscan friar Motolinía in the sixteenth century,
looking back at the pagan past of the Aztecs. He perceived clearly
the close relationship between Aztec war and Aztec sacrifice. Together they formed a single cult of astounding, original, and horrifying
power, one that may be said to have been the business of every Aztec city. A third element should be added to complete the picture of
this nuclear cult: cannibalism. This trinity of war, sacrifice, and cannibalism made up a combined religious service with all its parts carefully articulated. War, as we shall see, was thought to have been created to be in itself an act of sacrifice. The sacrifice of those captured
in battle validated the heroism which had been displayed on the field,
while cannibalism passed vigor and heroism along so there would be
further war, which in turn would produce further sacrifice, and so on.

This chapter introduces the subject of cult, which up to now has
not been our interest. We cannot, however, avoid some consideration of the cult of sacrifice, for it contains the congelation of the previ-

ous matter of this book. It has been kept to the last and given separate treatment because of its centrality. Sacrifice may in fact be said to have been the central fact in Aztec life.

The Origins of War

The Aztecs were fascinated by the subject of war. It molded many, perhaps most, of their institutions. It pervaded the social forms of their daily living and influenced the iconography which surrounded them. It colored the education of their young. It defined manhood and, by consequence, virtue. This absorption of Aztec culture in an ambient of war is clearly pointed out in their mythology.

Put summarily, war was created by the gods and came down from above.[2] There are several versions of this divine act which we have briefly noted before. A song composed by the great ruler Axayacatl in the middle days of the empire expresses this fact poetically:

> The flower death [war] came down to earth. It came here;
> It had been created in Tlapallan.[3]

The most sophisticated version of the myth of the origin of war tells how, in the beginning, the four creator gods paused before creating the sun, for they knew that such a supreme act would be vain and foolish if they did not give thought to what the sun might require to eat once he was created. And, because blood and hearts alone could satisfy such a hero as the sun, they decided to create war, which would provide that fare in abundance. Still, it took them two full years precedent to the creation of the sun to call forth such a mighty system as war. Where the Aztecs assigned the creation of war to a single god, that god is either Mixcoatl or Tezcatlipoca. In the case of the former we know that the war between the Five Mimixcoa and the Four Hundred was the first of all wars. And when we shift from the Chichimec mythology to that of the late Toltecs we find Tezcatlipoca acting in Tula in the person of his avatar the Enemy. As long as Quetzalcoatl had been ruling in Tula, humans had not been sacrificed; by implication there had been no war, only a reign of peace. But Quetzalcoatl's humiliation and exile at the hands of Tezcatlipoca gave free rein to the latter, who as the Enemy stirred men to fury and destruction. By the year 13 Reed, as the great capital of Tula was disintegrating, war had become an all-consuming activity.[4]

The three versions of the origin of war presented above are not alike. The first one, wherein war predated the sun himself, is a mythic exercise which surely came out of the *calmecac*, for it has a strong bias toward rational understanding: it wishes to *explain* warfare, not merely to state its origin. It is in other words a contrived myth. The Chichimec myth was the possession of all the Aztec groups entering from the north and west, and it presents war as simply the condition to which they were all willy-nilly committed. The Toltec version treats war almost historically, assigning it to a known passage in the annals of Tula and presenting it as an inexplicable outburst of rage and fury incited by Tezcatlipoca. These attempts by the Aztecs to understand through myth the presence of war were necessarily piecemeal, but all the myths did agree on the divine authorship of war. It was incontestably a heavenly institution.

War gods in the societies of Central Mexico go back to Teotihuacan times, and we may ask whether any connection can be seen between such early militarism and the later Aztec warfare. The answer must be a tentative yes. In one instance the Aztecs did project their thoughts back to Teotihuacan in trying to explain warfare when they agreed to assign the origin of their two knightly orders to that city. They did this in a tale which was an obvious variant of the myth of the creation of the fifth sun.[5] This told how in that early time the eagle and the jaguar contended for the honor of being the sun. The eagle was the first to hurl himself into the pyre and thus became the sun. The jaguar followed and became the moon, the spots on his coat recalling the incompleteness of his immolation. No doubt this myth was the property of the eagle and jaguar orders and validated their exclusive standing in Aztec society.

All such mythological justifications for war and explanations of its origins help us understand the several historic levels involved in Aztec militarism: that of Teotihuacan, that of the Toltecs, and that of the Chichimecs. But, more important for our purposes, they point out the ineluctable quality of war for the Aztecs. While war was indeed an activity of men, it was still nothing men could choose to do or not to do. It was simply incumbent upon them.

Aztec Concepts of War

The usual term for war among the Aztecs was *yaoyotl*, which means roughly "the warrior's business." There was, however, another and more revealing term which could be written as a glyph and which

The goddess Chantico with the glyph for war issuing from the back of her headdress (Borbonicus)

had profound religious connotations. This was *teoatl tlachinolli*, which meant "divine liquid and burnt things" or, more simply, "blood and fire."[6] It was this glyph which was customarily shown protruding from the eagle's beak as he sat on the cactus where Tenochtitlan was to be founded. The interpretation of that emblem is that an eagle (the sun) was seen screaming out the word for war to the Mexica as they were about to enter upon their imperial history. Considered under such a rubric, war to the Aztec was nothing abstract but was the very battlefield itself, red with blood and billowing with smoke and sparks from the burning temples of the enemy and from the cremations that followed. It was a term designed to evoke spasms of heroism.

The gods took an unholy and savage delight in the melee of battle, in the dust, the shouting, the terrible exertions, and the sudden fallings down. War, said the Aztecs,

> comes from the influence of the sun. He awakens it on earth
> as something strong and valorous, all so that warriors and brave
> men, men powerful and turned toward war, will find great con-
> tent and pleasure in it, seeing that many will die there and much
> blood will be shed and the field will be strewn with corpses and
> bones and skulls of the vanquished, and the surface of the
> ground strewn with hair wrenched from heads and rotting.[7]

Because the battlefield was beloved by the gods, it should be equally appreciated by men. Therefore, a euphemistic effort was made to conceal the fears which assailed the warrior's heart when he first looked out on the field. A gilded membrane of words, in fact, was placed over all things connected with it. The battlefield was a place "where spreads out the passionate divine liquid," "where the jaguars roar," "where feathered warbonnets heave about like foam on the waves." Perhaps the most poetic of all these concepts is that of the battle as a rain of blossoms wherein precious warriors, beautiful in their finery and splendid in their contempt for death, fall here and there on the field as if a wind had shaken a flowering tree in the springtime. And the death that went with this was the *xochimiquiztli* or "flower death."[8]

The presiding genius of war was sometimes said to be Tonatiuh, the sun, but his connection with the actuality of the battlefield is really secondary. He was indeed viewed as the ideal warrior, but his implication in physical combat is never mentioned. To all intents and purposes he is merely the exaltation of the warrior concept. His place as the spirit of war is taken by that more vulturine deity, Tezcatlipoca.

As the Enemy this god decides who shall die on the battleground and who shall live. Victory is his alone to give. The Aztecs, in short, viewed the battlefield as so focal and war as so imperative that they were constrained to place over these as supreme and sole arbiter Tezcatlipoca, the greatest god in their pantheon.

The Warrior

The Aztec warrior was surely unique in history, not in the fact that he was devoted to war, for many cultures have produced such men, but in the source of his devotion. It is difficult for us to grasp his fervid commitment and to realize that it was part of a cosmic vision—that it was the pinnacle of a very real faith.

We can understand the *teuctli*, the elite Aztec knight, as a kind of priest.[9] Just as a priest is trained in a peculiar and trying discipline and accepts an orthodoxy, so the *teuctli* took vows, accepted certain austerities, and lived under the constant injunction of his god. This is not to say that he did not relish the adventure, the color, and the rewards of a life of war, for he would not have been human if he had not done so. But the orthodoxy which he accepted was monstrous and demanding to an extraordinary degree, and only the most ardent faith could possibly have sustained it. All Aztecs shared in the cosmic vision, but only the *teuctli* lived it out in sustained action, anticipating constantly that he would end his life as food of the gods. That this warrior was psychotic in some sense seems evident.

To give him the disciplines and the daily support such a life required, there had arisen the various military orders of which the eagles and the jaguars were the two most elite.[10] The presence of these two leading orders back in Teotihuacan times is not proven but is probable. Certainly the two orders were well defined by the Toltec period, and it is almost certain that they had been adopted by the Chicomoztoc Aztecs early in their history. The orders probably existed among the Huaxtecs, and we know that they existed among the Tarascans. They formed, therefore, a very old and widespread Mesoamerican institution. Indeed, by all counts, they formed a true international order.

We do not know exactly what the requirements were for induction into these lodges. The presumption is that a member should have captured at least one of the enemy or performed some similar deed of valor, that he be a *tequihua*, "one who has [a share in the] tribute," in other words a recognized champion. Once a man possessed membership in one of these orders, he could go up the grades of heroic accomplishment. A warrior at these top grades was designated as an Otomí or as *cuachic*, "a shaved head"; such men wore only a scalp lock on the forehead which would then be adorned with tassels, each representing a special act of heroism. These men were the patricians of Aztec warfare and were generally held in reserve until a situation arose on the battlefield which called for their special combination of ferocity and granite courage. Not many of these survived to become "old eagles," as those warriors of past renown too old to fight were called.

Pressures on the young to rise to such heights of prowess were constant and cruel. A typical tale of the pride and passion of the Aztec warrior comes from the city of Tezcoco.[11] The two generals commanding the forces of that city against Chalco, a dangerous enemy, happened to be brothers. Just preceding the hostilities, they held a battle breakfast with their compeers. To this meal came uninvited a third and younger brother, Axoquentzin, seeking an opportunity to distinguish himself on the battlefield. As the youth reached out to eat, one of his brothers sent him sprawling into the dust, contemptuously informing him that only veterans were worthy to eat with other seasoned warriors.

It was customary for women to publicly deride those young men who had not yet made a capture. Youths were heckled and insulted with allegations of cowardice until they were forced into frenzies of heroism or death.[12] Instances occurred, and were undoubtedly not uncommon, where the young warrior might actually retire from warfare to escape from having to wear the untrimmed hair which indicated his mediocrity in battle. He would then turn to farming, apprentice himself to a merchant, or take up some other less lurid calling, though of course he would always be on call for the mass levy. Aztec culture in brief was one of superheated masculinity, where fathers would occasionally kill sons suspected of being effeminate or unwarlike.[13]

> You belong out there; out there you have been consecrated.
> You have been sent into warfare. War is your desert, your task.
> You shall give drink, nourishment, food to the Sun and the
> Earth.[14]

So was the perfect Aztec warrior created by a combination of early indoctrination, assiduous training in the skills and weapons of war, constant public scrutiny, and the possibility of public scorn. Once the warrior had been molded, all Aztecs knew what to believe of him. He was a man who contemplated death on the battlefield with equanimity; in fact he actually desired it and held it to be sweet. He went even further. Though he naturally savored the prestige and adulation accorded to his kind, he was restless and unhappy because of his great longing for death.[15] He longed for *itzmiquiztli*, death by the knife.

The prime example of such a model warrior is found in the story of Tlahuicole, a Tlascalan of legendary accomplishments.[16] After a series of brilliant exploits he was captured by the Mexica; because of his great fame he was brought before Moteuczoma II who, in a quixotic decision contrary to all usage, spared his life. The captive was offered an important command leading Mexican warriors against the unconquered Tarascans to the west. In this war he further distinguished himself for audacity and steadfastness but, on returning, covered with honors, he demanded that he be sacrificed according to a warrior's legitimate expectation. Moteuczoma assured him that he could be a captain of the Mexica for the remainder of his life, but he refused, insisting loudly on his right to be sacrificed. Moteuczoma finally gave in and ordered him to the gladiatorial stone. Here, with only the customary wooden club edged with cotton, he again performed wonders but was finally cut down and sacrificed.

Whether all the details of this story are true is immaterial. In the main it probably is true. The fact, however, that it was told at all reveals the orientation of the Aztec warrior contemplating death on the sacrificial stone. In any case, Tlahuicole could not have returned to his own people, for no Aztec city would ever receive one of its own knights who had escaped from captivity or may have otherwise succeeded in returning. Such a person would have been publicly throttled as a craven.

This desperate spiritual orientation of the Aztec warrior is made fully explicit in a Mexican account of an event that took place on the eve of the Feast of the Flaying of Men. Here, before the captive was sent to the gladiatorial stone, his captor was covered with white down, the sign of the doomed:

> The pasting on of feathers was done to the captor because he
> had not yet died here in the war, but was as yet to die and would
> pay his debt in war or sacrifice. Hence his blood relations greet-
> ed him with tears and encouraged him.[17]

The Aztec City at War

In Ochpaniztli, the eleventh month, an accounting was made of all the warriors, which of the neophyte braves were to be inducted into the *calpulli* companies, what awards for service would be given, and so forth. Harvest home had just been celebrated, streets and temples had just been swept and cleaned, and the Aztec city was ready for war.

Reports from spies were now in and had been assessed, maps had been drawn, the generals had been commissioned, and arsenals and warehouses had been ordered to provide the necessary array. The night before leave-taking, if the affair promised to be especially dangerous, the warriors gathered in solemn assemblies and, to the shrilling of flutes, drank *octli* with an infusion of the narcotic mushroom so they might see their fate or receive assurances from the god. At dawn the army left the city, and the women began their penitential customs. Until their men returned they would pour ashes on their heads and never wash.

On the march the Aztec army was a terror to friend and foe alike. Neutral states and even vassal states through which they passed shuddered and treated the warriors as gods, for their wrath was unpredictable. If the expected battle did not begin with an ambush, both sides had time to prepare for the great drama, the warriors putting on their war paint, their feathers, bells, and bracelets. The two sides closed with each other to the thunder of conch trumpets, the shouts of the commanders, and ululating war cries from all sides. And then came the flights of darts, barbed and deadly.

It is not our purpose here to describe an Aztec battle. Our interest is rather in the way battle reflected their beliefs, and this can best be appreciated by considering certain elements in the victory proceedings and the return of the army.[18]

Right after the battle a count was taken of the number of captives and the number of the dead. This report was rushed back to the ruler by runners, and it named all the nobles killed and captured as well as those alive who deserved special awards. A panel was then convened on the field to hear cases in which there were disputes concerning the facts of a capture—whether a captive should be adjudged to a single warrior, or to two, or perhaps to many. The importance of these findings is at once evident, for a warrior's advancement depended on that court's decision.

On the return march the Aztec army escorted its captives in files, their hands tied behind them and their necks locked in wooden collars. These prisoners wailed and expounded loudly on their coming sacrifice. Communities on the return route obsequiously served the army, and those that failed in anything were wrecked, their men murdered, their women raped, and their fields burned. Even towns desperately trying to accommodate the victors were sometimes savagely treated and sacked. As Father Durán wrote of the victorious warriors, "The earth trembled beneath them."

Preceding the army as it returned came the file of captives, each with his fully armed captor walking beside him. Lining the triumphal way into the city stood the veterans or "old eagles" dressed in their former war finery. They welcomed the captives, shouting and offering them flowers and cigars. The captives were escorted to the place where the ruler welcomed them as brothers and god offerings. Then, if the captives were not Aztec but foreign, they announced through an interpreter that they came to die and they thanked the ruler for the opportunity soon to be in the sun's company. When the ruler himself had taken a prisoner this captive, laden with jewels and richly attired, was borne back from the battlefield in a litter. As the "son" of the ruler he was accorded every honor and a particularly gala reception, while poets created new songs for the occasion. The populace greeted this captive even before they greeted their own commander, welcoming him to "his" city. And, from all around, other rulers came to add to the rejoicing. When finally sacrificed, this captive was dressed as the sun god himself, and his skin, stuffed with cotton, was kept in the palace for many years.

The main body of the army, loudly lamenting its own losses, had followed the captives into the city. The captives were next divided into groups and sent to the different *calpulli* in the city, where they were kept for fattening and assignment to certain sacrifices. Though they were, by our standards, cruelly guarded, they were treated with great honor and courteously addressed as children of the sun. Meanwhile, a formal lamentation for the city's fallen was made to the sun. The "old eagles" followed this up by going to the houses of the dead and missing and offering the widows set speeches of condolence.

An army that returned in defeat was ceremoniously welcomed in something of the same manner. After the memorable Mexican disaster in Michoacan, Axayacatl returned with the pitiful remnants of his forces and reported his appalling losses to the vicegerent Tlacaelel, who replied as follows:

Take heart, for your vassals did not die comfortably at home like women but on the battlefield, fighting to gain glory for you and honor for their city. They have gained the same fame dying there as they used to gain in victory. I thank the creator that he has allowed me to see these many deaths of my brothers and nephews.[19]

The Flower War

Wars for conquest were common enough in the Aztec world and some wars, such as the war between Chalco and the Three Cities, were fought with determination over many years. They were no different from similar conflicts with which all national histories have been studded. The Aztecs, however, knew of another and quite different kind of war, the justification for which was wholly religious. This was the well-known *xochiyaoyotl*, "war of the flowers," a type of tournament almost unthinkable to us who conceive of war as an exercise in hostilities with the sole objective of obtaining victory over the enemy. The flower war was not part of the policy or the international relations of any Aztec state; it existed solely to produce sacrificial victims.

Nobody knows how old the flower war was in Mesoamerica. We know of it only from the Aztec world and even there only from the period which began just before the Tepaneca War. The two greatest Aztec cities, Tezcoco and Mexico, both claimed it as their invention, but it, or some predecessor type of tournament, certainly antedated their claims. Tezcoco insisted that it was the great Nezahualcoyotl, after he had regained his throne, who instituted the tournament with his former allies, the cities of Tlascala and Huexotzinco. He did this not only to be able to feed his gods but to keep his nobles keen and tensed for war. Mexico countered that it was their own terrible Tlacaelel who had promulgated the institution during the calamities of the mid-1400s, thus tightening up Mexico's war psychology at a time when widespread starvation threatened. That both these notable men had a hand in expanding the institution cannot be doubted, but that either of them created it is highly improbable.[20]

The cities involved in these flower wars were almost without exception Aztec and, therefore, Nahuatl-speaking. Within the Basin all the cities dominated by the Three City League were involved in it, while outside to the east and southeast was another group, the cities of Tlascala, Huexotzinco, Atlixco, and others. The two sets of Aztec cities formed what were in essence two loose amphictyonic bodies existing solely to fight flower wars with each other. Outside this chivalric bond the cities were normally competitive and could easily be enticed into more serious hostilities where subjection was the object.

The typical *xochiyaoyotl* was set in motion only after the gods had complained to their priests of hunger and thirst.[21] The ruler would then issue a call for knights to make ready to march. Attendance, however, was purely voluntary and would thus attract only those knights who felt the need of new glory or further distinction. All the battlefields were known, for each of the larger cities had set aside out on its borders a field which was used only for such agreed-upon confrontations. These fields were held to be especially sacred.

The ruler of the challenging party sent an embassy to the city or cities thought also to be needing captives for sacrifice, and the day and the site were stipulated. In some cases arrangements were automatic: parties of knights from two cities would regularly meet on the first day of every month to replenish the gods' larder for upcoming festivals. In times of drought or other hardships, when the energies of a city were radically diminished or when it might be hard-pressed by some enemy, the antagonist city would call off the flower wars or even come to the aid of the threatened city until the flower wars could be reinstituted.

Each party was accompanied by a priest bearing an image of Tezcatlipoca, who as Yaotl was the ultimate arbiter of the battlefield. In the preliminary parleys the two parties addressed each other courteously as "brother" or "nephew." The numbers in the typical flower war were probably not exceptional. Unlike an army of conquest, which included veteran commoners, these battle groups included only knights, each contingent broken into small companies which represented each of the cities involved.

As the contest opened only a limited number of knights were sent in, perhaps two hundred in all, while the rest watched and admired. But as the fury and carnage increased others were fed in until all were committed. In numbers the two sides might be quite unequal, and many of the great champions preferred some underrepresentation of their side as offering more scope for their valor. The captains of the various contingents formed roving bands, men not out to take prisoners but to redress imbalances. The most renowned warriors were constantly running from one side of the field to the other, seeking the enemy's strongest positions or hunting down famous warriors to duel with. No one could leave the field without authorization, no matter how many of one's company were dying or captured. The priests acted in some sense as umpires, but bringing a battle to an end where one side was hard-pressed was extremely difficult. After years of such periodical encounters, the bitterness between the two sides might become so intense that a flower war was no longer possible, only a war of conquest.

When he was in his old age, the tigerish Tlacaelel put the ultimate gloss on the flower war by explaining it as a military "fair" or "market."[22] Just as merchants went to distant marketplaces to purchase luxuries and necessities, so he argued, the god, accompanied by his army, went to the flower war to purchase the food and drink he coveted. The knights thus symbolized both the god's food and the currency used to purchase that food.

The death of Tlacahuepan, which occurred in a memorable flower war fought between Mexico and Huexotzinco, was held to be the

The capture (Nuttall)

ideal death.[23] In the last years of the reign of his father Axayacatl this great warrior, who was the heir presumptive, led some Mexican knights against the Huexotzinca. His impetuosity was so great that he repeatedly rushed headlong into the enemy, dealing mighty blows and utterly careless of consequences. At last, however, he was surrounded and cut off from the possibility of aid. He was last seen standing on a pile of Huexotzinca corpses, too exhausted to lift up his sword, surrounded on all sides by the enemy. In a formal speech he surrendered but demanded to be sacrificed where he stood. The enemy accordingly closed in and slew him, cutting his body into a thousand pieces, which they made off with as sacred relics to be consumed later.

He was remembered in many poems. One has been taken out of Nahuatl, from which I excerpt the following lines freely translated:

> Banners flutter and become entangled in the field;
> Like flowers the obsidian swords of death mingle together;
> The chalk and the white down [of sacrifice] cause men to tremble.
> Tlacahuepan was there.
> O! Tlacahuepan, you came for your heart's desire—
> Death by the obsidian edge of the sword.
> You move about, your golden skin laced with jewels [wounds].
> And so you were happy in that meadow.[24]

Sacrifice and Its Attendant Concepts

The pivotal role of sacrifice in Aztec culture is displayed in the myth, already alluded to, of the birth of the flint knife of sacrifice which established the cosmic order of the fifth sun. What interests us is the desire of the Aztec mythographers to place sacrifice at the beginning of all things and to give it the status of a divinely established mode of action. Sacrifice was the Aztec decalogue, the touchstone of all virtue, the alpha and omega of the Aztec understanding of the world of the spirit.

Human sacrifice as a cult pervaded all of Mesoamerica. Legend had it that human sacrifice began in Tula as the Toltec empire was disintegrating and that Tezcatlipoca was its grand originator.[25] In those last days the Enemy stirred up Tula to fight a neighboring city and there, for the first time, taught people how to sacrifice those they had captured in war. And it was the Culhua, a Toltec people, who are said to have brought the custom down into the Basin. Alternatively it is said to have been acquired by the Mexica as they passed through Tula. One of our sources states that the Mexica practiced it to an extent never dreamed of by the Toltecs.[26]

The fact that the Aztecs believed they had acquired the cult of human sacrifice from the Toltecs explains why to them it was supported by an infallible dogma. The gods had originated it and the Toltecs had passed it on.

The cult of sacrifice was supposed not only to provide the ultimate test of the manhood of those offered up but also to renew the god for whom the sacrifice was intended. These two concepts interpenetrated each other for, the greater the test and the more valorous the mortal response to it, by so much more was the god pleased and renewed. The sacrificial cult, therefore, though it was maintained by man and was part of his culture, was also a necessary function in the supernatural world. The Aztecs could not conceive of the gods and their welfare without supportive sacrifice. To this extent—and only to this extent—did man count in the cosmic order.

Sacrifice was an alimentary cult with a rigid hierarchy of foods and drinks offered. The definition of this hierarchy lay not with the priesthood who served the food but with the elite warrior class who produced it. The heart and blood of a hero such as Tlacahuepan were more nutritious for the gods than the heart and blood of a slave bought and fattened by a merchant, and that in turn was better than the autosacrificial blood of a commoner.

One of the details in the field of Aztec religion which has not been sufficiently described is the importance of cactus in their mythology: the Mimixcoa fall upon cactus before they are sacrificed, the sun eagle designates the site of Mexico by perching on a cactus, Mixcoatl's mantle depicts five cactus plants, symbolizing the Five Mimixcoa, and so on. It was the *nochtli* or fruit of this plant which gave it its sacred connotation, for it was sweet, roughly heart-shaped, and often a lively crimson pink. The cactus thus stood for the lavish offering of hearts. In fact, in the cult of sacrifice, the heart torn from the body of the victim was designated as *quauhnochtli*, "eagle-cactus fruit." The eagle perched on the cactus which was the blazon of the city of Mexico can thus be glossed as the sun god feasting on hearts and calling for more.

Perhaps the most pervasive of all the concepts connected with the cult of sacrifice, however, is the equivalence of the god and the victim being sacrificed to him. We have seen something of the same identity attributed to the captor and his captive, who were supposed to be father and son. Captives belonged to the gods, not to any man. For instance, a warrior who had taken a young woman in an attack upon some city was killed if he had sexual relations with her; his crime was defined as a violation of the property rights of the god to whom she alone belonged.

We have already noticed the identity of god and victim when discussing the *ixiptla*, who, dressed in the god's regalia and with his face painted appropriately, was sacrificed to the god. In our logic we would have to say that the god is here sacrificed to himself. This is another way of designating renewal or resurrection, which naturally presumes a previous death. The Aztecs even inserted the god a third time in the cult, for the high priest performing the sacrifice was sometimes also equated with the god. Thus a total triune homogeneity could be achieved, where the god in person sacrificed himself as a third person. Nothing can so well illustrate the fact that the Aztecs were literally drowned in, and totally surrounded by, the supernatural. The sacrificial act at such a peak of conceptualization was thus removed from earth and became a wholly divine drama.

The Paraphernalia of Sacrifice

The actual instrument of sacrifice, the *tecpatl*, was divinized as the knife god and is often depicted in the codices. As a god it was accounted a transfiguration of Tezcatlipoca and was one of the so-called nine Lords of the Night. It was properly of flint and was a heavy and serviceable instrument with a jeweled or mosaic haft.[27] In the more brittle but sharper form of an obsidian blade, it is the very person of Obsidian Knife Butterfly, the terrible Chichimec goddess, which had been carried about wrapped in a sacred bundle on Mixcoatl's back. We also know of the *tecpatl* carried about swaddled like a papoose on the back of Snake Woman, the universal mother and the hungriest of all the goddesses. From the washings of this blood-encrusted knife came a magical drink which made one contemptuous of death; such a potion could be administered both to warriors going off to battle and to captives approaching the sacrificial stone.[28]

The *techcatl*, the stone of sacrifice, upon which the victim was stretched had no such richness of mythology, though it too was supposed to have dropped down from the heavens, originally as a prophecy of the doom which was to befall the Toltecs.[29] The *techcatl* was approximately two feet high and rose to a rounded point. The best-known one stood on the summit of Huitzilopochtli's pyramid directly in front of the god's shrine. It was placed only inches from the front edge of the upper terrace so that the body destroyed upon it could easily be tipped off to tumble down the steps to the bottom.

There was another and quite different sacrificial stone, the "eagle bowl," which we have mentioned in connection with the temple of the sun god.[30] This was wheel-shaped and lay on its side next to the gladiatorial stone. On its upper and therefore exposed side were engraved the armorial bearings and the name of the sun. It was conceived as a drinking bowl for the great solar deity; the shallow depression in the center collected the blood of the victim, which flowed inward through small channels. Only the most valiant warriors were sacrificed on this stone, and then only after they had performed on the gladiatorial stone next to it.[31]

The two stones represented two different traditions of sacrifice. The *techcatl* was widespread in Mesoamerica and goes back at least to early Toltec times. It could be used in the cults of any of the gods, being designed for ease in extracting the human heart. The eagle bowl, on the other hand, stressed the idea of the sun's drinking blood. But this latter stone could not be indiscriminately used. It was beautifully embossed and was the prized possession of the military orders of the knights of the sun. It could be used only in Xipe's cult and in the celebration of the sun's birthday. We are not informed as to its antiquity in Aztec cult.

Attached to many of the temples was customarily a *tzompantli* or skullrack, generally a high latticework construction of long poles horizontally arranged in tiers, one above the other. After a captor had offered his friends a feast of the choice parts of the body of his slain captive, the skull was defleshed if that of a commoner and taken to the temple where he had been sacrificed. If the skull belonged to a nobleman or a great captain, the skin and hair were left on. The priests knocked holes in the sides of all the skulls and strung them along the poles.

These ossuaries were of Toltec origin. Two of the conquistadors who were with Cortés in Tenochtitlan estimated that there were, at a minimum, 136,000 skulls on the single skullrack attached to the central temple.[32] The *tzompantli* was a permanent affair designed to display the people's assiduity in the feeding of the gods. Some, like the one in Tenochtitlan, were flanked by two high towers, one at each end, the walls of which were made of skulls cemented together cheek to jowl–giving, according to one observer, an interesting architectural texture. All Aztec cities had several skullracks. Periodically, when the *tzompantli* became full or the older skulls began to decay and drop away, they were cleaned out and a new beginning made.

Varieties of Sacrifice

The Aztec knew of at least six varieties of human sacrifice: heart extraction, immolation, shooting with arrows, beheading, the destruction of children, and autosacrifice. As the first of these, sacrifice by the knife, was by far the most common, we will present it separately in the following section. Here we need only note its close connections with the Chichimec stratum of Aztec religion.

Sacrifice by burning would appear to have been derived from the Otomí, who claimed the fire god as their first ancestor.[33] In the tenth month, the Great Feast of the Dead, the Mexica celebrated the day of this god, having taken him over from the Tepaneca. In Mexico a great bonfire, which was the divine presence himself, burned throughout the night to become a glowing mass of coals by the opening of the feast day. Bound hand and foot, five *ixiptla*, each representing a different god, were thrown onto the coals. Before they were thoroughly blackened and dead, they were hooked out of the fire to have their hearts torn out.

Tlacacaliztli, sacrifice by arrows, was widespread in Mesoamerica and the regions to the north. It was a unique style of sacrifice and had a special meaning. The victim was tied to a square wooden frame; thus spread-eagled, he represented the sun in the heavens. He was then shot at with arrows and killed; his blood pouring onto the ground may have been the equivalent of the sun's semen falling on the Earth Mother to impregnate her. The fertility aspects of the *tlacacaliztli* are suggested when we recall that the Mexica, after they had fled from Culhuacan, stopped at Mexicaltzinco, where they shot a victim to death with arrows while he was upside down on a rack, his genitals being thereby exposed.[34] An equally good interpretation of the role of that sacrificial victim at Mexicaltzinco, however, could be that he represented the sun past midday, hurtling downward into the earth, or perhaps that he represented the planet Venus.

In all cases of sacrifice, the head was severed from the corpse, as we have seen, to be strung on the poles of the *tzompantli*, a sign of the piety of the state. In two of the festivals, however, heads were additionally flourished by dancing priests. The exact meaning of cult decapitation is somewhat unclear. In the Codex Borgia, in a plate already alluded to, there is a depiction of the deification of human sacrifice wherein heads are prominently displayed.[35] In the center of a blood-red field sits the deified concept of·human sacrifice, there depicted as the *tecpatl* with two heads, each a blood-stained knife. The body of this grisly creature is painted with white and red vertical stripes, the customary identification of a sacrificial victim. The field of blood is embedded in a night sky and in each of the four corners can be seen a differently colored Tezcatlipoca, each carrying two newly defleshed skulls. In the four cardinal directions are four demonic figures, each dancing and holding two heads. The whole sky is enclosed in a palisade of knives.

The sacrifice of children belonged exclusively to the cult of Tlaloc and undoubtedly goes back to some of the La Venta practices in the pre-Classic period.[36] The children selected by the Aztecs were given the names of those mountains to which and on which they were to be sacrificed. This was in reference to the fact that the Tlaloque, the spirits of the mountains, were always conceived as dark-skinned dwarves or little people. The children had been purchased from their mothers and had to have favorable birthdates and bodily signs and, in some cases, had to be of noble birth. They were sacrificed in one of two ways: they were taken out in a ceremonial flotilla of canoes to a certain place in the lake and there drowned, or they were escorted in litters up into the mountains and sealed up by fours in certain caves which were opened only for these annual rites. These children became "human gods" and lived thereafter in great delight with the Tlaloque inside the mountain.[37] Such sacrifices were specifics for bringing rain during the growing season.

We note that in these sacrifices to Tlaloc the concept of feeding the god is not insisted upon; this distinguishes Tlaloc's cult greatly from the others. Here the idea of renewal through substitution is uppermost. The children were cast as *ixiptla* but, though in some ceremonies they might be eaten later by the nobles, no part of them was thought to feed the gods. Rather, in their juvenile figures and ritual purity, they were additional forms being offered to the Tlaloque. They reinforced the known diminutiveness of those gods, added to their numbers, and renewed them.

Autosacrifice among the Aztecs has a more complex motivation than any of the preceding; it was not directed solely at the gods but was also inward-oriented. According to some Aztecs it had been taught to men by Quetzalcoatl in order to accompany and fortify their petitions.[38]

Autosacrifice took a multitude of forms. The commonest consisted in piercing the lips, ears, legs, or arms with maguey needles and then collecting the blood on slips of paper which could be presented to the god. There were certain ritual times of the year when the entire population of a city was required to draw blood in a kind of corporate self-humiliation. The maguey thorns would be deposited finally in a certain holy place, where the gods could not help but become aware of their existence.

Such blood tokens were an occasional part of the penitential life of the common people, but for the average Aztec priest autosacrifice was constant and was of an unprecedented rigor. In Tehuacan, for instance, there were priests who volunteered for a four-year fast and penance so exacting that mental derangement and death must often have resulted.[39] Because sexual activity was unclean and an offense to the gods, the priests pierced their genitals and pulled knotted cords through the wounds; in some cases involving this form of humiliation they would string themselves on the same cord and would perform their cult duties. A common variant of this penance was to drill a large hole through the tongue and then to pull through it cords with spines knotted in them or long wands, sometimes four hundred in number, to produce superior holiness. After such heroic masochism, the mutilated priests forced themselves to sing hymns of praise to the god.

Such penances were thought to be surrogate self-mortifications for the whole people, and the priests who volunteered for them were considered to be of extreme holiness. There was a great variety of such penitential exercises, culminating in self-devotion to death, oftentimes by throwing oneself off a high temple pyramid. More formally a priest might devote himself to death in a four-year penance, during which he passed from city to city discoursing about the gods, principally Tezcatlipoca. He wore special garb indicating his intention and was correspondingly revered; at the end of the four years he was put to death and his heart offered up.[40]

Death on the Techcatl and the Cannibal Meal

Heart extraction was the most common form of sacrifice among the Aztecs and was surely one of the most dramatic and grisly skills ever created by the imagination of man. The subject is unpleasant but, without at least a cursory knowledge of this theater of the macabre, one can never know the Aztecs.

Spanish estimates of the extent of this institution naturally varied. Cortés judged that fifty persons were sacrificed annually in every Mesoamerican temple. On the Gulf coast alone he estimated three to four thousand persons a year,[41] which comports with another source giving two to eight thousand persons sacrificed in specific rituals.[42] This is also consistent with Acosta's statement that over twenty thousand were annually sacrificed throughout the land.[43]

Tlaxcala was known to sacrifice great numbers of men, eight hundred in the normal year, while every fourth year (the divine year) one thousand or more were destroyed. In Cholula, with its unusual number of temples, at least six thousand a year were killed.[44]

But it was in Mexico that the highest number was reached, Cortés' secretary reporting the annual total as twenty thousand.[45] In fact, in one festival there, eight hundred victims alone were slaughtered.[46] Certainly the figure of 136,000 skulls counted on the greatest *tzompantli* in Tenochtitlan is in agreement with the secretary's estimate. If we wish we can refuse to accept such gruesome statistics, but even the lowest number given by our sources speaks loudly.

We have seen that the captive who was taken in war was already, by the mere fact of capture, set apart for the god. He was now *teomicqui*, "one who dies for the god." His sacredness was taken for granted. This was true even if the captive was passed on as an item of tribute from one city to another; in such a case he was escorted to the imperial city by his original captor for delivery, but even there he could not be used in other than a sacrificial way.

The merchants could purchase slaves to offer to the gods at certain festivals; such slaves at that point also became persons devoted to the gods and were considered sacrosanct. They had first to be purified in a lengthy series of ritual ablutions, fattened, and taught to dance. The better ones were exceedingly expensive items in the famous slave market at Azcapotzalco.

The two groups, captives and purified slaves, were thus made up of sacred persons no longer having ties to the land of the living. In some Aztec cities these groups, gorgeously attired, went about the city singing and dancing in preparation for that festival where they would be sacrificed.

The captives destined for sacrifice were *uauantin*, "striped ones," a term alluding to the red and white stripes with which they were painted on the last day. White down was pasted on their heads, black circles were painted around their eyes, and their mouths were heavily reddened. For the final ceremony they were grouped at the foot of the *tzompantli* near the temple. One by one the victims were escorted up the steep stairway of the pyramid. As soon as they reached the top, they were thrust back over the *techcatl*, with great speed and precision. Their backs were bent backward under great tension, four priests bore down, each on an arm or a leg, while a fifth crushed the neck backward, pressing down on the throat with a long implement. The *quetzalcoatl* or high priest who wielded the *tecpatl* struck the blows that smashed through the chest. He then thrust his hand into the horrible cavity which he had opened to rip out the still beating heart. This he held high as an offering to the sun, after which he flung it into a bowl especially designated to collect hearts. The body was straightway tipped off the stone to go tumbling down the steps until it thudded to the bottom, where it was instantly collected by the captor and his adherents and taken away to his residence.

A demon presiding over a cannibal meal (Magliabecchiano)

The corpse was now a *cuauhtecatl*, an "eagle man," and joined the sun. In ascending the pyramid steps he had been the young sun in his rising, while being sacrificed on the *techcatl* he was the sun gloriously poised at his zenith. His tragic descent was the sun going down into the earth. It is of interest that, after slaves were destroyed on the *techcatl*, their bodies were not tumbled down in imitation of the westering sun but were carried down. In either case the victims, being escorted to the *techcatl*, met the mutilated body of the one who had just preceded them as it bumped down the steps. Some sources make mention of the fact that, at the end of a long day of sacrificing, the steps of the pyramid were so slippery with blood as to be almost impossible to mount. The serious problem of the disposal of the cadavers did not arise to plague the temples, for in most cases warriors and merchants individually claimed the bodies belonging to them at the bottom of the great stairway, taking them home to serve in a feast. The hearts, which had been presented to the god for his consumption, were later cooked and eaten by the priests.

Cannibalism was a pervasive aspect of the cultures of Mesoamerica. The Otomí, for instance, after sacrificing a victim, cut him up in slices and sold the chunks in the marketplace.[47] Before they had ever entered the Basin, the primitive Chichimecs killed men for the sole purpose of eating them; only later did they offer the victim first to the god to eat.[48] The taste for human flesh was well developed among the Aztecs, and the parts of the sacrificed person not claimed by the captor or the priests could be sold as protein in the market.[49] One thigh of every victim in Mexico was customarily reserved for the palace, and in all such matters Tlascala was equally greedy. As indicated above, commoners (including women) might occasionally partake of human flesh, but by and large its consumption was a privilege reserved for the nobility, the merchants, and the priests.[50] The meal was generally prepared as a corn stew with pieces of the flesh mixed in; this was the well-known *tlacatlaolli*, "human succotash," and could be particularly enjoyed with squash flowers as a savory. It was a favorite Aztec dish.

Summary

What we find difficult to understand in all this is how the Aztecs could have placed war and its corollary, sacrifice, at the very center of their universe.

We know that they did not hold a cosmological theory of a prince of light and a prince of darkness struggling against each other, of a divine duel, or of a principle of eternal opposites in heaven. The Aztec gods were not theologically opposed to each other, nor were they ordered into two camps. If Huitzilopochtli secured a victory over the Southerners, it was not because he stood for good and they for evil. He was in fact one of them, a Huitznahua. Similarly Mixcoatl, who as one of the Five secured a victory over the Mimixcoa, in no sense stood forth as their eternal antagonist. He was simply their leader. Tezcatlipoca admittedly overthrew Quetzalcoatl but there was no expectation that the quarrel, as one between equals, would ever be renewed.

War for the Aztecs was thus not a description of a situation in which there were only two opposites but was the one and eternal order itself, supremely right and supremely acceptable because it carried no possibility of a negation.

A people with this belief will readily accept human sacrifice as the end for which all wars are waged. They can even be led, through deepening piety and the increase of superstitious terrors, to draw out the drama of human sacrifice until, in its acceleration, it could become self-sustaining. There can be no doubt that as the Aztec population grew—as it was patently doing at the time of the Spanish entry—so did the incidence of human sacrifice.

But there is a cut-off point in the ability of a society to continually augment such nightmare practices, let alone to continue to insist upon them as being axial. Terrors beyond endurance will finally cause a society to crumble or revolt. The facts that have been displayed in this final chapter certainly raise the question whether such a point had not been reached and whether, indeed, the Aztecs were not beginning to feel that they were living in the banqueting hall of an ogre.

Three early Spanish sources were of the opinion that the Aztecs felt human sacrifice to be insupportable. Even the Aztec priests, said one source, "in their hearts desired to be freed of such an intolerable burden."[51] A well-known belief of theirs clearly reveals their suffocated horror and feelings of guilt connected with human sacrifice. We have already mentioned the Night Ax, one of Tezcatlipoca's disguises, a phantom which moved about only in the night. He could be heard in the distance as the thudding sound of a woodsman's ax. He was a headless man with a horrible wound in his chest which, with awful regularity, opened and then clapped shut again. It needs no perspicacity to see that this creature is simply a projection of the sacrificed and beheaded victim after he had been toppled off the *techcatl*. Obviously the ruined cadavers, so common a sight to all Aztecs, had returned to haunt them.

Epilogue

The Aztecs, I believe, produced one of the most astounding examples of piety in the whole history of man. Their passion for the supernatural may well be called extreme. They seem to have had a constant need to reach out and touch their gods, to see them walking about among them singly or altogether. No day went by in any of the larger cities without these presences, yet this familiarity did not produce any lessened feeling for the holy; indeed it seemed to further activate it, and that is the curious thing.

In looking at the physical world the Aztecs beheld a vast embodied logic. Under their feet was earth, whether green or dusty, fruitful or desert. Its surface rolled away in a series of mountains and steppe until it ended in great oceans, which curled up to become the sky. Gigantic lights, which were gods, slid neatly over the scene, each knowing its own mysterious course. In one recurrent nocturnal sorrow, a certain star, the greatest, fell from the sky and sank into the earth. It returned again in splendor, and then again sank down.

All the parts of this numinous world were held together with a web of bridges. Gods could impersonate other gods or sit in the orbits of other gods. There was enough homogeneity in the numinous to allow these slippings in and out of transfigurations, these puttings on and takings off of masks and parts of masks. But there was no bridge between men and the divine. They were nothing alike. Aztec men were not made in the image of a god.

It was probably this feeling of near total separation which induced the Aztecs' extreme piety for, in a situation where the gods are completely "other," men cannot impute injustice to them or any other human quality, good or ill. Nor could Aztec men consider themselves to be tragic objects, for the essence of tragedy is that man first imputes some part of the divine to himself.

This wonderful piety of the Aztec tended to demote his institutions and lessen the creative role they might have played in Mesoamerican history. Only the institutions of cult were given full credence. The anxieties raised by his total reliance on cult probably account for the ferocity with which he lived.

How different from some others! The ancient Egyptian claimed to live in the very valley where the god (who was the pharaoh) resided: he could, therefore, easily appropriate parts of the divine legitimacy and rest content. The imperial Roman was aware of the divine mission of Rome to be a mother to the world: all the legal and military institutions of the state were at his disposal to help further that great enterprise, so he remained confident. The Inca was a child of the sun god, who had given him a commission vague enough to allow him to substitute his own organization for the designs of the gods—so he was engaged in a possible enterprise. The Chinese possessed the mandate of heaven which, whatever the vicissitudes on his northwest frontier, always worked out to insure the continuation and the rightness of his humane way of life. In these and like cases peoples have been convinced that the human and the divine shared in some fashion a family likeness and that there consequently existed grounds for confidence.

Not so with the Aztecs. Their view of the divine was far more serious, far less familiar. To them the gods stood in the midst of the inane, unscrupulous and appetitive, while man stood only on the earth.

But they were never thoroughly at ease with this extreme vision and the subjugation it imposed. On the one hand they had knowledge of the pantheon of gods, who, if they lived catastrophically, at least lived heroically. In cult the Aztecs could find ways of participating in the divine lives. But there was, on the other hand, another world beyond that pantheon, unknowable and thoroughly alien, derived from a consecration of numbers and signs which revolved ceaselessly on each other. In that world the gods themselves were not always their own masters, for the luck of their own birthdate hung over them like the sword of Damocles.

The Aztecs made no attempt to reconcile those two aspects of the divine; in other words, they had no one myth which dealt with both at once and joined them together in a competent theology. The Aztec advance toward the divine was blocked by this unresolved ambiguity. In their more dispirited moods, the Aztecs lamented because they could not see life as a reality of memory, decision, and action but only ultimately as a hallucination.

The biblical view sees God as being both unknowable and participatory at once, but these divine qualities exist in a creative tension. The linked biblical myth of the Creation, the Fall, and the Atonement clearly explicates both the grace and the tragedy in human life. The Aztec had no corresponding and integrating myth.

Nonetheless their vision was one of mankind's notable religious formulations. Few people in history have acted out so deliberately the requirements of their beliefs. The blood of sacrifice that washes through the Christian cult and gives it meaning was present also in Aztec cult but was distorted by its derivation from the battlefield. And throughout Aztec history that blood poured forth in torrents constantly increasing because it satisfied hunger rather than love. We shudder at such views of the Divine, but it is certainly worth our while to consider this cosmic vision of the Aztecs at length so that we may compare it with our own, not invidiously and certainly not with self-congratulation but with wonder at us all.

Notes

1. The World, the Heavens, and Time

1. There are four major sources for the shooting of arrows at the four directions: Ixtlilxochitl, *Relaciones*, pp. 87f.; *Anales de Cuauhtitlan*, pp. 1, 21; Códice Xolotl, pl. 26; Veytia I, 236. The first makes clear that the meaning of the rite was the taking possession of the land. The version in the *Anales* is connected with the installation of a new tribal leader. The two versions are not, however, incompatible.
2. The pan-Aztec version of this myth is found in Sahagún 1950, VII, 6f. There was a Mexican version put forth by the priests of Huitzilopochtli; see LaFaye, p. 87, and Durán I, 22f.
3. Codex Telleriano-Remensis I, pl. 12.
4. The color symbols of the four directions were extremely variable. A frequently employed system is found in Durán I, 98; Sahagún 1950, X, 166. A differing set of colors is splendidly illustrated in Codex Féjérváry-Mayer, pl. 1.
5. The concept of the differing moral qualities of the five directions is not matched by a corresponding moral quality inherent in the five divisions of time, i.e., the five suns. In their temporal thinking the Aztecs accepted what was really a theory of improvement or progress, the fifth and last sun being the most perfect in a succession where each sun was an improvement on its predecessor.
6. Sahagún 1950, XI, 247.
7. Muñoz Camargo, p. 131.
8. The sea could also be called *teoatl*, the "marvelous water" (Sahagún 1956, III, 344).
9. Olmos, p. 32.

10. The thirteen heavens (common in Mayan lore) are widely attested in the mythology of the Aztecs. There was, however, a competing tradition (at home in Chalco and Tlascala) of only nine heavens (Muñoz Camargo, p. 130; Jonghe, p. 31). The nine-level concept is at least as old as the date of the interior of the Castillo, or temple of Quetzalcoatl, at Chichén Itzá, which has nine stages.

11. In Nahuatl the name of the Milky Way is simply the name of the goddess Citlalinicue (Molina I, 24; II, 23; Serna, pp. 168, 227, 274).

12. Tlazolteotl will thus have been allied to Ix Chel, the Putun Mayan goddess of the moon. The subject of the Aztec moon deity is complicated and quite obscure. The deity can be of either sex and when male is generally called Teucciztecatl. The moon was thought of as a jar, a conch, or a sacrificial knife in the sky. The first two conceits connect the moon with water and dew, as does his affiliation with Tlaloc and Chalchiuhtlicue (Olmos, p. 35).

13. All the great gods had their own particular star or constellation. There was, for instance, a star called Teoyaotlatoa Huitzilopochtli, Huitzilopochtli Who Calls to Divine War (Castillo, p. 98). The stars influenced the destinies of men on earth (Sahagún 1950, X, 168).

14. *Tlachco* could therefore be translated as "hellmouth"; see the *tlachtonco*, "little hellmouth," near Chapultepec (Durán II, 495; Alvarado Tezozomoc 1944, pp. 508–511).

15. In Mayan *uol* (*uolol*) denoted a ball or a sphere (Landa, p. 93). The presumption has been that this is somehow related to the Nahuatl *ulli*, "rubber" or "rubber ball," or that both may be derived from an Olmec prototype. *Ulli* itself would seem to be a derivative of *olini*, "to move," and thus to be a cognate to *olin*, "motion."

16. The *tlachco* is equated with the House of Night in Sahagún 1958a, pp. 151, 153, 167. For the midnight dedication see Cervantes de Salazar, p. 285.

17. Another interpretation has been advanced by scholars that the struggle represents the waxing and waning of Venus. An interpretation of this and the solar event is also possible. Statements about the religious orientation of the game should not obscure the fact that it was also played as a pure sport, as a gambling game, and as a way to discover the meaning of omens.

18. Amapan and Uappatzin (Sahagún 1950, II, 134, 162, 172; 1956, I, 210, 230, 237). They do not seem to be connected with Macuilxochitl, the god of games in general. Durán refers to the god of the game as "monkey-faced" (I, 207), which probably means Macuilxochitl. Amapan and Uappatzin most probably had positional or geographical references.

19. Torquemada II, 151; Sahagún 1950, II, 171. In one source Huitzilopochtli is even said to have invented the *tlachco* (Veytia I, 296).

20. Torquemada II, 79.

21. In one source (Codex Borbonicus, pl. 27) four gods form a complete cos-

mic cast in the ball game: Ixtlilton, Quetzalcoatl, Piltzinteuctli, and Cihuacoatl. If we translate each of these gods into that which they symbolize we have (1) a form of the night sun (see Sahagún 1950, I rev., 36), (2) the Morning Star, (3) the sun that rises at dawn (also the young corn), and (4) the dark Earth Mother. This comprises the scenario we have already opted for: a struggle in the night, under the earth a blackened and ominous sun, his last duel with the Morning Star, and his victory when he emerges again in glorious youth. But note that the reenactment of this game took place when the early harvest was being celebrated. Thus the *tlachtli* can be interpreted seasonally, i.e., as an identification of the heroic young corn (just beginning to tassel up) with the great solar champion—both sprung out of the dark Earth Mother.

22. I have here passed swiftly over the difficulties surrounding Aztec calendrics and the startling differences of opinion which have appeared among scholars. The most compendious way to enter the subject is through Caso. See also his short article in *Handbook of Middle American Indians* (hereafter referred to as HMAI) X, 13.

23. The *teoxiuitl*, "the divine year," was especially reported from the cities of Tlascala, Huexotzinco, Cholula, and Tehuacan (Motolinía 1967, p. 70; Mendieta I, 112–115). These expanded penitential rites were celebrated only in rabbit years—every fourth year.

24. The list is simplified, for in certain cases the months have variant names. A further complication lies in the fact that the Aztec states could, and did, begin their years with different months, Cuauhuitlehua here being only one possibility. The word for the calendar of 365 days was *ilhuitlapohual amoxtli*, "the book of the count of festivals" (Molina I, 23; II, 38). It contrasts therefore with the *tonalamatl*.

25. First propounded by Sigüenza y Góngora (Clavigero II, 132).

26. It is possible that we have an approximation to this hypothetical canon of deities in the list known as the Thirteen Lords of the Day, which begins with Xiuhteuctli (who lives at the lowest level in the earth's center) and ends with Citlalinicue (a form of the high goddess Omecihuatl) in the thirteenth and highest. However, Mictlanteuctli in the list poses a problem, for he is in no sense a celestial deity.

27. Mendieta I, 106. See also Sahagún 1950, IV, 4; *Anales de Cuauhtitlan*, pp. 3f.; Serna, pp. 122, 241, 252.

28. This concept of time is generally associated with the Maya, but Nicholson has noted that the concept was present in Central Mexico as well (*Estudios de cultura Náhuatl* VI, 143f.). The reference to the circular ritual promenade of the four *xiuhtonalli* or year-bearers in Sahagún certainly supports this (1950, II, 98).

29. Xiuhteuctli can be translated as Lord of the Year or Lord of Turquoise. The former, I think, is to be preferred. Anderson and Dibble, however, employ the latter (Sahagún 1950, I rev., 29).

30. He is put on the same level of venerability as Tonacateuctli (*Leyenda de los Soles*, p. 121). Once he is even said to be the father of Tezcatlipoca (Sahagún 1950, VI, 19).
31. Serna, p. 77.
32. For the god's domicile within the earth, see Sahagún 1956, II, 122; 1958a, pp. 91f.; Codex Féjérváry-Mayer, pl. 1. See also his interesting title Tlalxictentica, He Who Is in the Earth's Navel (Serna, p. 124; Sahagún 1950, IV, 87).
33. His horizontal title Nauhyoteuctli, or Nauhyoueue, Lord of the Four Directions (Sahagún 1950, II, 155), is completed by his vertical patronage as Chiuhnauhyoteuctli, Lord of the Nine [Underworld Levels] (Serna, p. 65). The colors of his four avatars are given in Sahagún 1950, II, 177.
34. Of interest in this regard is the identification by Christian Aztecs of fire as the Forerunner of Our Lord (Serna, pp. 62, 65). As the hearth fire at dawn precedes the light of day, so Xiuhteuctli preceded Christ.
35. The title Nauhyoteuctli can apply to time as well as space; see 33 above. Every fourth year the fire god's festival was celebrated with special rites, commemorating the fact that the god had not died in the four preceding world catastrophes, as had all the other gods (Codex Telleriano-Remensis I, pl. 12).
36. This myth is nowhere directly alluded to but is an inescapable inference from the mention of a mountain of Mixcoatl in Culhuacan (Sahagún 1958a, p. 192) and from the fact that the god was the first to make fire (Olmos, p. 33).
37. The year 2 Reed, which begins the new lustrum, was the year of the birth of Huitzilopochtli, an avatar of the sun (Caso, pp. 135, 138).
38. A convenient summary of the five ages along with useful tables can be found in Moreno, pp. 183–210.
39. This final collapse will occur appropriately enough on a day 4 Movement (i.e., earthquake) (Codex Telleriano-Remensis II, pl. 2).
40. Sahagún 1950, VI, 37.

2. Creation and the Role of Paradise

1. Mūnoz Camargo, p. 150.
2. Jonghe, pp. 28f.; Olmos, pp. 25f.
3. Jonghe, p. 25; Olmos, p. 32. This variant is found as one of the myths connected with the five aeons or suns and does not purport to describe the original cosmogony.
4. He was probably in origin a generalized agricultural deity identified with heat and summer (Serna, pp. 124, 247) and belonging to the Teotihuacan culture (Ixtlilxochitl, *Relaciones*, pp. 38f.). He was a god important to Aztec speculation, but his worship appears to have lapsed well before Aztec history. He can be depicted seated on a mat of maize tassels and presiding over the act of human copulation (Codex Vaticanus,

pl. 15). His female counterpart is a kind of Ceres (Serna, p. 319). Children who died very young were buried near bins of maize and were thought to go to the paradise of Tonacateuctli, which had abundant cornfields (Sahagún 1956, II, 144).

5. Olmos, pp. 23ff. Quetzalcoatl and Tezcatlipoca are always present in these lists, but the others sometimes vary (Torquemada II, 78; *Leyenda de los Soles*, pp. 120f.).

6. This myth can be found in Jonghe, pp. 29f.; Torquemada II, 37f., 76f.; Mendieta I, 83; Clavigero II, 63f.

7. She is identified with Teteoinnan, Mother of the Gods (Sahagún 1956, IV, 283), who wears the *citlalicue*, the star skirt, a kind of kilt belted on and made of leather straps ending in jingling seashells (Sahagún 1950, I rev., 16). She wears the same skirt when she appears as Ilamateuctli, Leading Old Woman (Sahagún 1950, II, 143). When not considered to be the Milky Way, Citlalinicue was one of the two sentinel stars guarding the approaches to the sky, her consort being the other (Olmos, p. 69).

8. Ilhuicamina, He Shoots Arrows at the Heavens. This name probably characterizes the sun as the one who destroys all the stars, i.e., the Four Hundred. It was an early and honorable name among the Aztecs (Alvarado Tezozomoc 1949, p. 15) and was carried by the greatest Mexican ruler, Moteuczoma I, thought to have been born as the sun appeared over the horizon (Chimalpahin, p. 183).

9. Mendieta I, 86.

10. Xippilli, the Jeweled Prince, was a god of verdant fields and summer (Alvarado Tezozomoc 1944, pp. 95, 211, 407, 410f.).

11. Cuauhtemoc.

12. Tlalchitonatiuh, literally Groundward Sun. He is shown being slain by the Evening Star in Codex Borbonicus, pl. 16.

13. On Yohualtonatiuh, the Night Sun, see Klein, pp. 77f. There is an excellent depiction of him in Codex Borgia, pl. 40.

14. *Chronicles of Michoacan*, pp. 63f.; Corona Núñez, p. 20.

15. Sahagún 1958a, pp. 151, 153, 166f.; 1950, II, 212. The reader should be aware that this myth has been extracted from a very obscure hymn. That Piltzinteuctli was a very ancient god can be seen from that other relationship credited to him, namely that he was of the second generation of gods and had mated with a goddess created from the hair of Xochiquetzal (Olmos, p. 27) or with Xochiquetzal herself (Sahagún 1958a, p. 110). Their son was Cinteotl, the maize. In this fertility relationship Piltzinteuctli as the vigorous spring sun cohabits with Mother Earth to produce corn.

16. Las Casas, p. 100.

17. For the pessimism with which the sun was often regarded in Aztec thought, see Sahagún 1950, I rev., 81ff. We have noted that half of the sun's career is spent in the underworld as a wrinkled and ominous being, the Night Sun.

18. Sahagún 1956, II, 258–262; Garibay 1961a, pp. 215–220; Sahagún 1950, VII, 3–8; *Leyenda de los Soles*, pp. 121f.; Jonghe, pp. 29f. The one god who consistently appears in the lists is Quetzalcoatl (either as Ehecatl or Nanahuatl); Tezcatlipoca is usually paired with him, but the other two creator gods vary. In Xipe's cult there are four officiants called the Four Dawns, each a different color (Durán I, 98, 140). Xipe is certainly a form of the sun god and so there may be some connection between his four officiants and the quadruple dawn in the myth of Nanahuatl.

19. Quetzalcoatl can substitute for Xolotl as the executioner of the 1,600 gods (Sahagún 1950, VII, 8); in other words either one of the two appearances of the planet Venus can act vicariously for all the other stars. The element of sacrifice is also found in the Huichol myth of the birth of the sun (Furst 1967, p. 66).

20. See the preceding note.

21. *Leyenda de los Soles*, p. 121.

22. In one curious version of the myth Quetzalcoatl hurled his son (who never had a mother) into the fire to become the sun (Olmos, p. 35). This would imply that the god sacrificed to become the sun (elsewhere Nanahuatl) was really a form of Quetzalcoatl, the Morning Star. Ergo Nanahuatl was himself a form of the Morning Star!

23. Thompson conjectures that Tamoanchan may be Mayan and mean At the Moan Sky, where the Aztecs would have borrowed the Mayan concept of the moan bird as a celestial being (Thompson, pp. 104f.). Nicholson agrees that it is a Mayan word but translates it as the Place of the Bird-Serpent (HMAI X, 408).

24. In a list given to Sahagún personally, Tamoanchan is seen as a sacred city comparable to Tula or Teotihuacan (Garibay 1961a, p. 248). This very accurately describes Xochicalco. It should be noted that the site in Morelos was called Xochicalco at the time of the Spanish entry (Sahagún 1956, I, 30). This therefore may have been its pre-Columbian name in Nahuatl. The identification of Xochicalco and Tamoanchan is based on Jonghe, p. 27, and is vaguely supported by Sahagún 1950, X, 191–194.

25. Sahagún 1956, I, 30f.; Codex Telleriano-Remensis II, pl. 23.

26. This tree was called either Xochitlicaca, It Stands Covered with Flowers, or the Tree of Tonacateuctli (Muñoz Camargo, p. 155; Sahagún 1950, VI, 115). It becomes the Tonacaxochincuahuitl of Aztec poetry (Garibay 1964, I, 106f., 118; II, 21ff., 139, xxvf.; 1953, I, 179, 181). The Maya had a similar Green Tree of the World (Landa, pp. 131f.).

27. For the attribution of the fall from grace solely to Itzpapalotl, see Codex Vaticanus, pl. 43.

28. Edmonson, pp. 4f., 20–23; Thompson, p. 44.

29. Codex Vaticanus, pl. 1; Codex Telleriano-Remensis II, pl. 14.

30. Serna, p. 122.

31. Codex Telleriano-Remensis II, pl. 22; Codex Vaticanus, pl. 43.
32. For the various items of culture sponsored by Oxomoco and Cipactonal, see Sahagún 1950, X, 167, 191; 1956, II, 172; III, 186f.; Serna, pp. 122, 241, 252.
33. Mendieta I, 106; Sahagún 1950, IV, 4; *Anales de Cuauhtitlan*, pp. 3f.
34. Because they purchased slaves to offer in sacrifice, merchants were also thought to go to Tonatiuh Ichan, the Sun's House (Sahagún 1956, III, 33).
35. Generally placed in the east (Sahagún 1950, I rev., 9; X, 187f.).
36. Alvarado Tezozomoc 1944, pp. 503f.; Durán II, 493f.; Sahagún 1956, IV, 97; 1950, XII, 26. Cincalco is also quite logically called Huemacco, the Place of Huemac (Chimalpahin, p. 69). Other gods present in this paradise were Totec Chicahua, Our Aged Lord, and two attendant deities: Ixtepetla and Acuacuauh.

3. The Quality of the Numinous

1. Swadesh and Sancho, pp. 65f.; Sahagún (in *Estudios de cultura Náhuatl* IX, 245, 250f.).
2. Sahagún 1950, XII rev., 11f. This is the same list of four gods as is portrayed in Codex Magliabecchiano, pl. 89.
3. When the ambassadors arrayed Cortés they seem to have given him items of the regalia of all four of the great gods (Sahagún 1950, XII rev., 15), though one source insists that they dressed him as Quetzalcoatl (Torquemada I, 381f.).
4. In discussing the *neteotiliztli* ceremony Durán states that the Aztecs believed that, underneath, all the gods were one (I, 96f.). To my knowledge no other source makes this assertion. Siméon translates the word as "a latrian cult" (p. 300). I do not think there is any basic contradiction. A people able to abstract an idea of "divinity" (which is an absolute) are not necessarily obliged to give up polytheism.
5. The word for face or mask is *xayacatl*. Mask is more specifically the *tlachichiualli* (adorned, false, feigned) *xayacatl*. The entire array of a god (mask, regalia, face and body paint, sandals, etc.) is more properly *nechichiualiztli*. Thus my use of the word "mask" in this work is a translation of the latter.
6. For the extreme idolatry practiced by the Aztecs, see Ixtlilxochitl, *Relaciones*, p. 457; Clavigero II, 83; Torquemada II, 64. The Maya were scandalized by the idolatrous propensities of the invading Toltecs (Landa, p. 23). In Aztec times the proliferation of idols reached a point where the great cities had to organize them; see, for instance, Nezahualcoyotl's move in this respect (Pomar, p. 13).
7. Sahagún 1950, VI, 175, 183, 202; X, 169; 1956, III, 188; Hernández, p. 19;

Clavigero II, 164f. Note that the "two" gods are equated with Citlallatonac and Citlalinicue (Torquemada II, 37f.).

8. Seler 1960, I, 64.

9. Codex Telleriano-Remensis II, pl. 1 (see also pl. 15).

10. See n. 6.

11. The common word for idol is *tequacuilli*. It can also be used to mean the
particular priest or priests who had charge of the image. A stone idol
is *teteotl*. When carved out of wood the idol is *cuauhximalli*. *Toptli* is
the ark or coffer containing the sacred image and by extension can
mean the image itself. *Tlachichihualtin* (pl.) are all shaped idols. The
tlaquimilolli ("wrapping" or "mantle") was a cloth bundle containing
the sacra and therefore generally portable. A household figure was a
nenetl ("doll" or "female genitalia"). Envisaged as small female guardians of the home, these figurines were also called *tlazolteteo* after the
Great Mother; undoubtedly they go back into pre-Classic times (Serna, pp. 315, 324). The Tlaloc cult produced the *tepicme* or *tepictoton*
("little molded ones"), squat dough images of mountains, and the
ecatotontin (also dough but molded over twisted, snakelike armatures),
representing the airs and winds.

12. Sahagún 1950, II, 167.

13. This is my considered opinion and not a fact. I believe that a very good
case could be made in support of this statement, though I have not
had time to work it out in detail.

14. A widely held opinion. For a late statement on it see the excellent article by Klein, pp. 81f.

15. Torquemada II, 286.

16. The deity appears as one, four, or multiple. As single she is the night
sky demonically conceived (Jonghe, pp. 27f.), or she is even death itself (Codex Vaticanus, pl. 3; Codex Magliabecchiano, pl. 76). As fourfold the deities were the directional atlantes who supported the sky
(Olmos, p. 32; Garibay 1945, p. 125). They are also called *ilhuicatzi-
tzque* (Durán II, 229; Alvarado Tezozomoc 1944, p. 159). Their clear
connection with the collapse of the sky at the end of time would support this (Sahagún 1956, II, 83). The temple of Huitzilopochtli in Mexico had carved *tzitzimime* at the corners as supporting pillars (Durán
II, 333). As multiple beings they were female demons (*tezauhcihua*) of
the sky, awaiting the end of the aeon, when they will dive down to
eat all men (Olmos, p. 69; Sahagún 1950, VII, 2).

17. Codex Magliabecchiano, pl. 76.

18. Olmos, p. 69.

19. Olmos, p. 23.

20. Codex Borgia, pl. 21.

21. Mendieta I, 83.

22. Sahagún 1958b, p. 73.

23. The *teopatli* (Clavigero II, 105) was also called *teotlacualli*, "divine food"

(Durán I, 51f.). It was a paste made of soot, tobacco, poisonous snakes, scorpions, morning-glory seeds, etc.

24. Ixtlilxochitl, *Relaciones*, pp. 253, 324, 496; Olmos, pp. 21, 228, 243f.; Veytia I, 343, 354.

25. Literally Yohualli Ehecatl, Night and Wind. This is the most difficult and interesting of all his titles, for it was also characteristically applied to Quetzalcoatl, who of course was Ehecatl in any case and therefore was invisible (Sahagún 1956, III, 194).

26. Torquemada II, 528. Tzontemoc was one of the four avatars of the god of death (Codex Vaticanus, pl. 3). He is also called Cuezalli, which appears to mean Flaming Thing (Sahagún 1950, VI, 4, 21; 1956, IV, 331). He was called Acolnahuacatl after the ward in Tenochtitlan where he was worshiped (Sahagún 1950, III, 39; 1956, I, 293). His temple was called Tlalxicco, after his place in the underworld (Torquemada II, 148).

27. For representations of Itztlacoliuhqui, the god of frost, see Seler 1963, II, 202–205. This god unexpectedly turns out to be an avatar of Cinteotl (*Estudios de cultura Náhuatl* X, 187; Sahagún 1950, II, 112f.; VII, 19).

28. Amimitl was an old Chichimec god reputedly from the homeland in Aztlan (Sahagún 1950, II, 210; 1956, III, 212; Barlow, pp. 104f.). He was a form of Mixcoatl, being specifically his dart or harpoon (Olmos, p. 40; Sahagún 1958b, p. 139).

29. The Olmec origins of Tlaloc are scarcely to be doubted. One of his names was Epcoatl, Seashell Serpent (Torquemada II, 147; Sahagún 1950, II, 43; 1956, I, 232). Rubber, a lowland and coastal product, was featured prominently in his cult (Sahagún 1958b, pp. 89ff.; 1950, II, 80; Torquemada II, 267). He can be poetically referred to as Lord of the Sea (Garibay 1964, II, 15). His cult was intimately connected with children, again an Olmec religious theme. Furthermore, in Olmec iconography the god sits within his cave as does Tlaloc, his priests wear buccal masks, and his eyes are rimmed with the rain god's goggles (Gay, pp. 38–45, 47, 66–69, figs. 11, 17).

30. See Pasztory.

31. Tlaloc's original identity as an earth or mountain deity is clearly attested in his title as Tlalteuctli, Earth Lord (Torquemada I, 290; Olmos, p. 26; Sahagún 1958a, p. 191). We must not confuse this aspect of Tlaloc with the demonic goddess Tlalteuctli.

32. Oztoteotl, the god of caves, who was worshiped in Chalma and had children offered to him, was almost surely a form of Tlaloc (Garibay 1953, I, 269). Tlaloc is depicted as living inside the mountain in Codex Vaticanus, pl. 67.

33. The Tlaloc behind Tezcoco is identified as a god of the ancient race of giants, the Quinametin, who are clearly the late folk memory of the Teotihuacanos (Ixtlilxochitl, *Relaciones*, pp. 18ff., 30).

34. The Tlaloque were thought to carry the rattlestaff called *chicahualilizti*, "that which makes things strong" (Sahagún 1950, VI, 39). This was a cult instrument, symbolizing the erect penis and/or the digging stick. When thumped on the ground it called forth the rain clouds and thunder. Gods of fertility, such as Cinteotl and Xipe, carried it as well. There is undoubtedly an identity between it and the sacred tree called Chicahuazteotl, the god of vigor or ripeness, worshiped by Quetzalcoatl (Ixtlilxochitl, *Historia*, pp. 23f.).

35. On Popocatepetl in cult, see Durán I, 163–166; Chimalpahin, p. 147. Until very recently the caves on the south side of that mountain were still processionally entered and the winds called *ehecatzitzintin* were worshiped.

36. Olmos, p. 26.

37. I have here used the translation of Thelma Sullivan in *Estudios de cultura Náhuatl* V, 37–55.

38. From a hypothetical word *xipitl* or *xipilli*, judged to mean penis (Garibay's suggestion; Sahagún 1958a, pp. 177f.). A word *xipintli*, "foreskin," is known and is probably cognate. The usual translation of the god's name is the Flayed One (Durán I, 95), but Torquemada (II, 58) gives "bare" or "bald" or "blackened."

39. Alvarado Tezozomoc 1944, p. 389.

40. Durán II, 173; Codex Vaticanus, pl. 56. Xipe wears a kilt of sapodilla leaves (Sahagún 1958b, p. 128; Garibay 1953, I, 370). The zapote even today is connected with bravery (Robelo, p. 287).

41. Note that Durán implies that his feast, the first of the year, is a feast of the sun (I, 102). The circle device on his shield may well be a depiction of the sun (Codex Vaticanus, pls. 10, 12).

42. Tlatlauhquitezcatl (Pomar, p. 17; Durán I, 95).

43. These gods could be referred to as "the heart of the people" (Codex Vaticanus, pl. 5).

4. Tezcatlipoca

1. Sahagún 1956, I, 37.

2. The name when properly spelled out is Tezcatl Ipoca, Mirror That Smokes, but it is almost always found run together (Andrews, p. 469). An early Mexican prince bore the god's name with the verb intensified: Tezcatlpopocatzin (Alvarado Tezozomoc 1949, p. 104). A related man's name, Tezcapoctli, is not to be confused with this. *Tezcapoctli* is the name of the black obsidian with a reflecting surface used for making mirrors.

3. Torquemada II, 150.

4. In Aztec times mirrors presaged war, witness the bird called *cuatezcatl* (Sahagún 1969, pp. 123–125).

5. Jonghe, pp. 36f.

6. Sahagún 1958a, pp. 253f. The verb *ixcehualpopocatimani*, from which I have taken my paraphrase, is very expressive. Inasmuch as the speech scroll and the smoke emitted by Tezcatlipoca's mirror are often indistinguishable, we are tempted to further gloss the object as a "speaking mirror."

7. Pomar, p. 14.

8. Xiuhteuctli also carries this as a sort of lorgnette (Sahagún 1956, I, 58).

9. He was called Opoche, He Who Has Left-Handedness (Sahagún 1950, VI, 34). One of his priests is appropriately called "his left hand" (Torquemada II, 149).

10. Sahagún 1950, V, 180; Serna, p. 224.

11. Codex Telleriano-Remensis II, pl. 6; Codex Vaticanus, pl. 21.

12. Sahagún 1950, XI, 1f.

13. Little is known about this ancient deity (Codex Telleriano-Remensis II, pl. 4; Codex Vaticanus, pl. 19; Garibay 1964, II, 47). He is shown as a form of Tezcatlipoca in Codex Borbonicus, pl. 3. Typically he is a jaguar sitting on a hill hollowed out and full of stars (Codex Borgia, pl. 63).

14. Sahagún 1950, V, 157ff.

15. Sahagún 1950, II, 214; Veytia I, 288f.

16. LaFaye, p. 95.

17. *Selden Roll*, pp. 15f. and reproduction.

18. Tlatlauhqui Tezcatlipoca, the red Tezcatlipoca, is said to be either a younger brother of the black Tezcatlipoca (Ixtlilxochitl, *Relaciones*, p. 47) or less powerful (Olmos, p. 23). The intent is plainly to emphasize the superiority of the Night Sun over his counterpart in the sky of day. Both transfigurations are said to have been worshiped by the Toltecs and the invading Aztecs (Ixtlilxochitl, *Relaciones*, pp. 47, 140). The red Tezcatlipoca can be transfigured as Camaxtli (Olmos, p. 23) or Xipe (Motolinia 1967, p. 44). It is interesting to see him once depicted as a jaguar (Codex Telleriano-Remensis II, pl. 31).

19. Sahagún 1950, I rev., 5; IV, 33f.; VI, 11. It was he who caused the breakup of the Toltec empire by inciting internal dissension, according to the *Historia Tolteca-Chichimeca*.

20. Sahagún 1950, VI, 11.

21. Codex Borgia, pl. 14. In connection with this, see his name Itzcaque, He Who Has Obsidian Sandals (Sahagún 1950, VI, 34).

22. Sahagún 1956, IV, 287. He was the patron deity of both the northern and the southern arsenals (Codex Magliabecchiano, pl. 36).

23. Codex Vaticanus, pls. 59, 66; Codex Telleriano-Remensis I, pl. 6.

24. Ixquimilli literally means "a blindfold" (Codex Vaticanus, pls. 37, 39). He is presented as a spirit of night or darkness in Codex Cospi, pl. 12; Codex Borgia, pl. 15; Codex Laud, pl. 13. Thompson finds him in the Dresden Codex (pp. 15, 35, 69) but considers him to be a form of the deity of the planet Venus.

25. Torquemada II, 40f.; Sahagún 1950, VI, 33. Sahagún also insists that

Nezahualpilli was another name for Tezcatlipoca (1950, I rev., 67; III, 12). I strongly suspect that this epithet (Fasting Prince) is connected with his avatar Telpochtli.

26. Sahagún 1956, I, 299.
27. Torquemada II, 278.
28. Torquemada II, 220f.
29. Torquemada II, 151, 281. Tlamatzincatl is equated with Telpochtli in Sahagún 1956, I, 197; 1950, II, 118; Serna, p. 188. He of course had a cult in Mexico (Sahagún 1950, II, 21, 26, 129).
30. On this god see Sahagún 1956, III, 353; Torquemada II, 245; Serna, pp. 142f. It is the latter source who describes Telpochtli as *tlaca*, "chaste" or "virgin" (Siméon, p. 506; Swadesh and Sancho, p. 67).
31. We note that his feast was in the month of Tepeilhuitl, which is consonant with his character as a Tlaloc (Sahagún 1950, II, 176).
32. We must beware of confusing this god with the fourfold avatar of Xiuhteuctli known by exactly the same name.
33. Chimalpahin, pp. 100, 147.
34. The full story of this interesting cult episode is found in Chimalpahin, pp. 78ff., 154, 177ff.
35. Sahagún 1956, II, 67.
36. Codex Borbonicus, pl. 6.
37. The day was 1 Death (Sahagún 1950, IV, 33–36).
38. The day 2 Reed was even more intimately associated with Tezcatlipoca than was 1 Death, for it became deified as one of his avatars (Serna, p. 178; Sahagún 1950, II, 38; IV, 56).
39. Torquemada II, 78.
40. Sahagún 1950, IV, 33.
41. Sahagún 1956, II, 86.
42. Tlatocateotl (Castillo, pp. 66, 89). Tezcatlipoca's rulership is made visual on Tizoc's *cuauhxicalli* (HMAI X, 125), where he is depicted as a conqueror for the city of Tenochtitlan. This does not deny that Huitzilopochtli (an avatar of Tezcatlipoca) also gives the victory.
43. Monenequi has been variously translated; see the footnote in Sahagún 1950, VI, 11. I have adopted Andrews' translation (p. 457).
44. Alvarado Tezozomoc 1949, p. 15.
45. It is nowhere definitely stated that Macuiltotec is a form of Tezcatlipoca but, considering that he was a god of the arsenal in both Tlatilulco and Tenochtitlan, it seems to be a fair assumption (Sahagún 1950, II, 178; 1956, I, 241; IV, 65).
46. Torquemada II, 38.
47. Pomar, pp. 23f.; Ixtlilxochitl, *Relaciones*, p. 324. It is highly probable that this claim of the god's exclusiveness is a product of the city of Tezcoco (the city where Tezcatlipoca was peculiarly honored), and I have so stated it.

48. Torquemada II, 78.
49. Olmos, p. 30. The fact that elsewhere (Sahagún 1950, VII, 66) the Great
    Bear appears as a scorpion constellation does not militate against its
    identification with Tezcatlipoca. Seler prefers to identify the god, how-
    ever, with the constellation Citlallachtli (1963, I, 216f.). See also Beyer
    on Aztec imprecision in the identification of constellations (1969, p.
    103).
50. Codex Borgia, pl. 32.
51. Durán I, 11; Torquemada II, 79; Codex Telleriano-Remensis I, pl. 9.
52. For Tezcatlipoca as a seducer, see Codex Vaticanus, pls. 40, 52; Codex
    Telleriano-Remensis I, pl. 9. It is probably this sexual aspect of Tez-
    catlipoca which prompted Serna to think of him as Cupid (pp. 176,
    184).
53. *Chronicles of Michoacan*, p. 184; Corona Núñez, p. 23. Note that both Taras
    Upeme and Tezcatlipoca are closely connected with strong drink in
    their respective myths.
54. Olmos, p. 34.
55. Olmos, p. 33.
56. Tlacahuepan was a Toltec war god considered by the later Aztecs to be a
    younger brother to Huitzilopochtli (Torquemada II, 265). His name is
    ambiguous. It could mean Pillar of the Lord, Support of Men, or
    Man Log; see n. 61. He had close connections with Tezcatlipoca (Tor-
    quemada II, 46; Sahagún 1950, II, 73; III, 25f.).
57. Torquemada II, 79; Mendieta I, 88.
58. Olmos, p. 32.
59. Sahagún 1950, III, 17–20.
60. Sahagún 1950, III, 21f.; Torquemada I, 37f.
61. This tale is etiological, for Tezcatlipoca is here his avatar Tlacahuepan
    (whose name contains the element *huepantli*, "log" or "rough-hewn
    timber") (Sahagún 1950, III, 25f.). The figure being dragged along by
    the Toltecs and crushing them is stated to be a *huepantli*. The story of
    the rotting giant is told somewhat differently in the *Leyenda de los Soles*,
    pp. 125f.
62. Huemac was a *tlachichihualli* or phantasm of Tezcatlipoca (*Historia Tol-
    teca-Chichimeca*, pp. 14f.; Torquemada I, 255; Muñoz Camargo, pp.
    5f.).
63. Ixtlilxochitl, *Relaciones*, p. 29.
64. *Leyenda de los Soles*, pp. 126f.
65. The four goddesses married to the *ixiptla* were Xochiquetzal, Xilonen,
    Atlatonan, and Huixtocihuatl, representing respectively sexual plea-
    sure, food, drink, and salt.
66. The geography of the area of the sacrifice of the god's *ixiptla* is curiously
    coincident with the territory sacred to Huitzilopochtli on the south
    shore of the lake (Sahagún 1950, II, 10; 1956, I, 155; Chimalpahin,

p. 56). Tezcatlipoca was important in the Chalco area just adjoining (Serna, p. 63; Chimalpahin, pp. 100, 130, 147; Alvarado Tezozomoc 1944, p. 366; Durán II, 366).

67. Durán I, 38, 44.

5. Quetzalcoatl

1. The buccal mask was modeled on an aquatic bird's beak, according to some sources; see Durán I, 62. There was, however, a wide variety of buccal masks in Mesoamerica, especially those worn by the Tlaloque (Codex Vindobonensis, pl. 26). It is almost certain that the Aztecs themselves did not know what to make of it.

2. The *ehecailacacozcatl*. This was also well known in Tarascan culture, where it seems to have represented, as it did among the Aztecs, the winds that precede the downpour (Corona Núñez, pp. 90f.).

3. The *xonecuilli* may also refer to the lightning because of its serpentine shape (Sahagún 1956, I, 50). It is called a *coatopilli* or "snake staff" in Alvarado Tezozomoc 1944, p. 265.

4. Torquemada II, 48.

5. One of Quetzalcoatl's names, Ocelocoatl, is found, as far as I know, only in Cervantes de Salazar, p. 51. It is probably to be connected with his black or nocturnal form.

6. Marquina, p. 32.

7. Durán I, 14.

8. For his title Tlilpotonqui, Feathered in Black, see Sahagún 1950, III, 59f.

9. Molina has thirteen entries under *viento* (I, 118) and fifteen under *ehecatl* (II, 28).

10. See also the entry under *ecacouayo mixtli*, "a twister" (Molina I, 90).

11. The goddess in the scene is Tlazolteotl (Codex Laud, pl. 16).

12. This does not mean that the two deities could not adopt parts of each other's regalia; they could and did, as witness Codex Telleriano-Remensis II, pl. 12. One source even tells us that Quetzalcoatl was occasionally referred to as Tlaloc (Codex Magliabecchiano, pl. 34).

13. Torquemada II, 47, 52; Sahagún 1950, I rev., 9.

14. It may be that the identification of Quetzalcoatl with Ce Acatl (whom we equate with the Morning Star) began in Teotihuacan times. For this see the beautiful illustrations of the Plumed Serpent with the Venus glyph spotted at intervals on his body (Miller, p. 165).

15. Corona Núñez, p. 18.

16. Codex Telleriano-Remensis II, pl. 14. The heavens were supposed to have been created on the date Ce Acatl (II, pl. 33), not on the date signifying the sun.

17. *Leyenda de los Soles*, p. 122; Mendieta I, 85.

18. Jonghe, pp. 34f.

19. *Anales de Cuauhtitlan*, p. 11. See the marvelous sets of illustrations of the carnage caused by the Morning Star in Codex Cospi, pls. 9–11; Codex Borgia, pl. 53f. The Toltecs introduced this concept of the ominous rising of Venus to the Maya (Thompson, pp. 64, 67, 69ff., pls. 46–50).
20. Torquemada II, 152; Veytia II, 241; Sahagún 1956, I, 237; Clavigero II, 93.
21. There is a good translation of this important myth in Garibay 1953, I, 317.
22. Note that the Codex Borgia plainly shows the two as distinct and even opposed deities (pl. 19).
23. Topiltzin can be translated either as Our Revered Prince or as the word "scepter," with a possible derived meaning of the "justiciar" (Veytia I, 186). The former is preferred.
24. They were called *tlanquacemilhuitime* (Sahagún 1950, III, 14; 1956, I, 278; Torquemada II, 48). The translation is "knees last an entire day," which can only mean "untiring travelers."
25. *Leyenda de los Soles*, pp. 124f.; Olmos, pp. 113f.
26. The sources that deal with the legendary life of Topiltzin are so numerous and well known that I am not citing them here; I have made a composite account of all of them. The standard version exists, I suppose, in Sahagún 1950, III, 13–16, 31–36.
27. The vandalism of his temple in Tula is a matter of archaeological record.
28. One source says he became the Evening Star (Jonghe, p. 38). Other interesting variations on the disappearance exist. One motif is that, on arriving at the coast, Quetzalcoatl by his word opened a fissure in a mountain and entered, whereat it closed behind him and he was never seen again (Durán I, 12). The other tale was that he shot an arrow into a tree which split open. He inserted himself into the cleft and disappeared. The tree was then burned (Olmos, p. 116). These display the complexity of the god. In the first version he is a stellar god, in the second he is a Tlaloc, and in the third he is a god of a tree or pillar cult.
29. Codex Vaticanus, pl. 9.
30. Other gods invoked by Topiltzin do not appear in the Aztec pantheon to my knowledge. They are Tecolliquenqui, Yeztlaquenqui, Tlallamanac, and Tlallichcatl (*Anales de Cuauhtitlan*, p. 8).
31. Nacxitl is translated in one source as Caminador (Alvarado Tezozomoc 1944, p. 523). Garibay translates it more literally as He Who Has Four Feet (1961a, p. 306).
32. Chimalpahin, p. 62; Garibay 1964, III, 1.
33. Garibay 1964, III, 1. I have made some slight changes in Garibay's translation.
34. There are many references to the return in our sources. For the popularity of the belief, see Torquemada II, 51.
35. Codex Vaticanus, pl. 13.
36. This date is an inference from Chimalpahin's *Segunda relación*, signed and attested in that year; see Chimalpahin, p. 62.

37. Ixtlilxochitl, *Relaciones*, p. 55; Torquemada II, 52; Durán I, 12. Note that the tradition that the god is inside a mountain is parallel to the tale that Huemac disappeared into the rock of Chapultepec.
38. Sahagún 1950, X, 190f.; 1956, III, 208.
39. A mythological scene in Codex Vindobonensis (pl. 49) shows two Xolotl twins in existence before Quetzalcoatl descends from the heavens (pl. 48). This is not conclusive evidence that Xolotl is an older deity than Quetzalcoatl, but it is suggestive.
40. Swadesh and Sancho, p. 75; Sanford, p. 150. The Aztec use of the word *tlacaxolotl* (Muñoz Camargo, p. 174) to identify the Spanish horse and horseman is composed of two words which have to be translated as "man" and "beast." Thus *xolotl* probably does carry the meaning of "beast" or even "monster."
41. Sahagún 1956, II, 261.
42. The *tlalcoyotl* (Sahagún 1950, XI, 8).
43. Mendieta I, 85.
44. Sahagún 1950, VII, 8.
45. Mendieta I, 83f.; Torquemada II, 77; Jonghe, p. 27.
46. Codex Borbonicus, pl. 16.
47. Codex Magliabecchiano, pl. 34.
48. Sahagún 1958a, pp. 151ff.
49. Yacateuctli is translated by Anderson and Dibble as Lord of the Vanguard (Sahagún 1950, I rev., 41). This derives the element *yaca* from the noun *yacatl*, "nose," "van," and is to be preferred to Garibay's derivation from *yahqui*, "a goer," "one who goes forth" (Sahagún 1958a, p. 204). Note that the god can be characterized for his cunning as Yacacoliuhqui, He with the Aquiline Nose (Torquemada II, 57, 272), and as Yacapitzahuac, Pointed Nose (Sahagún 1956, I, 198).
50. For the material on Cholula's past, see Marquina.
51. Sahagún 1950, VI, 141.
52. For these claims made by the mythographers and priests of Quetzalcoatl, see Codex Telleriano-Remensis II, pl. 2; Sahagún 1950, VI, 31, 181, 183, 185, 202; Torquemada II, 222; Motolinía 1967, p. 347.
53. *Leyenda de los Soles*, pp. 120f. There is a version with some interesting differences (Olmos, p. 106). Here the gods are reduced to two, Ehecatl and Tezcatlipoca, of whom only the first descends into the underworld to retrieve the bones of men. It is Xolotl who finally raises and nourishes men.
54. *Leyenda de los Soles*, p. 121. That part of the myth involving Nanahuatl is probably depicted in Codex Borgia, pl. 43.
55. Jonghe, pp. 27f.
56. Alvarado Tezozomoc 1944, pp. 247, 490.
57. The nobility is referred to as the sons and servants of Quetzalcoatl (Sahagún 1956, II, 118f.). Quetzalcoatl's movable feast on the day 1 Reed was celebrated in the *calmecac* by the lords and leading men of Mexico

(Sahagún 1950, II, 36f.; Serna, p. 175). In this celebration the god appears as a protector of lineage and therefore as opposed to the common people.

58. Torquemada I, 380.
59. Such an instrument is reproduced in Seler 1960, V, 491. The thunderous tones of the god's voice are often alluded to (Durán I, 170; Sahagún 1950, III, 34).
60. Michael Coe has recently stated that Mesoamerican religion is basically a dualism (Benson, p. 13).

6. The Making of Huitzilopochtli

1. I am following Di Peso's definition of the geographical term Gran Chichimeca (I, 48–55).
2. Garibay 1961a, p. 248.
3. *Anales de Cuauhtitlan*, p. 30.
4. Our sources regarding Chichimec religion fall into two distinct categories: those insisting that the sun was adored as the father of man and the earth as mother, and those insisting that Mixcoatl and Itzpapalotl were the leading god and goddess of the Chichimec pantheon. It must be obvious that the two versions are not contradictory but parallel, in other words that Mixcoatl *in some sense* is reducible to the sun, while Itzpapalotl *in some sense* represents the earth. The myth of Mixcoatl and the Four Hundred is found in Olmos, pp. 36f.; *Anales de Cuauhtitlan*, p. 3; *Leyenda de los Soles*, pp. 122f.
5. The five were Mixcoatl, Quauhtliicohuauh, Tlotepe, Apanteuctli, and Cuitlachcihuatl. Their names may be translated as Cloud Serpent, Eagle Twin, Hawk Mountain, Lord of the Watercourses, and Wolf Bitch. This follows a frequent pattern of four male gods and one female.
6. There is no doubt that the Mimixcoa were cast as the ancestral Chichimecs (*Anales de Cuauhtitlan*, p. 30). The Four Hundred were definitely thought of as denizens of Chicomoztoc, the Chichimec homeland (*Leyenda de los Soles*, p. 123; Sahagún 1950, II, 209; 1958a, pp. 93–97). They are also characterized as northerners (Garibay 1961b, p. 49; Sahagún 1950, IX, 10). It is quite probable that the term "cloud serpent" was an early equivalent of "warrior."
7. Torquemada says that the name Mixcoatl refers to the flight of arrows through the air (II, 280). Siméon gives it as meaning "tornado," apparently thinking of it as a synonym of *ehecacoatl* (p. 247).
8. Olmos, p. 33.
9. *Leyenda de los Soles*, p. 124.
10. The identification of Tetzauhteotl (or Tetzahuitl, the Omen) with the Chicomoztoc appearance of Huitzilopochtli is common in our sources.

Torquemada (II, 42) and Sahagún (1956, I, 273) both accept the identification but connect it with Coatepetl rather than with Chicomoztoc. In line with this name of the god is his appearance as Omiteuctli, Lord of Bones, and as the two-headed maquiz snake which prophesied a person's death (Olmos, pp. 23f.; Sahagún 1950, XI, 79).

11. Chimalpahin, p. 68.

12. Neither Mecitli nor its variant Mexitli, as they stand written, can mean Navel of the Maguey, as Torquemada claims (I, 293). Andrews gives Navel of the Moon (p. 453). I have the highest regard for his expertise in the matter, but for other than linguistic reasons I cannot agree with him here. The name Mecitli can mean Maguey Hare, as Sahagún says (1950, X, 189). It may just as easily mean Maguey Grandmother, which is what I opt for here.

13. *Leyenda de los Soles*, p. 122.

14. Andrews reads the city name Mexico as meaning In the Middle of the Lake of the Moon (p. 453). I know of no reference to Lake Tezcoco as anciently called the Lake of the Moon.

15. Found in several sources. Perhaps the standard version is Sahagún 1950, III, 1–5.

16. On Coyolxauhqui see Justino Fernández in *Estudios de cultura Náhuatl* IV, 37–53. This includes León-Portilla's translation of the myth cited in the previous note.

17. Alvarado Tezozomoc 1944, pp. 13f.

18. Sahagún 1950, II, 130–138, 161f.

19. *Leyenda de los Soles*, pp. 126f.

20. One source says that the Mexica had to surrender their god to the Culhua (Olmos, p. 52), another that they buried the idol to prevent its seizure (*Relación de la genealogía y linaje*, p. 249). It is plain that a spiritual trauma of profound importance struck the Mexica at this point.

21. Sahagún 1950, XI, 24; Motolinía 1967, p. 333.

22. Torquemada's rendering of the name as a "cosa de pesca o de caza en agua" (II, 59) connects it with a weapon used in lake hunting. It is depicted as essentially a dart or *tlacochtli*, but the god carries no accompanying spear thrower (Sahagún 1958b, p. 139). The text calls it *ytzihuactlacoch*, "his cactus dart," and shows it as having a specially heavy kind of head, probably obsidian. Olmos (p. 40) calls it a *vara*.

23. Barlow, pp. 104f.

24. Sahagún 1950, I, 37; II, 199.

25. Sahagún 1958b, p. 103.

26. Sahagún 1950, I rev., 37. Note that the three-pronged fishing and fowling spear was the *minacachalli*, obviously not the weapon referred to above in n. 22.

27. Olmos, p. 47. For this famous spring see Sahagún 1956, I, 207.

28. Olmos, p. 47.

29. This important tale has not been recognized up to now for what it is—a propaganda disguising of a serious religious upheaval and reorientation. It is referred to in Durán II, 51f., 399; Alvarado Tezozomoc 1949, pp. 52, 81.
30. Olmos, p. 54; Chimalpahin, p. 71; Códice de 1576, pp. 35ff.
31. Olmos, p. 54; Torquemada II, 116, 118, 276; Durán II, 42, 463; Alvarado Tezozomoc 1949, pp. 54f. We note that the name of the goddess is variously given as Toci, Yaocihuatl, Teteoinnan, etc.
32. The major sources for this difficult tale are Olmos, pp. 48f., 51; Chimalpahin, pp. 54ff., 153; Durán II, 37f.; Alvarado Tezozomoc 1949, pp. 31, 41–44; *Anales de Tlatelolco*, pp. 34f. For Garibay's translation see Garibay 1953, I, 278ff., 322ff., 466. Details differ in these sources. I give what I consider to be an acceptable version.
33. Códice de 1576, pp. 39ff.; Torquemada I, 288f.; Chimalpahin, p. 94. For Garibay's translation see Garibay 1953, I, 302f.
34. The name Axolohua means He Who Has the Axolotl Salamander [as a *Nahualli*]. For the axolotl, an edible, lacustrine salamander, see *Estudios de cultura Náhuatl* VIII, 157–173. In the tale Axolohua is clearly a sorcerer from the southern part of the lake. He is said to have died in Tizaapan near Culhuacan (Alvarado Tezozomoc 1949, pp. 70f.).
35. Durán II, 333. This head is preserved today in the National Museum as one of the great Aztec works of art.
36. The festivals of the fifth, the ninth, and the sixteenth months are the ones referred to. Some of the major sources for the Panquetzaliztli are Sahagún 1950, I rev., 67; II, 130–138, 161f.; 1956, I, 128, 206–213; Mendieta I, 109, 112; Torquemada II, 281ff.; Motolinía 1967, p. 47. These have provided the basic material in the account given here. The interpretations of the various phases of the ceremony are, of course, mine. Because of the close political alliance between Mexico and Tezcoco the Panquetzalliztli was celebrated in both cities (Motolinía 1967, pp. 57f.).
37. Sahagún 1950, III, 15.
38. Sahagún 1950, III, 4; Torquemada II, 42.
39. See n. 56, chap. 4. In Tenochtitlan Tlacahuepan as Cuexcoch was worshiped in the barrio of Huitznahuac (Sahagún 1950, II, 161; Torquemada II, 155). Here he was presented to the people as a dough statue who, along with Huitzilopochtli and Painal, formed a close-knit trilogy (Torquemada II, 281f.; Clavigero II, 79). But his perfect equation with Tezcatlipoca brings this threesome inevitably into the usual quadruplicate structure. For Tlacahuepan as a younger brother, see Torquemada II, 265. As we might expect of a transfiguration of Tezcatlipoca, he was especially revered in Tezcoco (Sahagún 1950, II, 73).
40. Torquemada II,151; Sahagún 1950, II, 171.
41. Sahagún 1950, II, 73; III, 7.

7. The Goddesses

1. The Mexica considered the mountain mass southwest of Chapultepec to be their mother. As a topographical feature it was known as Zacatepec, Grass Mountain, but as a goddess it was known to be Ixillan Tonan (Sahagún 1956, I, 126, 204). The beautifully rounded mountain overlooking Teotihuacan was also Tonan, as well as others.
2. Commonly referred to as Tepeyacac, the Promontory.
3. Codex Telleriano-Remensis II, pl. 1.
4. Cihuatzintli means Female Buttocks. For her title Techyahuallotoc see *Anales mexicanos*, p. 59. This is the only reference to this goddess that I am aware of.
5. Tlalliiyollo is appropriately associated with the *temazcalli* or sweatbath (Sahagún 1956, I, 91), one of her titles being Temazcalteci, Grandmother Sweatbath.
6. There can be no doubt that the Mexica found the cult of Toci in Culhuacan (Durán II, 42, 463; Torquemada II, 116, 276; *Anales de Cuauhtitlan*, p. 29). However, it was that aspect of her as the goddess of discord that appealed to them most (Herrera IV, 107; Alvarado Tezozomoc 1949, p. 54).
7. Sahagún 1956, I, 218. She had two avatars. One was Ilancueye, She of the Old-Lady Skirt, where the reference is possibly to the withered husk around the dried maize cob (Caso, pp. 129, 133). The other was Cozcamiahuatl, Cornflower Necklace (Jonghe, p. 30; Serna, pp. 132, 140, 142, 193; Sahagún 1956, I, 129). In these two avatars she is clearly associated with the stored corn.
8. See n. 5.
9. One of the most important of the deities. In myth she was the first to cook food (Sahagún 1956, I, 47).
10. Olmos, p. 110.
11. For the Basin people Chalchiuhtlicue was the mountain Iztaccihuatl (Sahagún 1958a, p. 258) or Popocatepetl when it was viewed as the source of flowing water (Durán I, 165). Appropriately she could be depicted wearing Tlaloc's mask (Codex Magliabecchiano, pl. 92).
12. *Leyenda de los Soles*, p. 122.
13. Sahagún 1950, X, 179; Codex Vaticanus, pl. 29.
14. Jonghe, pp. 27f.
15. Seler's thesis that these pulque gods were symbols of dying and resurrection is very convincing (1963, I, 107).
16. Durán I, 193f. Her festival was a farewell to flowers (151).
17. Codex Magliabecchiano, pl. 41.
18. Nicholson has a list of the myths involving Xochiquetzal in HMAI X, 431; consequently I need give no source references here.
19. There is a confused Yucatec counterpart to this myth of the origin of flowers which proves how widespread it was (Roys, pp. 104f.). Briefly

it is as follows. Bolon Mayel, accompanied by two honey-sucking bats, descends (into the underworld?) to create flowers. These flowers are somehow connected with the "sin" of a deity of the nine underworlds. Then Ppizlimtec, a god of music and poetry (no doubt a Mayan Pil-tzinteuctli), descended in the form of a hummingbird and mated with the goddess (of the plumeria?), producing thereby a beautiful flower, probably representing the sin of lust. A wicked, blindfolded god is also involved in this myth, but nothing about him is clear. He could be the equivalent of Tezcatlipoca; see chap. 4, n. 52.

20. This tree was the *xochitliicacan* (Muñoz Camargo, pp. 154f.). It is illus-trated as a broken and bleeding tree in Codex Telleriano-Remensis II, pl. 23.

21. Codex Telleriano-Remensis II, pl. 7; Codex Vaticanus, pl. 22.

22. See the translation by López Austin in *Estudios de cultura Náhuatl* VI, 106ff. This myth is glancingly alluded to in Sahagún 1958a, p. 151; 1950, II, 210.

23. Durán I, 154f.

24. Codex Telleriano-Remensis I, pl. 5; Torquemada II, 134. I believe the physical and sexual implications of the name are as important as the philosophical. See n. 4 in this connection.

25. An adulteress was known as *tlazolteocihuatl*, "a woman of the sex god-dess" or "nymphomaniac" (Molina I, 88; II, 119). Much is said in the secondary literature about her connection with the moon. This may well be true (I have assumed it is) but I know of no primary textual source which supports it. Her iconography, however, appears to sup-port this identification with the moon or the night (Codex Borbonicus, pls. 12, 55).

26. Sahagún says that *ixcuina* is the name of an animal like the wolf (1956, I, 91). The word does not appear in the dictionaries.

27. Sahagún 1956, II, 261.

28. Olmos, p. 110.

29. See n. 6, chap. 2.

30. This myth of the northern provenience of Coatlicue is contained in the fascinating chapter in Durán II, 215–224.

31. *Anales de Cuauhtitlan*, p. 12.

32. Sahagún 1950, II, 127.

33. This figuration of the great female deity was specifically associated with the Huitznahua people (*Leyenda de los Soles*, p. 124). In pre-Aztec times she was important enough to have been taken by those groups, influenced by the Toltecs, who invaded the Guatemalan highlands and became the Quiché (Edmonson, pp. 36, 38).

34. Alvarado Tezozomoc 1949, p. 18; Barlow, p. 105; Códice de 1576, p. 20.

35. Sahagún 1950, II, 55. Coatlan was a ward in Tenochtitlan as well as in Tlatilulco. The name of the goddess' temple in Coatlan was the same as her sacred mountain in myth, Coatepec. The fact that Huitzilopoch-

tli's temple was also known as Coatepec is something of a difficulty. The temple of Huitznahuac (i.e., Huitzilopochtli as conqueror of the Huitznahua) was in Coatlan, as we might expect. In the year preceding the entry of Cortés, Moteuczoma dedicated the new temple of Coatlan with an impressive number of human sacrifices (Torquemada I, 228). This temple of the goddess (Alvarado Tezozomoc 1944, pp. 454, 457, 459f.) must not be confused with the Coacalco, where all the captive gods were kept (Sahagún 1950, II, 168).

36. Itzcoatl erected a temple to Cihuacoatl shortly after he had conquered Xochimilco, one of the centers of her worship (Durán I, 125; Torquemada I, 150). She was also of great importance in Culhuacan and Chalma (Olmos, p. 52; Sahagún 1950, II, 211f.). From the statement in Olmos we can infer that in her Culhuacan cult she was definitely an infernal goddess and a patroness of war. We have speculated that it was at this time in the career of the Mexica (right after the final defeat of the Chinampaneca cities) that the great reformulation of the deity Huitzilopochtli was made official.

37. Sahagún 1950, I rev., 11.

38. Mendieta I, 98.

39. The essential references to the Tlillan are in Sahagún 1956, I, 233; Torquemada II, 146f.; Durán I, 125f.; Gómara, p. 165. The Tlillan (also called the Teccizcalli in Sahagún 1956, I, 233) was an integral part of Moteuczoma's palatial complex (Sahagún 1956, II, 292).

40. Durán I, 130.

41. She also appears as Quilazteotl (Sahagún 1950, II, 213).

42. I am here using Sullivan's translation of the name in *Estudios de cultura Náhuatl* VI, 77. See also Sahagún 1958a, p. 139; Garibay 1953, II, 406.

43. Olmos, p. 40.

44. The myth appears in the *Anales de Cuauhtitlan*, p. 3; *Leyenda de los Soles*, pp. 123f. Garibay's translation is perhaps better (1945, pp. 32ff., 133). Heyden brings together the scattered material on Itzpapalotl and rightly emphasizes the fact of her near exclusion from the Mexican pantheon. I am inclined to doubt the resemblance which Heyden sees between her and Tlazolteotl, but her statement that she represented "los viejos tiempos, los tiempos Chichimecas" fits her properly into her place. As an authentic Chichimec deity she was never tamed.

45. Codex Vaticanus, pl. 22; Codex Telleriano-Remensis II, pl. 22.

46. The goddess Itzcueye, Obsidian Skirt, who was Camaxtli's consort, is undoubtedly an avatar of Itzpapalotl (*Historia Tolteca-Chichimeca*, p. 91).

47. These shrines were the *cihuateocalli* or the *cihuateopan* (Sahagún 1950, II, 37; Serna, p. 170).

8. Man

1. *Leyenda de los Soles*, p. 120. For another translation, see Garibay 1953, I, 293f., 390. Quite similar is the Huichol myth that one man survived the flood by making a canoe out of a great world tree (an amatl tree) which stood in the underworld (Furst 1967, p. 60). Clavigero has rescued an interesting variant of the tale (II, 61). Here only the goddess Xochiquetzal and her consort Teocipactli (also called Coxcox) were saved from the flood. They landed on top of Mount Culhuacan, where they had many children. A dove flew from a great tree and gave each child a different speech. This reminds one of the myth of Oxomoco and Cipactonal, who made all men and gave them the fate of toiling and having few pleasures (Olmos, p. 25).
2. *Tata* is a small child's word for father (Molina II, 91). *Nenetl* is the word for idol, doll, or vulva and obviously was an old generic name for woman or girl.
3. Sahagún 1950, VI, 176f.
4. Sahagún 1950, VI, 105.
5. The idea of the transitoriness of life was expounded throughout Aztec society, among commoners and nobles both. See, e.g., Nezahualcoyotl's lament (Ixtlilxochitl, *Historia*, pp. 235f.) or the address to the dead (Sahagún 1950, III, 39).
6. Garibay 1964, I, 85f.
7. Sahagún 1950, V, 161.
8. Codex Vaticanus, pl. 21.
9. The *tonalpouhqui*, "he who reads or counts the day-signs," was an essential member of Aztec society, far more so than the astrologer ever was in the European world. It was he and his predecessors in the Mesoamerican world who created and elaborated the *tonalamatl*, the book of destinies, which was fundamental to his calling. See Sahagún 1950, IV, 1, 142; VI, 197ff. The *tonalamatl* was reputed to go back, through Quetzalcoatl, to Oxomoco and Cipactonal (Sahagún 1956, I, 315, 319).
10. For the possibility of a person's changing his fate, see Sahagún 1950, IV, 34, 100; VI, 95.
11. Sahagún 1956, II, 67.
12. Sahagún 1956, II, 128.
13. Sahagún 1950, II, 158.
14. Andrews derives *nahualli* ("a thing interposed, like a mask or disguise") from a possible verb *nahua*, which would appear to mean the interposition of something between the natural and the supernatural (p. 455). There is an extensive literature on the meaning of the word *nahualli*.
15. Serna, pp. 90f.
16. The following interesting example of the *nahualli* was given me by Dr. David Stuart (presently at the University of New Mexico). In the spring of 1966 he arrived at a village near Huamanguillo, Tabasco.

The cacique there was a middle-aged man in good health but with only one eye. A party of Americans left the town with a native guide early in the evening to hunt jaguars. That night the cacique suddenly and inexplicably died. Before dawn the hunters returned with a jaguar which they had just shot. The fact that it had one wasted and useless eye aroused the people of the village to a pitch of fury. The Indian guide was pommeled and the American party, fearing for their safety, left hurriedly. The villagers believed that the Americans had killed the jaguar which was their cacique's *nahualli*. With the death of the jaguar the cacique also had to die.

17. Ponce de León, p. 379.
18. Garibay 1961b, pp. 103f.
19. Sahagún 1950, XI, 130.
20. Codex Vindobonensis, pl. 24.
21. See Furst 1974. The Aztecs called the morning glory *coatl xoxouhqui*, "green snake" (Sahagún 1956, III, 292f.). We note that there was a deity so named in Sahagún 1950, II, 103.
22. Durán mentions a fiesta of visions where the magnates all took the *teonanacatl* (II, 416).
23. Sahagún 1950, VI, 175.
24. Sahagún 1950, VI, 51.
25. Sahagún 1950, I rev., 23.
26. There is an excellent account of the rite of confession in Sahagún 1950, I rev., 23–27.
27. Durán I, 155f.
28. Sahagún 1950, VIII, 81.
29. Garibay 1964, I, 132; *Estudios de cultura Náhuatl* X, 82f.
30. We have to depend mainly on Molina here. For "soul" he gives *toyolia* or *toyolitia* (I, 9; II, 95, 149). This would imply a nominative **yoliatl*, an assumption which Siméon makes (p. 173). The word for spirit Molina connects with the Nahuatl words for breathing, blowing, or breath (see *ihiyotl, tlalpitzaliztli, ehecatl*; I, 60). Sahagún says that *ihiyotl* is given to a person from heaven (1950, VI, 203), but this does not help much inasmuch as it might have only its literal meaning, breath. Another word for soul is *tonalli* (Molina II, 151; Sahagún 1950, X, 169), which appears to be used interchangeably with the preceding words. The heavy Christian overlay in the dictionaries has probably closed the possibility of distinguishing the words properly.
31. Motolinía 1967, p. 31.
32. Sahagún 1950, X, 192.
33. Sahagún 1950, X, 192.
34. Clavigero gives us an interesting insight into Aztec burial when he states that the dead were arrayed with a god's insignia, referring either to their status or occupation or to the manner of their death—i.e., disease, drowning, etc. (II, 173f.; Motolinía 1967, p. 247). Thus a mat maker

would be buried with the appurtenances of Nappateuctli, an emperor with the regalia of Tezcatlipoca, and so on. The implication is that death was not a homogeneous cosmic condition but, like the mask pool, was broken up into categories, each god being provided with one. Such a reading of the situation has no support in our sources, however.

35. Ixtlilxochitl, *Relaciones*, pp. 55f.

36. Garibay has collected most of these allusions to Mictlan (1953, I, 195f.). He has, however, misread and therefore mistranslated Apochquiauayocan, which means Place of No Smoke Hole; see Sahagún 1950, XI, 277; Alvarado Tezozomoc 1944, pp. 285, 390. There may be confusion between this and Opochhuayocan, the Left-Handed [i.e., sinister] Place; see Alvarado Tezozomoc 1944, pp. 244, 264.

37. Sahagún 1950, XI, 277.

38. The connection between the dog and the god Xolotl seems self-evident, but no source spells it out.

39. I suspect that Motolinía's statement that each level in the underworld was reserved for a certain sin or manner of dying has been contaminated by Christian thought (1967, p. 246).

40. Torquemada II, 79.

41. Durán II, 295–300; Alvarado Tezozomoc 1944, pp. 240–244.

42. Ceremonies connected with the death of a warrior were naturally very elaborate (Durán II, 153–155, 287–290, 435–436; Alvarado Tezozomoc 1944, pp. 232–235; Motolinía 1967, p. 247). Yahualiuhcan, where the Mexica buried the ashes of their dead warriors, was the knob just southeast of the Hill of the Star (Alvarado Tezozomoc 1944, pp. 95, 234f.).

9. The Nuclear Cult: War, Sacrifice, and Cannibalism

1. García Icazbalceta I, 272.

2. Olmos, p. 34. The descent of war is depicted in Codex Cospi, pl. 6r.

3. León-Portilla 1967, p. 145.

4. Garibay 1953, I, 461.

5. Garibay 1945, pp. 15f.

6. There is a further refinement of interpretation possible with regard to this Aztec phrase, namely that the word *tlachinolli* refers to the cremations that immediately followed the carnage on the battlefield. There will thus be a double reference to the word: one to the incineration of the enemy's homes and temples, the other to the apotheosis of the dead warriors through cremation; see Garibay 1964, I, 80f. I have used this additional meaning in the text. We note that in Codex Vaticanus Tezcatlipoca's mirror foot has the *atl tlachinolli* glyph issuing from it (pls. 59, 66). This may mean that in his name the element "smoking"

may particularly refer to the dust and billowing smoke of the battle-field; see nn. 4 and 6, chap. 4.

7. Sahagún 1956, II, 83f.

8. Most of these poetic references are found in Garibay 1953, I, 19f., 76; 1964, II, 11.

9. Properly the Nahuatl word for warrior is *yaoquizque*, "he who goes to war," or *yaochihuani*, "he who makes war." *Teuctli* means lord or nobleman, but it implies martial renown as man's highest quality. I have there-fore loosely used it as the medieval word *varon* or *baron* was used. A commoner could be and indeed was a soldier in the Aztec armies, but only if he was also a *teuctli* was he granted privileges and honors.

10. There is a real doubt that lesser orders under the eagles and the jaguars actually existed. Some sources imply or even say that there were three orders (Veytia I, 267, 271; Codex Ramírez, pp. 100f.; Torquemada I, 565), the third being pumas. Once four orders are mentioned (Acosta, p. 314). The stellar myth adverted to in n. 5 above mentions only the eagle and the jaguar as archetypal. *Miztli*, the puma, is of small mo-ment in the thought of the Aztecs and is not mentioned in any of their mythology.

11. Torquemada I, 152.

12. Sahagún 1956, II, 331; 1950, II, 62.

13. Pomar, p. 12.

14. Sahagún 1950, VI, 171.

15. There is plenty of evidence for this statement; see Sahagún 1950, VI, 23; 1956, II, 65; Codex Telleriano-Remensis II, pl. 30; Garibay 1964, II, 54, 95.

16. Muñoz Camargo, pp. 125–128; Torquemada I, 219f.; Durán II, 456f.

17. Sahagún 1950, II, 48.

18. Durán is especially informative on the return of the army; see among other passages II, 159–161, 169f., 182, 188f., 203, 274, 287–290, 305f., 423f., 441, 482.

19. Durán II, 285.

20. The outstanding victory of Tezcoco and Mexico in the Tepaneca War was certainly a crucial point in the development of the flower war. Nezahualcoyotl was apparently the one who gave it its special Basin/transmontane pattern, with the three major Basin cities–Tezcoco, Mexico, Tacuba–directed against the three major cities east of the sierra–Tlascala, Huexotzinco, and Cholula (Ixtlilxochitl, *Historia*, pp. 207f.; *Relaciones*, pp. 51f., 321, 492; Pomar, pp. 41f.). This semimili-tary, semireligious understanding between the two great Aztec re-gions was accepted and standardized in Mexico by Tlacaelel (Codex Ramírez, pp. 82f., 181f.). The earliest reference I can find to the flower war is to a year 1 Knife (1324 or 1376), when the Chalca and the Tlacochcalca fought in this fashion (Chimalpahin, pp. 74, 177). The significant feature is that the flower wars were kept exclusively among

the Nahuatl-speaking groups. The gods, in other words, preferred Nahua blood (Durán I, 32f.).

21. Our best sources on the flower wars are Durán I, 33f.; II, 433–436; Pomar, pp. 41f., 45ff.; Alvarado Tezozomoc 1944, pp. 462, 482; Chimalpahin, p. 152.
22. Durán II, 232f.
23. There are several conflicting versions of the Tlacahuepan story. I have used the account in Durán II, 433ff.
24. Garibay 1953, I, 204.
25. Garibay 1953, I, 461; *Anales de Cuauhtitlan*, pp. 13f.
26. A tale was propagated by the Mexica and believed by other Aztec people that Huitzilopochtli had taught the Mexica the rite of heart sacrifice at Coatepec (Torquemada I, 81f.; II, 115; Codex Ramírez, p. 27; Olmos, p. 45). Neither the Tepaneca, the Chinampaneca, the Acolhua, nor the Aztec groups across the Sierra Nevada succeeded in so closely identifying with the practice.
27. Serna, p. 168. The full designation of the heavy sacrificial knife was *tecpatl ixcuahua*, literally "the knife with the broad forehead or face," an anthropomorphic title (Molina II, 93; Sahagún 1950, II, 47).
28. Sahagún 1950, IX, 87f.; Torquemada I, 177.
29. Sahagún 1956, I, 287f.
30. Durán I, 100, 107.
31. The gladiatorial stone, or "stone wheel," was the *temalacatl*.
32. García Icazbalceta II, 583.
33. The common name of this god was Otonteuctli, Lord of the Otomí. He was also known as Ocoteuctli, Lord of the Pine (Olmos, pp. 40f.), and Cuecuex (*Anales de Cuauhtitlan*, p. 46). The latter name seems also to have specified the male dead (Sahagún 1950, X, 192).
34. Alvarado Tezozomoc 1949, pp. 58f.
35. Codex Borgia, pl. 32.
36. We note that the Huaxtecs, living along the Gulf coast, also sacrificed children on mountaintops (HMAI XI, 600).
37. *Tlacateteotin* (Sahagún 1950, I rev., 68) or *teteopohualtin*, "those accounted to be gods" (Torquemada II, 151).
38. Quetzalcoatl is that god identified, through his mask, with penitential rites. He is often depicted holding the bone or thorn used to draw blood. He invented autosacrifice even before the tearing out of hearts became acceptable (Codex Vaticanus, pl. 18). The contradictory assignment of the institution of autosacrifice to Camaxtli (Olmos, p. 36) is not as startling as it looks when we recall that the Aztecs believed Camaxtli (Mixcoatl) to have been Quetzalcoatl's father.
39. The penitential priests of Tehuacan were simply the most famous college; there were many others (Torquemada II, 182f.; Las Casas, pp. 69f., 93f.; Motolinía 1967, pp. 69ff.). Durán was appalled at the rigor with which the Aztec priests carried out their exercises (I, 48).

40. Hernández, p. 176; see also López Medel, quoted in Landa, p. 222.
41. Cortés in his first letter is presumably including the figure of the twenty thousand children thought to have been annually sacrificed to Tlaloc; in drought, of course, the figures would have risen dramatically (Torquemada II, 120).
42. Durán II, 415.
43. Acosta, p. 253; Torquemada II, 120.
44. For the figures cited in this paragraph, see Gómara, p. 120; Hernández, pp. 186f.; Torquemada II, 290; Herrera III, 193.
45. Gómara, p. 95.
46. Alvarado Tezozomoc 1944, p. 460. Durán pretty well agrees with the figure given by Cortés when he tells us that on Xipe's day alone above sixty men were offered up (I, 96). And we must remember that those who died on the *temalacatl* were carefully selected from the valorous few.
47. Clavigero II, 114.
48. *Anales de Cuauhtitlan*, p. 30.
49. García Icazbalceta I, 365.
50. Codex Magliabecchiano shows women eating human flesh (p. 73). This is the only reference I know to this feature of Aztec cannibalism.
51. Acosta, p. 254; see also Torquemada II, 134f.; Herrera IV, 124.

Bibliography

Acosta, José de
1962   *Historia natural y moral de las Indias*. Ed. Edmundo O'Gorman.
            2d ed., rev. Mexico City: Fondo de Cultura Económica.

Alvarado Tezozomoc, Hernando
1944   *Crónica mexicana*. Mexico City: Editorial Leyenda.
1949   *Crónica mexicayotl*. Trans. Adrian León. Mexico City: Imprenta
            Universitaria.

Anales de Cuauhtitlan
1945   In *Códice Chimalpopoca*. Mexico City: Imprenta Universitaria.

Anales mexicanos: México-Azcapotzalco, 1426–1589
1903   Trans. Faustino Galicia Chimalpopoca. Mexico City: Anales del
            Museo Nacional, VII.

Anales de Tlatelolco
1948   Trans. Heinrich Berlin. Mexico City: Editorial Porrúa.

Andrews, J. Richard
1975   *Introduction to Classical Nahuatl*. 2 vols. Austin: University of
            Texas Press.

Barlow, Robert H.
1949   "El códice Azcatitlan." *Journal de la Société des Américanistes de
            Paris* 38 (Paris).

Benson, Elizabeth P. (ed.)
1972   *The Cult of the Feline*. Washington, D.C.: Dumbarton Oaks.

Beyer, Hermann
1965 *Mito y simbología del México antiguo*. Mexico City: Sociedad Alemana Mexicanista.
1969 *Cien años de arqueología mexicana*. Mexico City: Sociedad Alemana.

Carrasco Pizana, Pedro
1945 "Quetzalcoatl, dios de Coatepec de los costales, Guerrero." *Tlalocan* 2 (Mexico City).

Caso, Alfonso
1967 *Los calendarios prehispánicos*. Mexico City: Universidad Nacional Autónoma de México.

Castillo, Cristóbal del
1966 *Fragmentos de la obra general sobre historia de los mexicanos*. Trans. Francisco del Paso y Troncoso. Ciudad Juárez: Editorial Erandi.

Cervantes de Salazar, Francisco
1914 *Crónica de la Nueva España*. Madrid: Hispanic Society of America.
Chimalpahin, Francisco de San Antón Muñón
1965 *Relaciones originales de Chalco Amaquemecan*. Trans. S. Rendón. Mexico City: Fondo de Cultura Económica.

Chronicles of Michoacan
1970 Trans. E. R. Craine and R. C. Reindorp. Norman: University of Oklahoma Press.

Clavigero, Francisco Javier
1958 *Historia antigua de México*. 4 vols. Mexico City: Editorial Porrúa.

Codex Borbonicus
1974 Graz, Austria: Akademische Druck- u. Verlagsanstalt.

Codex Borgia
1976 Graz, Austria: Akademische Druck- u. Verlagsanstalt.

Codex Cospi
1968 Graz, Austria: Akademische Druck- u. Verlagsanstalt.

Codex Féjérváry-Mayer
1971 Graz, Austria: Akademische Druck- u. Verlagsanstalt.

Codex Laud
1966 Graz, Austria: Akademische Druck- u. Verlagsanstalt.

Codex Magliabecchiano
1970 Graz, Austria: Akademische Druck- u. Verlagsanstalt.

Codex Ramírez
1944 Mexico City: Editorial Leyenda.

Codex Telleriano-Remensis
1964   In Vol. I of *Antigüedades de México, basadas en la recopilación de Lord Kingsborough*. 4 vols. Mexico City: Secretaria de Hacienda y Crédito Público.

Codex Vaticanus #3738 (Codex Ríos)
1964   In Vol. III of *Antigüedades de México, basadas en la recopilación de Lord Kingsborough*. 4 vols. Mexico City: Secretaria de Hacienda y Crédito Público.

Codex Vindobonensis Mexicanus I
n.d.   Graz, Austria: Akademische Druck- u. Verlagsanstalt.

Códice de 1576 (Codex Aubin)
1963   Trans. Charles E. Dibble. Madrid: José Porrúa Turanzas.

Códice Xolotl
1951   Trans. Charles E. Dibble. Mexico City: Publicaciones del Instituto de Historia.

Corona Núñez, José
1957   *Mitología tarasca*. Mexico City: Fondo de Cultura Económica.

Di Peso, Charles
1974   *Casas grandes*. 3 vols. Flagstaff: Northland Press.

Durán, Diego
1967   *Historia de las Indias de Nueva España e islas de la tierra firme*. 2 vols. Mexico City: Editorial Porrúa.

Edmonson, Munro S. (trans.)
1971   *The Book of Counsel: The Popol Vuh of the Quiché Maya of Guatemala*. New Orleans: University of Tulane.

Estudios de cultura Náhuatl
1959–1976   Vols. 1–12. Mexico City: Instituto de Historia, Seminario de Cultura Náhuatl, Universidad Nacional Autónoma de México.

Fernández, Justino
1963   "Una aproximación a Coyolxauhqui." *Estudios de cultura Náhuatl* 4. Mexico City: Universidad Nacional Autónoma de México.

Furst, Peter T.
1967   "Huichol Conceptions of the Soul." *Folklore of the Americas* 27, no. 2.
1974   "Morning Glory and Mother Goddess at Tepantitla, Teotihuacan." In *Mesoamerican Archaeology*, ed. Norman Hammond. Austin: University of Texas Press.

García Icazbalceta, Joaquín (ed.)
1971   *Colleción de documentos para la historia de México*. 2 vols. Nendeln, Liechtenstein: Kraus Reprints.

Garibay, Angel María
1945   *Épica Náhuatl: Divulgación literaria*. Mexico City: Universidad Nacional Autónoma de México.
1953   *Historia de la literatura Náhuatl*. 2 vols. Mexico City: Editorial Porrúa.
1961a   *Llave del Náhuatl*. 2d ed., rev. Mexico City: Editorial Porrúa.
1961b   *Vida económica de Tenochtitlan*. Mexico City: Universidad Nacional Autónoma de México.
1964–1968 *Poesía Náhuatl*. 3 vols. Mexico City: Universidad Nacional Autónoma de México.

Gay, Carlo
1972   *Chalcacingo*. Portland, Ore.: International Scholarly Book Services.

Gómara, Francisco López de
1964   *Cortés: The Life of the Conqueror by His Secretary*. Trans. Lesley Byrd Simpson. Berkeley and Los Angeles: University of California Press.

Hernández, Francisco
1964   *Antigüedades de la Nueva España*. Mexico City: Editorial Robredo.

Herrera, Antonio de
1944–1947 *Historia general de los hechos de los castellanos en las islas y tierra firme de el mar océano*. 10 vols. Asunción, Paraguay: Editorial Guaranía.

Heyden, Doris
1976   "La diosa madre: Itzpapalotl." *Boletín INAH*, época II, num. 11.

Historia Tolteca-Chichimeca
1968   Ed. and trans. Konrad Theodor Preuss and Ernst Mengin. New York and London: Johnson Reprint Co.

Ixtlilxochitl, Fernando de Alva
1965a   *Historia de la nación chichimeca*. Vol. 2 of *Obras históricas*, ed. Alfredo Chavero. Reprinted Mexico City: Editora Nacional.
1965b   *Relaciones*. Vol. 1 of above.

Jonghe, M. Edouard de (ed.)
1905   "Histoyre du Méchique." *Journal de la Société des Américainistes de Paris*, n.s. 2, no. 1.

Klein, Cecilia F.
1975   "Post-Classic Mexican Death Imagery as a Sign of Cyclic Completion." In *Death and the Afterlife in Precolumbian America*, ed. Elizabeth Benson. Washington, D.C.: Dumbarton Oaks.

Krickeberg, Walter
1966   "El juego de pelota mesoamericano y su simbolismo religioso."
            In *Traducciones mesoamericanistas*, vol. 1. Mexico City: Sociedad
            Mexicana de Antropología.

LaFaye, Jacques (ed.)
1972   *Manuscrit Tovar, origines et croyances des Indiens du Méxique*.
            Graz, Austria: Akademische Druck- u. Verlagsanstalt.

Landa, Diego de
1941   *Relación de las cosas de Yucatan*. Ed. Alfred M. Tozzer. Papers of
            the Peabody Museum. Cambridge, Mass.: Harvard University
            Press.

Las Casas, Bartolomé de
1966   *Los Indios de México y Nueva España, antología*. Ed. Edmundo
            O'Gorman. Mexico City: Editorial Porrúa.

León-Portilla, Miguel
1967   *Trece poetas del mundo azteca*. Mexico City: Universidad Nacional
            Autónoma de México.

Leyenda de los Soles
1945   In Códice Chimalpopoca, trans. Primo Feliciano Velázquez.
            Mexico City: Universidad Nacional Autónoma de México.

López Austin, Alfredo
1966   "Los Temacpalitotique." *Estudios de cultura Náhuatl* 7. Mexico
            City: Universidad Nacional Autónoma de México.

Marquina, Ignacio
1970   *Proyecto Cholula*. Mexico City: INAH.

Mendieta, Gerónimo de
1945   *Historia eclesiástica indiana*. 4 vols. Mexico City: Editorial Chávez
            Hayhoe.

Miller, Arthur G.
1973   *The Mural Painting of Teotihuacan*. Washington, D.C.: Dumbarton
            Oaks.

Molina, Alonso de
1944   *Vocabulario en lengua castellana y mexicana*. Reprinted Madrid:
            Ediciones Cultura Hispánica.

Moreno de los Arcos, Roberto
1967   "Los cinco soles cosmogónicos." *Estudios de cultura Náhuatl* 7.
            Mexico City: Universidad Nacional Autónoma de México.

Motolinía, Toribio de
1951   *Motolinia's History of the Indians of New Spain*. Trans. Francis Bor-

gia Steck. Washington, D.C.: Academy of American Franciscan History.

1967   *Memoriales*. Ed. E. Aviña Levy. Facsimile of the Pimentel edition of 1903. Guadalajara.

Muñoz Camargo, D.
1966   *Historia de Tlascala*. Ed. E. Aviña Levy. Facsimile of the Chavero edition of 1892. Guadalajara.

Olmos, Andrés de
1965   *Historia de los Mexicanos por sus Pinturas*. In *Teogonía e historia de los Mexicanos: Tres opúsculos del siglo XVI*, ed. Angel María Garibay. Mexico City: Editorial Porrúa.

Origen de los mexicanos
1971   In *Nueva colleción de documentos para la historia de México*, ed. Joaquín García Icazbalceta. 2 vols. Nendeln, Liechtenstein: Kraus Reprints.

Orozco y Berra, Manuel (ed.)
1944   Códice Ramírez. Mexico City: Editorial Leyenda.

Pasztory, E.
1974   *The Iconography of the Teotihuacan Tlaloc*. Washington, D.C.: Dumbarton Oaks.

Pomar, Juan Bautista
1891   *Relación de Tezcoco*. In *Nueva colleción de documentos para la historia de México*, ed. Joaquín García Icazbalceta. Vol. III. Nendeln, Liechtenstein: Kraus Reprints.

Ponce de León, Pedro
1965   *Tratado de los dioses y ritos de la gentilidad*. In *Teogonía e historia de los Mexicanos: Tres opúsculos del siglo XVI*, ed. Angel María Garibay. Mexico City: Editorial Porrúa.

Relación de la genealogía y linaje de los señores que han señoreado esta tierra de la Nueva España
1971   In *Nueva colleción de documentos para la historia de México*, ed. Joaquín García Icazbalceta. 2 vols. Nendeln, Liechtenstein: Kraus Reprints.

Robelo, Cecilio A.
n.d.   *Diccionario de Aztequismos*. 3d ed. Mexico City: Ediciones Fuente Cultural.

Roys, Ralph L.
1967   *The Book of Chilam Balam of Chumayel*. Norman: University of Oklahoma Press.

Ruiz de Alarcón, H.
1953   *Tratado de las supersticiones y costumbres gentílicas*. In *Tratados de
            las idolatrías, supersticiones, dioses, ritos*, etc., ed. Francisco del
            Paso y Troncoso. 2d ed. 2 vols. Mexico City: Librería Navarro.

Sáenz, César
1967   *El Fuego Nuevo*. Mexico City: Universidad Nacional Autónoma
            de México.

Sahagún, Bernardino de
1950–1976   *General History of the Things of New Spain* (Florentine Codex).
            Trans. Arthur Anderson and Charles Dibble. 12 vols. (first and
            last vols. revised). Santa Fe: School of American Research.
1956   *Historia general de las cosas de Nueva España*. Ed. Angel María Gari-
            bay. 4 vols. Mexico City: Editorial Porrúa.
1958a   *Veinte himnos sacros de los nahuas*. Trans. Angel María Garibay.
            Mexico City: Universidad Nacional Autónoma de México.
1958b   *Ritos, sacerdotes y atavíos de los dioses*. Trans. Miguel León-Por-
            tilla. Mexico City: Universidad Nacional Autónoma de México.
1969   *Augurios y abusiones*. Trans. Alfredo López Austin. Mexico City:
            Universidad Nacional Autónoma de México.

Sanford, T.
1966   *Linguistic Analysis of Music and Dance Terms*. Offprint studies 76.
            Austin: University of Texas.

Selden Roll
1955   Ed. Cottie A. Burland. Berlin: Verlag Gebr. Mann.

Seler, Eduard
1960   *Gesammelte Abhandlungen*. 5 vols. and index vol. Graz, Austria:
            Akademische Druck- u. Verlagsanstalt.
1963   *Comentarios al Códice Borgia*. 2 vols. Mexico City: Fondo de Cul-
            tura Económica.

Serna, Jacinto de la
1953   *Manual de ministros de Indios para el conocimiento de sus idolatrías*.
            In *Tratados de las idolatrías, supersticiones*, etc., ed. Francisco del
            Paso y Troncoso. 2d ed. 2 vols. Mexico City: Ediciones Fuente
            Cultural.

Siméon, Rémi
1965   *Dictionnaire de la langue nahuatl ou mexicaine*. Graz, Austria:
            Akademische Druck- u. Verlagsanstalt.

Sullivan, Thelma D.
1965   "A Prayer to Tlaloc." *Estudios de cultura Náhuatl* 5. Mexico City:
            Universidad Nacional Autónoma de México.
1966   "Pregnancy, Childbirth and the Deification of Women Who Died

in Childbirth." *Estudios de cultura Náhuatl* 6. Mexico City: Universidad Nacional Autónoma de México.

Swadesh, Mauricio, and Sancho, Madalena
1966   *Los mil elementos de mexicano clásico*. Mexico City: Universidad Nacional Autónoma de México.

Thompson, J. Eric S.
1972   *A Commentary on the Dresden Codex*. Philadelphia: American Philosophical Society.

Tira de la peregrinación (Codex Boturini)
1944   Mexico City: Librería Antiquaria, G. M. Echaniz.

Torquemada, Juan de
1969   *Monarquía indiana*. 3 vols. Mexico City: Editorial Leyenda.

Veytia, Mariano
1944   *Historia antigua de México*. 2 vols. Mexico City: Editorial Leyenda.

Wauchope, Robert (ed.)
1964–1976 *Handbook of Middle American Indians*. 16 vols. Austin: University of Texas Press.

Index